BENNY

John Burrowes is the author of seven books. They range from his 'ghosting' of the autobiography of an Australian Olympic champion cyclist, which was a bestseller in that country, to a novel on the Middle East where he worked as an editor of a daily newspaper. It was his research on BENNY which gave him the inspiration for his well-known Glasgow novels, the JAMESIE'S PEOPLE trilogy, about life and times in the Gorbals from the 1930s to the 1970s.

MAINSTREAM SPORT

BENNY

THE LIFE AND TIMES OF A FIGHTING LEGEND

JOHN BURROWES

MAINSTREAM
PUBLISHING

EDINBURGH AND LONDON

First published in Great Britain in 1982 by
MAINSTREAM PUBLISHING COMPANY (EDINBURGH) LTD
7 Albany Street
Edinburgh EH1 3UG

ISBN 1 84018 661 5

This edition, 2002

A catalogue record for this book is available from the British Library

Printed and bound in Great Britain by
Cox & Wyman Ltd

For Benny Lynch . . . and the Gorbals.

Contents

Acknowledgements

Many people made this book possible, not the least of them those old men of the ring, the Fifty Bob Fighters of the Thirties, who are still alive today in Scotland. It was a pleasure for me to have dealings with them in my research for Benny. And my particular gratitude also goes to Sammy Wilson Junior; Mrs Anne Docherty, of Bramalea, Ontario, widow of Benny Lynch, and her family; Mr James Foley, for his great knowledge of the Gorbals; Mr Joe Aitchison for his great knowledge of the sport; Mr Harry Dingley, brother of George Dingley; the Lynch family of Carnamoyle, Co. Donegal, from where Benny's family originated; Father Joseph Walsh of Mount Melleray Monastery, Co. Waterford; the ever helpful staff of the Glasgow Room of the Mitchell Library; and numerous colleagues on the *Daily Record* too many to name for their own expertise. Finally, I should like to express my gratitude to *Boxing News* for permission to reproduce their photographs of Paddy Docherty, Tommy Steele, Johnny McGrory and Jim Warnock.

Preface

B enny Lynch was Scotland's first World Boxing Champion. He was the most talked-about sportsman in Britain in the Thirties. He became a legend in his own lifetime.

This is the first book which fully encompasses his life and times as well as depicting the great characters and great character of life in Glasgow in the years between the two world wars.

To fully understand the Benny Lynch story is to know of the rich complexion of life in that period brought about by living and working conditions which, by comparison with today's standards, seem of another century. There was in abundance a redoubtable spirit among the people whom they labelled "the working class". They were hard times and they produced hard people. Boxing was the big sport and there were hundreds of professional fighters. To most of them it was a chance to escape from the prevailing poverty. For ten rounds a man could earn himself fifty shillings—and fifty bob was the average worker's wage. If a man was really good he could earn £4 or £5 for a fight and the chance to go on one of the travelling booths during the summer and get a steady wage for a couple of months challenging all-comers. It was the heyday of Scottish boxing and such was the competition that anyone good enough to become a local champion was qualified to take on the best in the world. Benny Lynch was one of them. He battled his way through the fifty bob men to become the champion of Scotland, the champion of Britain, Europe and the World and one of the greatest pugilists of all time.

Although his career was tragically cut short, it was in a way a miracle that he lasted as long as he did. For Benny had an affliction. He was an alcoholic. They didn't understand alcoholism then. . . which is why they didn't understand him. And as the disease destroyed him, he was abandoned and deserted by his countless followers. Only death restored the fallen idol to the status of legend again.

The story of Benny Lynch is also the story of the Gorbals, an area of Glasgow which became Scotland's most cosmopolitan community with its influx of political and racial refugees and the deprived from a variety of countries. The Gorbals also became the scapegoat suburb for Glasgow's reputation as a violent city. Like Benny Lynch, it was misunderstood, misrepresented. Although the area is still settled, it had its heart and soul ripped out in a drastic redevelopment scheme which appears to have been masterminded by someone who had a vengeance on the once colourful community. All that is left is the memory of a diminishing number of people who remember the old Gorbals for fonder things and who recall its great sporting son for reasons other than the cheap portrayals which dwelt on his weaknesses. It is the hope that this book preserves some of these better memories.

The characters and events in the book are all as near the truth as was humanly possible for me to obtain. A few names have been changed to prevent embarrassment; dialogue which was not recounted to me by the person involved is based on the facts of the event.

1

Children of the Street

A raw, ragout of a breeze would fan down Florence Street, damp and chill after its long journey across the Atlantic. On its way it would bend every tree into a premature senility, sweeping in over the rich Ayrshire pastures to the south west, then up over the high moors of heather and bog, where the curlews shrilled and peewits panicked and rich men shot their grouse. Then it would descend on Glasgow, gathering with it the sulphurous stench from J. & J. White's Chemical Works, whose waste dyed the earth in strange hues, then mixing with the black and brown belching smoke and the hot steam that constantly screamed from Dixon's Blazes Iron Works, the perpetual beacon of the South Side of Glasgow.

Not even deepest night brought silence to the Gorbals. There was always the din from Dixon's, the place that generations of fathers had warned their children was the bad fire itself where they would be sent if they misbehaved. Dixon's Blazes was perpetual noise and fire. Puggy engines would clatter with their lethal load of molten slag along the uneven track which would screech in protest as it bent and strained with another passing load of wagons on their way to the dump at Mallsmyre where each truck would side-tip its contents in a spectacular volcano, spewing another cloud of putrid fumes into the air. The steam valves at Dixon's would deliver another symphony; shunting coal and ore trains would rattle in and out of the yards, each shunt ricocheting through the cars, a bumper to bumper tympany that would reverberate through the Gorbals.

Night was never still. And the mornings would dawn in agony. Consumptive coughs. Emphysemic endurances. Bronchitic breathlessness. All the hallmarks of the warren tenements where they were crammed, multiples to a bed, decimals to a room.

Once the long rows of gaunt tenement houses had been the pristine hues of the Braidbar, Orchard, Flag, and Williamwood Quarries at Giffnock from where they were cut and shaped into oblong blocks of honey-coloured stone which the masons termed as white freestone. But now they were uniformly black. Soot black and pitted black from half a century of the atmospheric torture spewed out by the coal fires which warmed every household, their blue, brown, grey and black smoke rising and mixing with the acrid and heavy fumes from the tall industrial chimneys of the district. Together they formed a nauseous gas cloud which rose slowly, trying to escape to the heavens, only to be rejected by the thick cold blanket of air which sat atop the sea-level city for the long months of the late autumn, winter, and early spring. From there it would spill back down from whence it had risen, a noxious niagara of yellow, choking fumes swirling through the gaunt, canyon streets fouling everything it touched, acne-ing stonework and tormenting the insides of bodies.

Daytime could bring happier hours, especially if it didn't rain. Then the children could be liberated from their overcrowded homes, a seething mass of them—so many that if you had a vantage point at the Dixon's Blazes end of Florence Street, the end that some would boast was the high, and better, end of the street, and looked down the quarter mile length which ran straight to the stinking river sewer fondly called the Clyde, all that could be seen was a constant moving body of countless children, engaged in a culture of their own, a culture that dictated happiness and competition, fun and frolic; a culture which was exclusive to them. The older ones once had it, but in their age and wisdom—or was it weariness?—had abandoned it.

Their culture was the unwritten legend of the streetgames, passed to them, word to word, deed to deed, action to action, game to game, by the children of continuing generations who had played and enjoyed these same games for longer than anyone knew.

The wee girls, in their cheap print frocks, had their rhymes for their skipping games, rhymes in which they would extemporise topical additions and which, in turn, would become part of the child lore legend.

> Gypsy, Gypsy Caroline,
> Washed her face in Turpentine,
> The Turpentine will make it shine,
> Gypsy, Gypsy Caroline.
>
> . . .
>
> I had a little monkey, his name was Jungle Jim
> I put him in the bathtub to see if he could swim
> He drunk all the water, he swallowed up the soap
> He died last night with a bubble in his throat.

Others would chant their counting-out rhymes, pointing as they did at the one on the receiving end of the last word which meant they were out—or   O . . . U . . . T   —and had to leave the game.

> Eenty, teenty, figgery, fell,
> Ell, dell, dominell,
> Arky, parky, taury rope,
> Am, tam, tousy Jock
> . . . You are OUT.

or a longer one like . . .

> My mother and your mother were hanging out some clothes,
> When my mother gave your mother a punch on the nose,
> Guess what colour the blood was? "Blue!"
> B . . . L ... . U . . . E spells blue and that's the colour it was,
> And you are OUT, with a dirty washing clout,
> Over your face like . . . THIS!

They had their formalised chants for their chase and contest games like Release and Relieve-Oh which meant running from one side of the street to the other, using the black tenement walls for their start and finishing points,

> My granny had a fiddle
> And she cut it through the middle,
> One . . . two . . . three . . . GO.

Others just sang for singing sake, parodies of the old songs their fathers and grandfathers had brought back from wars or adventures or from bits they had heard from the Back Court Entertainers, the adult minstrels who cheered the community life with their popular songs.

> Goodbye Gartnavel, farewell Barlinnie Square
> It's a long way to Campsie, but by Duke Street you'll get there
> There's a wee convict waitin'
> Wi' a big ball and chain
> He's been in Gartnavel fifteen years
> But now he's out again.

They played chuckies and jorries, rounders and film stars, girds and hoops, ring a ring a roses, in and out the dusty bluebells, kick the can, shops, beds and peever . . .

> I'm a little Brownie dressed in brown,
> See my knickers hanging down
> One, two, three, four
> Shove the tiger oot the door,
> Five, six, seven, eight,
> Here she's coming in the gate.

Their playgrounds were the grid-iron streets of the Gorbals built on a mid-nineteenth century formula, roads a uniform seventy feet wide, pavements, slabbed and ten feet wide, transforming the district from mediaeval to modern times . . . as they knew them. The children's best friends were the roadmen who had covered the cobbled streets with compressed natural rock asphalt, ram-finished so smooth that a spinning pirie would transmit endless chalk patterns from its flat top for what seemed an eternity before wobbling to a drunken demise. The same chalk they used for their pirie tops could be used on the surface of the street, blackboard smooth, to draw their "beds" for peever, the hopping game they played with clay chalk, or for expressing their artistic qualities, like the pavement artists did in Argyle Street by the Tron Church, only their drawings would be mammy and daddy and wee brother by a cottage they had never seen with a huge red sun in the sky, a memory from the holiday they once had at Saltcoats. And at night, when the rain fell and the chalkmarks rainbowed into the gutter, the smooth streets would shine and mirror walking images in the dancing gaslight.

Adventure, if you were old enough, was to wander to other streets and see the other "tribes" at play or go to the big shops in Crown Street and Rutherglen Road, with all their hustle bustle of electric tram cars and lines of mastodon Clydesdales and get "hudgies" on the rear ends of the big carts they pulled. If you weren't old enough you could climb to the top of the midden shelters and even though the rough concrete roofs scratched and tore bare limbs, it was always great to shout you were the king of the castle and everyone else was a dirty wee rascal.

They were the children of the closes. Most people in Glasgow at the time lived in a tenement with a close entranceway. Some were grand and were flanked by gardens. Some were wide and airy and were expensively tiled and were called a "wally" close. Some had doors, others had wrought-iron gates. Some were approached by a stairway which made them imposing. But the closes of Florence Street and the other streets roundabout were totally functional; oblong slits, unadorned and dark, some so narrow only one person at a time could use them. Up one close, on average, would live sixteen families. The overcrowding was so bad that in an effort to curb it the Sanitary Department fixed round metal plates which they called tickets to their entry doors. On the plate were the details of how many adults and children were permitted to live there. But it was easy to get round that. For when the officers came to check the tickets against the number of occupants, the cry would go up, "The sanny men are coming!" And the extra dwellers would immediately decant to other houses. Or some would do what old Jake McNulty did when he lived with his big family in a ticketed house. He would remove the metal ticket plate and when the Sanitary called he would tell them, "It's they bad boys up the street; stole it so they did; terrible so it is."

Just one close could produce enough children to make up two full-size football teams, field a rounders squad, and have a group kneeling after their brightly coloured marbles in the gutter game the boys loved called "jorries". If you emptied two closes of its children, you would have enough entrants for a Festival.

Numbers 107 and 103, Florence Street, neighbouring closes, were typical for their numbers of children. Number 107 had the MacDonalds, with eight, who lived with their parents in a "but-and-ben" house. This meant that as well as entering the close and climbing the· narrow stone stairs, you also had to go along a dark lobby at the end of which was the kitchen, serving also as living room, lounge and washroom, and off it, through another door, was the bedroom. The O'Briens had five kids; the Curleys five; McGuires three; Murtaghs two; Hills four; Kerrs two; Kellys five; Cavanaghs four; Humphreys three; and the Grants two.

Number 103 had the Eadies with five, living in a room-and-kitchen; McLarens, four, and Lambies two, living in single-ends (solitary rooms); Todds six; Meechans three; Lamonts four; Welshs five (one of their girls being called Suvla because her dad had died there in the Gallipoli campaign). That was seventy-nine children in two closes. There were seventy-eight closes in Florence Street and at number 71 there were twenty-six families. No one ever got a final count of the little ones who lived up the street's most populous close.

Once they tried a count at number 99, the next close down from 103. The McIntosh and Tasker families, both in "but-and-ben" houses had five between them. Then they came to old Mrs Lavell's. To help her in her old age she had made some honest pennies by taking in immigrant Irishmen as lodgers. Not that she had the space: the house was only a small room and kitchen. But for the Irishmen who tumbled off the boats at the Broomielaw in their wide-eyed innocence from the backblocks of Donegal, Derry, Fermanagh and Sligo in the North West, places like Mrs Lavell's were home from home.

When the counter came to her house he looked in to his astonishment. For sitting round the walls of the small room were countless Irishmen, all nicky tams and bright cotton neck scarves, listening to fiddlers scratching out some Donegal reels. Suddenly, the window was raised from the outside by another Irishman, wild-eyed and drunk, who launched a verbal assault on the room's occupants concluding with . . . "Up Mayo . . . ya bastards!" He then turned on his heels and ran for his life . . . and at the window they were fighting and struggling to get out, clay pipes, fiddles and all and yelling. "Ye Mayo swine ye." Like the emptying of *The Jolly Beggars* of its merry core o' gangrel bodies. The counter had never known anything like it. He looked on in dismay, shook his head, and reported back to his office that there was nothing untoward at number 99 Florence Street.

Often the same kind of instant violence could erupt with the children of the street. Their regulated and centuries-old lore games dominated, but from time to time other more primitive forces would overtake. The Irish-Scots-Gaelic temper rode on a short leash. Breach it and the leash snapped, even among the young ones of the street. One would cheat at a game, whether release, jorries and face or bluff, which they played with the cards from the sea-dog faced packs of Players cigarettes. A boy would say face, when in fact it was bluff. He would be caught. And the pot boiled over, bubbling and furious, instant logic and calm abandoned, violence the only thought—some age-old fury they knew nought about but which took over whenever they considered they were wronged. Wee Benny Lynch, from number 17 Florence Street, saw his first combat that way. A happy game, the competition stiffened, the other side weakened and cheated, the ire was raised, and the character forged by centuries unknown to him emerged. The other boys were older and bigger. But that didn't deter. The punitive battle was short and swift. And the littlest Lynch became a marked man. One to be watched. To be aware of. Not to be crossed. And he was nine years of age.

2

They Came to the Gorbals

In 1806 there were just five streets—Rose, Crown, Thistle, Hospital and St Ninian—in the little village of huts, shops and cottages with mud and heather roofs, at the other end of the bridge over the river Clyde from the busy Fishergate in the bustling town of Glasgow. Because of that they called it Bridgend. Later, when it was to become a much bigger place, it was given another name. The Gorbals.

In the upsurge of the tenement developments just before the middle of the nineteenth century, Rose Street was extended southwards. But they gave the extension to the street another name . . . Florence Street. Later they were to discover that several streets throughout the booming city had the same name, including some in the Gorbals. They rationalised and many were to have their names changed. Rose Street became Florence Street in its entirety. South Wellington became Lawmoor Street: South Shamrock became Camden Street. Main became Gorbals Street. Once Gorbals Street had been the main route to the south. The Regent Moray had ridden at the head of his big army, 600 Glasgow men among them, as it marched to the nearby hillocks of Langside to meet and defeat the forces of his half-sister, Mary Queen of Scots. Bonnie Prince Charlie rode up and down it several times, the last on his fateful journey to Culloden and the end of Scottish dreams. And Burns knew it well. By the time he got there after a long ride in from the Ayrshire moors he knew he was only minutes away from the bridge over the Clyde and the Black Bull Hotel in Argyle Street.

The Gorbals had a painful birth. Glasgow was several centuries old when a place sufficiently out of the way was needed to keep the growing number of lepers. Across the river there was land owned by the town, the townland or if said in the Gaelic, the *Gorbaile*. It was the ideal place for the lepers. They remained there for more than two centuries while across the bountiful waters of the Clyde, the salmon and brown trout darted round the heavy black oak pilings of Bishop Rae's stone bridge.

Despite the presence of the lepers, others had come to stay at Bridgend. But they were the poorer and rougher elements, so poor and rough that their immoralities deeply worried the authorities. At the beginning of the eighteenth century a special proclamation was issued in an effort to better the behaviour of the Bridgend citizens. They were warned that their "abominable vices, blaspheming, swearing, excessive drinking and profaning the Sabbath" had to stop. The drinking shops were ordered to close at ten in the evening. Stern punishment was taken against the offenders. One Charles Stewart was convicted of theft and the magistrate ordered that the punishment be "that he be burned upon the face and scourged through the streets". Anna Ramsay and Margaret Barclay, another two locals, stole from a blind man. They too were ordered to be scourged through the streets, then banished from the Gorbals.

Better days were to come. Good building sites for the rich merchants' houses near to the city had all gone. It seemed such a pity that the rough and poor occupied one of the best sites just across the river. So they were moved out and the best of Italian tradesmen were imported to help build the fine terrace of Carlton Place which promenaded on to the Clyde and where the wealthy were to come and live with views over the river to their places of commerce. Other fine streets were built around Carlton Place, streets like Abbotsford Place, a long tenement row with a handsome Italian Renaissance-style frontage and dominated at the rear by massive brick stair towers resembling some mediaeval castle .

But other less splendid tenements had to be built adjoining the fine houses, as homes for the massive influx of people flooding into Glasgow. The city and the other towns around it had become throbbing powerhouses of activity. Forests of tall chimneys belched the waste of boilers and furnaces. It was the industrial revolution and the West of Scotland was the workshop of the British Empire. The port was jammed by the big merchantmen loaded with tobacco, sugar, cotton and dyestuffs from America, India and the West Indies. They turned them around as fast as they could in order to carry off the products of Scottish industry. Locomotives, steam engines, ships, footwear, machine tools, architectural ironwork, refinery machinery, sanitary appliances, bridges, piers, gas-works apparatus, cloth and all forms of manufactured products . . . the world couldn't get enough of them.

The lairds were clearing the people from the Highlands because they needed the land for something more important than people. Sheep. So the Highlanders came to the town they called Glass-go and many of them came to the Gorbals.

Victims of other masters came too. There were the Jews, hunted and burned from their homes just like the Highlanders had been. After them came waves of Poles and Lithuanians, escaping their homelands for a variety of reasons; political oppression, a plunge in the grain market which pushed thousands of small farmers into drastic penury, wicked taxation levels, and population explosions in areas which could not provide for them. Many of them, as well as many Jews, had paid their fares in the Baltic ports for transportation to America but had fallen foul of unscrupulous shippers who left them at Leith in the East of Scotland, told them they were just outside New York and that if they walked westwards they would come to their California and more riches than they had ever seen in their lives. Their California was to be Glasgow. Their home in the new world was to be in the Gorbals.

But the biggest number that came to the Gorbals came from another homeland which couldn't keep them. Their potato crops had failed and when they fled from the south and west to other even poorer parts of their island home, the soil they discovered wasn't deep enough to hold their crops; their spades and primitive ploughs smashed on the grey stone that was everywhere and where there wasn't stone there were peatbogs deep enough to swallow a man and beast. The poor land could not support all of them so they had to flee to other lands; their destination depended on the size of their purse.

Scotland was no new land for them. The bonds between them and their nearest neighbour were the closest of all lands across the water. They had been coming and going to Scotland for centuries. And the old men who knew all the legends would recount the tales from the rich fabric of their history, tales that were handed down from father to son to son to son; tales that went back to times when there existed in their land a civilisation with its own literature and music and laws and when they were ruled by kings and princes. And that was many hundred of years before Christ. Yet the tales lived on, rich and glorious, of those Gaelic Celts enlightened enough in the dark dawn of history to have created the legends that were still spoken of 2000 years afterwards.

Above all else their glorious forefathers valued two qualities in their race . . . courage in battle and beauty of person. Their learned poets, masters of the word, were there to record the great deeds of the courageous and the beautiful and such was their prowess of prose that those deeds were to live on forever. And the greatest of all their tales was about the greatest of all their warriors . . . Cuchulain.

The four provinces of Ireland, as they were at that time, Ulster, Munster, Leinster and Connaught, had their own kings with their

own courts, each contributing to the legends that were to be passed
to posterity. The most colourful of these was the Court of King Conor
of Ulster; it was in his court that Cuchulain lived . . . Cuchulain, the
hero of the Gaels, just as Ulysses had been the hero of the Greeks.
The old men of Donegal would tell his story because he was from
their county and it was always a good time to retell the legend when
they heard that another of them was going over the seas; particularly
if it was to Scotland, for Cuchulain had great connections in the
history of that country.

"Aye, Cuchulain . . . now there was a warrior," they would say. "A
real fighting man if there ever was one and right from the time he
was a wee boy . . . Aye, greatest fighting man ould Ireland has ever
seen . . . Man, d'ye know, he had the courage of ten men when he
was in battle."

They gave him the name Cuchulain, Hound of the Smith, for
standing his ground as a young boy when a great dog of the King's
blacksmith had gone for him. With its huge mouth gaping and yelling
as it charged, the young Cuchulain carefully took aim with his
hurling stick and aimed a ball right into its throat . . . then as the
animal convulsed in a screaming frenzy he went in and finished it off.
From then on the tales about Cuchulain grew and grew as he
defended his northern province of Ireland from all invaders and
travelled to Scotland too where he performed even more great
warrior feats, and where he was to fall in love with with Aoife, the
Queen of Scotland. A son was born, but Cuchulain was never to meet
him . . . until they met in combat. The son only revealed his identity
with his dying words to the father who had mortally wounded him.

"Aye, tis a right sad story," they would say when they recounted
the tale. "But as Cuchulain himself told the King . . . 'Short Life, Long
Fame.' Sure and we'll be talking about him and the harps will be
playing about him forever."

Cuchulain was of myth and legend. But myth and legend did little
for empty stomachs. The farms were small and the families were
often large. A small farm could feed a man and his wife and their
children. But when the children had children the only alternative to
starvation was to leave the green land they loved and held so dearly
that they could still speak about their illustrious forefathers of a
thousand and more years ago as though they knew them themselves.

A little community of townlands near Derry in North Donegal
called Carnamoyle , Sappagh and Iskaheen was just one of innumer-
able other rural outposts which had to give up its children to other
lands. Some trekked over Grainne's Gap in the mountains to the
shore road that took them to Moville at the head of Lough Foyle

where the big ships came that could transport them to the great land to the west they called America where, letters had told them, there were riches beyond their wildest dreams. Others walked down the lanes, high-walled with flowering fuschias, hawthorn and whin, to Derry, where there were smaller ships which would take them to Scotland, the nearest land to the east and where so many had gone before them. There weren't the riches there that they had heard about in America, but their friends and relatives had told them that there was work and they wouldn't starve.

They had a special bottling which they called The Big Night for James Lynch and his wife Rebecca on the night before they set out to walk to Derry for the ship to Scotland. James Lynch was brought up in a house they called The Rocks at Meenamault in the townland of Carnamoyle six miles from Derry. Rebecca Gallagher, the girl he was to marry was from Burdoway in the same townland and when they married they lived together at The Rocks. Their limewashed stone cottage was high on the mountain they called The Rocky Hill in the part of Donegal known as Inishowen, the lonely and beautiful peninsula bounded by Lough Swilly and Lough Foyle in the most northerly knuckle of land in all Ireland.

They were hard but happy years at Meenamault. They grew oats to feed the horse, donkey and hens. They had two cows which gave them milk, butter and cheese. The pig they killed in the autumn did them through the winter. They pulled the lint, soaked and dried it, and it gave them a warm roof for their house. And they had turbery rights for the peat which they sliced from beneath the springy moss on the high hills behind their cottage. They would journey to these high lands on the Scalp Hill in the spring months with a horse and slean and donkey and creels to cut the turf which they needed for a year's cooking and warmth. In the good years it would be heavy and oily and they would stack it, two across two across another two, on the land beside the cuttings. The women would bring the bread they had baked and other food and they would light small cooking fires from the dried turf that always lay there to make their men's dinners. A week of hard work at the turf would give enough fuel for up to three cottages for a year. The state of the turf would always be a great talking point with them. If the weather was fine and it came out solid and dark and could be dried quickly in the stacks it would last them longer and their fires would be warmer. But in bad years they often had to leave it where it had been cut for up to a whole year and when they took it in the "goodness" would have been thinned by the rain which could fall day after day for months on end.

Their talk was of their labours, the happy times, the hard times.

The old ones would remind them always to clean their cutting spades and their hands on the spongy moss above the turf before they left the bog. If they didn't no amount of scrubbing would remove the dark essence of the turf from their hands, nor would it be scraped from their cutting tools if allowed to dry. "Did you hear about the men who were being annoyed by two ducks when they were cutting over the way there? They couldn't get on with their work for them so they tied two praities with string and one duck swallowed one and the other swallowed the second one and that was them tethered thegether and helpless."

And they roared and laughed at the ingenuity of it.

The Lynch's had survived the disastrously wet season of 1877 and the near famine of '79 when only a quarter of the normal potato crop was available for consumption. But by the end of the Eighties when young James had married Rebecca and they had a young family of their own, including a son called John, they were forced to leave the family home. There wasn't enough land around The Rocks to keep all of them. Between them they had less than £3 in savings, but that would be enough for their fares to Scotland where lots of others had gone from their district. There were even boats going from Derry over to Greenock charging less than two shillings for the one-way sail. So that's where they would go.

There were tears at the prospect of going over the sea and leaving their loved ones. Their lovely Inishowen was one of nature's masterpieces. When they had cut the turf high on the Scalp there were the shining waters of the Foyle on one side of them and the Swilly on the other and it seemed as if Inishowen really was the Island of Owen. In the distance below them was the town where they went for the bustling market and to pray in its cathedral, the town the English had come to and had renamed Londonderry, but to them would forever be Derry. God had sculpted for them one of his finest works.

The Big Night was a special bottling. A bottling was a regular affair at which they would go to each other's houses for singing, dancing and storytelling and to which each would carry a bottle with victuals of his own liking. Big Nights were different. They were for weddings or christenings or a good harvest . . . . . or for dear ones about to depart.

For bottlings and Big Nights in the district they would to to The Rock Public House at the junction where their track met the road for Muff, or else to Molloys at Burnfoot. There they could buy their whiskey or Guinness. Others would bring bottles that were got neither at Molloys or The Rock. For they were from their own little pots, which was why they called it poitin. Having their own little pots, as they would say, was as commonplace as having a cow in Donegal, particularly over in the west. But they were great poitin people too in Inishowen. At bottlings or Big Nights they would exchange their recipes and taste each other's poitin. It was a fine art getting the proportions of barley and sugar and yeast correct and an even greater art keeping it at an even temperature.

"D'ye know," they would say, "it really is magical stuff. You can use the first run singlings and rub it on any pain, even the rheumatics, and to be sure they just vanished. And if you fed your cow on the mash that was left over it would take the top price in the market, so healthy would it be looking. But have nothing to do with these bad fellows who're mixing it with sulphuric acid to convert it into ether. There's an awful amount of this ether drinking going on and to think they could be drinking lovely poitin instead."

All their friends and neighbours in Carnamoyle and Sappagh and Muff were invited to the Lynch's Big Night . . . . . the McColgins and McLaughlins, Dohertys, Platts, and McIvors. They drank from their bottles. They danced for a last time the quadrilles and lancers on the ash and lime floor of the cottage.

They spoke about the old days. "You'll need to watch, James, that you're not like the other Lynch that left from Carry just up the road there. Great man, so he was. Sat in his cottage up there thinking up inventions and sure did he not invent the first vacuum brake. He took it with him over to England and d'ye know what the Ould Queen did? Had him committed to an institution as a madman . . . . . and they had his invention stolen from him."

They spoke about the legends. About Cuchulain and his travels in Scotland. And the next day they walked down the winding track to the quayside at Derry and a new life in Scotland.

Like the Jews and the Baltic peoples, the Irish too were to make more fortunes for the grasping shipping merchants. Shipping humans, whether slaves from West Africa or the unfortunates whom other countries didn't want or couldn't afford, was the most profitable cargo of all. Unlike bulky machinery which took valuable time to load and required skilled packers and attendants, humans loaded themselves. They only required the minimum of food and water for the journey; and if they died they could be disposed of . . . . overboard. You couldn't do that with more valuable things . . . . like goods and commodities.

A flotilla of small ferry boats, varying between 200 and 500 tons did the bulk of the trade between Ireland and the North British ports. People were herded and crammed into the little ships in an orgy of exploitation unrivalled since the days of the slave hulks. So concerned was the Inspector of Vagrants in Glasgow that he issued a special report on the numbers being uncaringly shipped into the burgeoning city.

"On 6 August 1847 there were landed from the *Shamrock* steamer from Derry, being one deck load, 1233 persons; on the 7th of the same month, from Belfast, by the *Aurura* 705 persons; on the 8th from Derry by the ship *Londonderry* 454; on the 9th by the Ardrossan railway and steamer from Belfast 741; on the 10th, by the *Aurora* from Belfast 1000; on the 11th by the *Londonderry* from Derry 1778; on the 12th by the *Tartar* from Belfast 717; on the 14th by the *Londonderry* from Derry 746; on the 14th by the *Shamrock* from Derry 1130; on the 14th by the Ardrossan railway and steamer 1410; on the 14th by the *Aurora* from Belfast 940; on the 17th by the *Aurora* from Belfast 531; and on the 18th by the *Londonderry* from Derry 1105. The foregoing facts I can prove as I had officers attending these vessels night and day during their arrival and I leave it for you to judge if it had come to blow [a storm] what the result would have been with from 1000 to 1700 human beings crowded on the deck of a small vessel of perhaps not more than 200 tons burden.

Later that year the Inspector's report was tragically underscored. It happened on board the *Londonderry*, the regular Derry to Glasgow trader, and which in ten days noted by the Inspector had brought 3383 Irish to Scotland. It was on another run this time, from Sligo, further down the North West coast of Ireland, to Liverpool. On board was a cargo of emigrants bound for England in order to re-ship for the United States. And on this voyage, as the Inspector had said he feared, there was indeed "a blow".

The mist lay sombrely and forbodingly on flat-topped Benbulbin and over the Dartry Mountains as their little vessel, a mere 277 tons, cleared Rosses Point and Drumcliff Bay out of Sligo Port and troughed into the deepening swell of the Atlantic. They were off the coast of Donegal, Aran Island being their nearest point of land, when the huge waves threatened to wash off the deck cargo of hopeful Irish families on their way to the New World where their cousins had written to say the potatoes could leap out of the ground twice a year aye, and to be sure, they were lining the pavements with gold such was the wealth of the place.

The storm was such that everyone had to be cleared from the decks. The master and his rough crew drove the 174 steerage passengers down the vertical ladder into the hold. They pushed and shoved them into the black depths of the ship, the only access to light and air being the ladder area which they descended. But even that had to be covered lest the water breaking over the ship get into the hold and swamp them. The hold measured 23 by 18 feet with a headroom of just over six feet. All hatches were battened and the *Londonderry* headed into the fury of the Atlantic night. Inishowen Head, the guardian of Lough Foyle, greeted them in the morning, the lighthouse guiding them through the narrow channel at Magilligan Point and into the calm and sheltered waters of the big lough. When they opened the hatches there was a strange stillness below, in stark contrast to the screams of mercy from the women and children the night before.

They unloaded the corpses from the hold of the coffin ship and laid them in neat rows on the long quay at Derry. There were seventy-two of them; souls who had hoped for so much just hours before, exiling themselves so that their sons and daughters would have the chance of better fortune than they had.

Thus the Irish came to Scotland too; and with the Jews and the Poles, the Lithuanians and the Highlanders, and Lowland Scots fleeing the miseries of rural peasant life, they came to the Gorbals for a new way of living. And for years the Gorbals was good to them. It gave them work and trading. It gave them houses. The village they had once called Bridgend was now a thriving, self-contained town and when the wealthy moved out of the big apartments of the handsome-fronted tenements, they were sub-divided so that they could crowd as many in as possible. But such was the demand for houses, they even carved up some of the smaller ones to make even more profits for the landlords. So the long, slow, and tortuous decline of the Gorbals began. By the 1920s it had become the most over-crowded district in the metropolis they were calling the Second City of the Empire. Six times more people lived there to the acre than any other area of the over populated city. Fifty thousand of them played, worked, traded and slept in the geographical wedge they called the Gorbals . . . . just 272 acres of it, the size of a small Ayrshire dairy farm. Most of the houses were one room and one kitchen. Many of them were just one room, for that was all that could be afforded or obtained while 130,000 of the men were without a job and dole money was set at starvation level.

But from Scotland's deepest social depths and from the slumland that only Naples could rival, a new type of Scottish character was to emerge, a product of the intense and pressurised international mix in which the people lived; the devil-may-care of the Irish; the shrewd-ness of the Jew; the solidarity of the Eastern Europeans; the native wit and industry of the Scot.

Each grafted a little of their own on the other. Being from the Gorbals gave them a national blend which was different from other areas of the city. The successful ones had an edge that made them border on the brilliant, whether by brain or brawn. Taking on the world was a lot easier if you came from the little world they called the Gorbals.

Thomas Lipton from Crown Street did it. And he became the world's richest grocer. Allan Pinkerton, from Muirhead Street on the very site of the leper hospital, headed west and guarded Abraham Lincoln, before becoming the founder of the world's biggest private detective agency. John Buchan, from Bedford Street, wrote books and became the Governor General of Canada. Kennedy Jones, another from Crown Street, founded a newspaper in Fleet Street and became a wealthy politician. And Isaac Wolfson, from Thistle Street, went to London and founded one of the biggest stores groups in the country. They were just some who were to become legends in their own time, and for all time.

Others were to do it different ways.

3

Corner Boys All

They called them the corner boys, mainly because they stood at street corners. But even though they didn't meet there and met instead at some regular place along the street, they were still corner boys. The corner boys could be any age. Some were in their late teens, others in their fifties and over. Many of them had been the victorious fighters of the Great War, the Ladies from Hell, who had come back to their homeland of freedom to discover that freedom didn't include the right to get work and people were saying a depression was coming and life was going to get worse. Some of the corner boys wouldn't have worked even if there had been jobs for them. They had been to the real hell of mud and blood and had lost their best mates. They never again wanted a master to give them orders. The corner with mates, real mates, was an infinitely better place to be.

The corner was tribal. There were bad boys in other streets but the men of the corner were the best vigilantes the city ever had, although few realised them in that role. If the corner boys were there you could go shopping and leave your key in the door and you never gave it a thought that anyone would invade your premises. For no one would. The corner boys consisted of a whole variety of characters. There would be the younger members, the initiates, anxious to proclaim their manhood. The older men had done that by baring their legs for the kilt of the Highland Light Infantry, the regiment they called Glasgow's Own. The new members of the tribe would have to show courage and daring in the only fashion that was available to them. Often they would have vicious clashes with other corner boys, sometimes for no other reason than territorial bravado; but if it was a clash with other corner boys from over the river and the East End then it would be for a more sinister reason. Religion.

The East End was the stronghold of the Protestants, the Billy Boys, Billy for their King Billy, King William of Orange who had chased the Catholics at the Boyne and Aughrim, and Billy for their own great street leader, Billy Fullerton, the toughest and hardest street man from across the Clyde. The South Side corner boys were predominantly Catholic, first and second descendants of the human tide that had poured over, mainly from Donegal and the North West of Ireland in the wake of the Potato Famine.

Like every other street, Florence Street had its men of the corner. Some gathered at the Moy Public House, where Florence cornered with Cumberland Street. Others stood further down the street towards the river near a bookie, whose presence with his street stance was as good a reason for a gathering place as a corner. The Florence Street crowd that made their focal point the bookie's pitch consisted of all the types and characters that made up a corner boy group. There were the hard men who when angered could look at you, cold and mean, and say, "Want yer fuckin ears cut aff!" The threat was used for just one simple reason. They meant it. The spectrum ranged from hard man to fly man, chancer and speculator to joker and jester, patter man and philosopher, opportunist and optimist, the talented, and the untalented, the romantic and the romancer, and the fighter.

Life for many of the corner boys was a daily existence with little thought of tomorrow. A long lie in bed in the morning; when you've only the time of day to pass, why hurry? If there was a shilling or two from the day before, then the luxury of an early drink. Maybe the gods would be kind to them in the afternoon and bring a win from the bookie; if their sixpenny double came up they would be millionaires for the night. The prospect of that was much better to contemplate than the future; what was the future anyway? Wages or dole, neither provided real relief for the struggle that was survival: only drink could do that.

They would always be cheered when someone like Trouble Donnachie joined them, cupping his hands and rubbing them with a beam on his face which could mean he had a good story to tell them from his adventures of the day before or that he was planning to get up to something on the day. Trouble was one of the jokers of the pack; any kind of jest, no matter how adventurous, was his way out of what could be a monotonous routine. Devising them gave him hours of delight. Achieving them were great moments of amusement. And recounting them was a treasured experience.

"Howzitgaun, Trouble?" they would say when they met. "Oh ya beauty," he would reply. "What a fuckin laugh I had yesterday." Which meant he had one of his adventures. He would then recount the full adventure, detail by detail; often long elaborate stories of his endeavour to satisfy his sometimes bizarre sense of humour; but always his stories, even though the joker did go wild, were better in the telling and gave Trouble much more satisfaction than the actual perpetration of the deed.

They spoke for years about his escapades as a phoney gaffer. Trouble loved the gaffer joke. Maybe he had nurtured a secret longing to have been one . . . . had he worked, that is. He had a dozen variations of his gaffer joke, each one worked out in elaborate detail, told in even more graphic detail.

He would go to great lengths to play the role right. Brush and press his dark suit, same with the old soft hat he had; gaffer's never wore cloth caps. A collection of lead pencils in his top pocket, a notebook, a piece of chalk and a joiner's ruler he borrowed from a man in the close. That was Trouble a gaffer. Then he would go on a walk towards the city, just a mile away over the Clyde. There were always gangs working on the cobbled roads or digging up the flagged pavements repairing gas and water main leaks. He would look for a gang that hadn't dug too far down and with no gaffer in sight. Then Trouble would descend. He would fuss about them without saying a word making a variety of measurements from the building line to the pavement edge then to where the men were digging. Then he would make copious notes in his book after pedantically folding his measure. Only when he had finished his note taking would he speak to the men. "Right," he would say, "whose yer gaffer?" "Oh him," he would reply in disgust when they told him. "Well, he's tell't you the wrang place tae dig. Christ, yer nearly three yards out. He would flourish the ruler once again, this time making a series of crosses with his chalk at a point some feet from the squad. "Right . . . . this is supposed to be where you're digging. Get that hole filled and start o'er here. I'll be back later to dae more checks . . . . and see that gaffer o' yours." And with that he would be off.

He played the gaffer game like that at a variety of such work sites and each one became another lustre in the legend that surrounded Trouble. The joke may have been the same, but the situation and the reaction of the workmen always varied and Trouble could make every one sound like a first-time performance. Once he played the gaffer game at Dixon's Blazes. But only once for it caused so much confusion and he ran the greatest risk he had ever done to his own life and limb.

Gangs of newly-arrived Lithuanians and Poles used to gather at the big gates on the north side of the noisy iron works. Trouble stood and watched them. They were milling around waiting for news of some kind, any kind; that there was work for them . . . or no work . . . or that there might be work later. It was too much for Trouble to resist, despite the implications. "Right men . . . pay attention," he

announced in a loud voice. "Now do youse know what a gaffer is?"
The men silenced at his command and when he asked the question
they gave a nodding answer, a few of them shouting, "Yes." One
shouted. "Bossman." They knew. "Right," said Trouble. "Bossman is
the gaffer. Am the gaffer and ah've got work . . . for the lot of you.
See a' that pig iron piled in the yard there. Well, it contains water.
Hundreds of gallons of water. We need a lot of men to get the water
out. D'ye understand? That's your jobs. Get a' the water out of a' that
pig iron." Trouble stood his ground till the last man walked into the
big yard, looking for tools and other gaffers to give them more
precise instructions. Then he headed back to Florence Street.

Trouble had the boys in convulsions of laughter as he described
the scene at Dixon's. They were still laughing when Harry, who
joined them most afternoons, told them a story that had happened to
him the day before when he gone for a walk with Trouble to the city.

"Tells me he's going to the tailors," says Harry, "so I walks into
Argyle Street with him. Round all the big shops, the London Clothing
Company, and the like. And there he has them dragging out bolts of
cloth by the dozen, assistants, under-managers, the lot. We were half
an hour in the London Clothing Company and they're out with every
bit of blue serge they had in the shop and he insists they take it to the
door so that he can match it up wi' that auld bloody suit he's wearing.
Just when the guy thinks he's at last got a sale he asks yer man here
what kind of suit he would like. Christ, and does he no' just laugh
in their face saying . . . 'Suit! Am no here for a suit.' Then he turns
about, shows them his behind . . . and says 'All I want is a bit of cloth
to repair this tear in the arse o' ma trousers.' "

They laughed at that one even louder than Trouble's own story of
his gaffer joke at Dixon's. For in the tailors he had demonstrated
what, to them, was the ultimate in effrontery; laying the foundation of
a joke, carrying it through, then executing the final wound. That was
face to face combat, the kind that the men of the corner really
appreciated. Bravery in the face of the enemy, it was. And it needed a
special kind of courage. Trouble had it.

When Harry had finished telling them about Trouble at the tailors,
Trouble kept up the happy banter by telling them about his meeting
with another well-known member of their fraternity, although he had
never stood with them in the street.

"Never guess who we clocked yesterday. Bandit Rooney. Aye, the
Bandit in person. He's still at the ring game. Selling they young yins
groanies as they study a' the big-time diamonds outside Fred Hill's . .
bigtime diamonds; are ye kidding? half of them no bigger than a bat's
fart. Anyway, there's the auld Bandit waitin' for the right couple

then he pounces, a' honest and respectable like. Which is hard for the Bandit. Whit! Wae a face like his and that old soft hat. S'that greasy you could boil it down and make enough soap to last ye a year out of it. Then he sees the right couple and puts the bite on them. Keeps his groanies in new ring boxes he buys at Chisholm Hunters. When he flashes them at the young yins a' they see is that wee bit of yellow silk inside the red box; dead flash. I don't think they even bother to look at the ring, the box is that impressive. Then Bandit gie's them the patter. Same every time. 'Scuse me son. But would your lady'— get it . . . lady; whit he means is tart but he's being a' nice—'aye, would your lady like to have a look at this lovely ring. It was bought here less than a fortnight ago. Cost £35 so it did. You see it's my daughter's. She was engaged to get married and her boy got the ring here. But the boy died suddenly last week and the shop will no' take the ring back. She wants the money to gie to the boy's mother . . . funeral an' that, ye know; they're broke. She says if I could only get £10 for it she would be that happy. But I know money's tight. What I'll do is if I get five for it, I'll put another five·to it masel'. What do you think son? Does your lady like it?' I'm telling ye. It's a pure star performance. See that George Arliss. He couldnae compete. I saw him take two in a row and away they go wi' their wee bits a shiny glass."

One story about Bandit led to another. They all knew him, and many had experiences of him.

"He's no' just small time, you know," said someone else in the group after Trouble had told his story. He does the odd big yin now and then. Did a beauty in Howard Street. You know, in that pend just up from Sawyers the fish shop where the bowler hat toffs go for what they call their lunch . . . oysters and a bottle of Guinness on a stool next to the women cleaning the Finnan haddies. Imagine doing that for yer dinner? Aff their heids. Better in Knotts any day. Anyway, Bandit is touting round the pubs in St Enoch Square looking for a couple of mugs. . . but the right kind; fly men themselves that'll get up to tricks and are able to raise a few quid. So he spots a couple and gets on the chat wi' them. The patter's as good as it is outside Fred Hills. Does the educated gent bit. 'Terrible about all those unemployment riots down in Bristol . . . it was Bristol wasn't it? Hard times we're living in and that.' Being fly men, of course, the other two know he's up to something and are waiting for the bite. Then he pulls a half bottle of Red Hackle from the coat and asks if they're interested. They laugh and tell him it's pish. 'My friends,' says the bandit, 'might I suggest you take the bottle to the toilet and put it to the test.' When they return he knows he's got them hooked. And

when you get that far, then you can afford to play wi' them. 'Any
more of it,' they inquire. 'Oh yes,' says the Bandit. 'But . . . you see,
I'm not in the small order business. I represent a wholesaler who
needs some quick capital . . . a little tax problem; know what I mean,
like? So he's willing to sell off job lots at cut price. Stuff the
customsmen won't be knowing anything about like. And d'ye blame
us? We give them 8/5½d out of every bottle. That's why you're
paying as much as twelve and a tanner for a bottle. So we're selling
our stuff off at £6 per 12 bottle case, minimum order ten cases. Still
interested boys?' They were hooked and a deal was struck for ten
cases and he tells them to meet him at the pend in Howard Street the
next day and to bring their own van and the cash. Aye, but no afore
he gets his half bottle back and the pair of them buy him a couple of
big yins . . . wi' pints as well. Dead on time, the Bandit is there at the
pend when the happy lads turn up the following day. He's standing
there in his shirt sleeves and tells them that he's just come down
from his office above the wholesaler's in the pend. He gets them to
back the van into the opening, collects their £60 and tells them to
keep sitting in their van as he's got his own porters to bring down the
cases. And off he goes. They watch him going into the building and
think everything is all right. But there's a corridor that takes you
along the building and you can come out at the far end of the back
lane, then out into Howard Street again through another pend. And
that's what he does. He had his jacket hidden in one of the toilets and
off he goes. That was the last your men saw of him. At the same time,
the Bandit made sure he kept out of town for a while, and he never
went near Howard Street or St Enoch Square for about a year. Christ,
if they had caught him they would have cut his heid aff."

They called the police the Busies. Busy about this, busy about that
and, as far as they were concerned, too busy about them and what
they were—or were not—up to. Sometimes they would harass them
for loitering, but only rarely. There were other things in which they
were more interested . . . like illegal betting and illegal booze; the
bookies and the shebeeners. There was no shortage of either in the
Gorbals, particularly the illegal bookies.

It was against the law to bet . . . unless, that is, you were a person
of sufficient means so that a city turf accountant would put you on his
books as an account holder and then, in all respectability, you could
bet on the horses or dogs at your will. But if you were a man of no
property and had no goodwill or collateral then neither were you
allowed the sporting thrill of a bet. They said there was one law for
the rich and another for the poor. They were right.

So the illegal street bookmakers flourished. They had their pitches

and stances throughout the Gorbals, and the rest of the city. Had the
police enforced the law properly they could have been cleared from
the streets. But a blind eye was turned to them for most of the time;
the fact that the police, from beat constable upwards, were paid by all
the bookies agreed protection money wasn't the only reason they
were allowed to practice. But it helped. From time to time there
would be a raid. They would be tipped off, of course, and stand-in
runners would be hired for the day so as not to record a conviction
against one of the regular men, and as little betting money as possible
would be confiscated by the law enforcers. The arrested men would be
taken to the upstairs court at the Central Police Office in Turnbull
Street, opposite St Andrew's in the Field Church with its unique
steeple that sits on the roof without support columns and which
Bonnie Prince Charlie used for his recruiting campaign for Culloden.

In the court, the handsome, white-haired Police Procurator Fiscal
would read out in an accent they called pan-loaf the full terms of the
betting laws. He knew the words by rote, but held the charge sheet in
front of him as he spoke the words: "You are charged under the Street
Betting Act of 1906 in that any person frequenting or loitering in
streets or public places on behalf thereof himself or any other person
for the purpose of bookmaking or betting or wagering or agreeing to
bet or wager or receive or settle bets shall for a first offence be
liable to a fine not exceeding £10 and for a second offence be liable
to a fine not exceeding £20 and for a third or subsequent offence and
were it proved that there was a betting transaction with someone
under 16 years of age be liable to a fine not exceeding £50 or to
prison with or without hard labour for a term not exceeding six
months how do you plead?"

It was all said in the one tone, the one breath and there was never
a pause between the end of the charge and the question regarding
plea. The answer was invariably the same. Guilty. And the fine would
be minimal. It was their mock demonstration that the law was being
upheld. It would be reported in the *Times*, *News* and *Citizen* that night.
The statistic would be recorded and if anyone breathed suspicion that
the police were corrupt and were not really trying to clean up the
street bookies, they would have the facts to show that they were. But
the corner boys and the men of the street knew better.

There were also double standards about liquor; not so much on the
part of the law, but in the attitude of society, through years of indoc-
trination on the subject. To make liquor, under licence, of course, was
highly respectable. People were knighted for it, made Barons and
Lords for it. Selling it, under licence, of course, was a lot less
respectable. But nevertheless, it was an entirely acceptable pursuit.

But to either sell or make it, without licence, was the transgression of the code of society that brought total opprobrium on the transgressor. There was little chance to make it illegally in the Gorbals. But there was plenty of opportunity to sell it for the law dictated that it could only be sold on certain days and between certain hours. The law and people's demands on the subject didn't coincide. Which is why the shebeens were born. The shebeeners were the liquor entrepreneurs. In America they were speakeasies with a club atmosphere. In Glasgow they were basic and Dickensian. The Gorbals had no shortage of shebeens. There was Oily Greigs at the corner of Ballater and Crown Streets, near the Busy Bee store. You could get a drink in Oily's, a room and kitchen house which in some closes was accommodation for a family of ten, sometimes even two families, unless the sanitary men got to find out. Oily paid the police good protection money and could usually be relied on for a drink when the pubs were closed. Red Nose Andrews ran the shebeen at number 14 Camden Street. He operated it there for years undetected and therefore didn't have to pay protection money. But the police set out to get him . . . and found that was easier said than done. They knew for sure there was a shebeen at 14 and that Red Nose was connected with it. Informers had told them for the price of a drink that there was a shebeen there. People had been seen coming from that part of Camden Street when the pubs were closed and carrying the big screwtop bottles of McEwan's—"The Best of Brewin', that's McEwan"—which hissed, frothy and brown when their heavy black stoppers were unscrewed. Somebody had even dropped a parcel of three bottles of Keystone Burgundy, four and a tanner from the pub's Family Department, five bob from the shebeen, and it had stained the greyslab pavement dark red and rent the Sabbath air with the carrier's sacrilegious oaths. There was proof galore, but still number 14 carried on its illicit trade.

Raids were carried out at 14 and houses roundabout, but nothing illegal was uncovered, except some cases of gross over-crowding which were matters for the sanitary men, not the police. Once they even broke into the very house where they "knew" the shebeen was being operated and they didn't even find an empty bottle, let alone some alcohol. The big Inspector at Oxford Street Police Station was furious. "I KNOW there's a bluidy shebeen there," he stormed. "You know there's one," he said to the Sergeant who had led the previous raid, "every corner boy knows there's one, every bugger in the Gorbals knows there's one. I want those premises watched . . . night and day."

The Busies couldn't move in the Gorbals without being known. So they had to plan what was to be their final assault on number 14 with meticulous care or else word would get to the liquor operators. They decided to try a rearguard operation for a change and men were despatched to hide among the ancient gravestones of the Old Gorbals Burial Ground where the oldest bones were those of the lepers. From the graveyard they could see all that happened at the rear of the Camden Street houses. The shebeeners had heard, however, of the latest police move and ceased trading till the heat was off them. After a while, they resumed business but nothing untoward was observed until police with binoculars positioned themselves in the back courts of houses at the lower end of Florence Street. Each house at the rear of the number 14 close was scrutinised. Eventually they saw a sight which astounded them for its simplicity, at the same time illustrating how they had been deceived for so long.

The window of a house on the first floor lay open, as did one on the second storey. And, at regular intervals, a big galvanised bucket was lowered, slowly and carefully, from the second floor house to the one below it on the first floor. After a few seconds it was raised again, much more quickly this time. That was it. The shebeen had never kept the liquor. It had been stored in the house above and orders written on a slip of paper were taken up on the bucket, then lowered gently down from the big supply permanently stored on the second storey house. They were caught red-handed at number 14, summonsed and prosecuted. And the talk the next day among the corner boys was the two new shebeens which opened up in its place.

4

Sammy the Riveter

Sammy Wilson was as Gorbals as Dixon's Blazes. Maybe even more so. His family had lived there long before the fiery and fuming iron works. They even said the family were descended from Robert Burns' acquaintance John Wilson (Dr Hornbook) who for the last thirty years of his life was the Session Clerk of Gorbals Parish and who is buried in the Old Gorbals Graveyard. Sammy was of classical Gorbals mix. Shrewd, hard-working, enterprising, loquacious, witty, daring, cheeky, rough and tough. Exceptionally tough.

Sammy was born at the lower end of Florence Street just before the turn of the century and when the street at the time was called Rose Street. Few families were more well known. His father was John Wilson, Auld Jock, and the men of the street relied on him for that little chance that the regularity and monotony of their arduous daily routine could not give them. Auld Jock was the street's illegal bookie, one of the very first in the Gorbals. The women of the neighbourhood knew Sammy's mother equally as well. For she was Fish Jean and her call "Loch-figh-yen-herrrr-rrrrennnn" for the silver darlings was known by everyone and without as much as batting an eye she could use the flat of her big filleting knife to thwack the backs of the hands of her Jewish customers who liked to handle the fish before buying. "Other folks has tae eat them, ye know," she would scold. As well as her barrow stance at the junction of Florence and Cumberland Street—Stead and Simpson's corner—Fish Jean also ran a shop in Crown Street as well as two carts which toured the Gorbals streets with herring and haddies and pulled by two horses whose names everyone knew—Peggy and Hackenschmidt, the latter after the famous wrestler.

Despite the fact he was called Auld Jock, he wasn't really old. For John Wilson died when he was thirty-nine and Fish Jean was left with seven children to rear . . . John, Hughie, Sammy, Harry, Agnes, Amelia and Mary. No one knew Mary by her Christian name. She was always called Star. Like his father before him, Sammy was to become

the most famous of his particular generation of Wilsons. When he
was young and at school he told everyone that when he grew up he
would be a champion boxer. He practised hard at it when he was at
Camden Street School, just a street away from his own house at
number 29 Rose Street. And when he grew up he used to take great
delight in showing friends the scar on his leg inflicted by the school
jannie, the janitor, with the giant key he carried for locking the
school's heavy iron gates. "Caught us fighting one day and he let me
have it with that big key; bloody nearly broke my leg so he did."

Apart from wanting to be a fighter, Sammy's other ambition was
to leave school as soon as he could. His early wile helped him
achieve that. He was thirteen at the time and it was the last day at
school for the fourteen-year-olds; they left then to go to work for
their wages were badly needed by their parents. The thirteen-year-
olds shared the same class as the fourteen-year-olds. Just before
lessons were finished for the day, the teacher asked all those who
were leaving to line up and be signed off the register. Sammy Wilson
joined them and got signed out. . . a year early. They never saw him
back again at the Camden Street School.

Sammy was free now. Free to be a fighter. Free to be champion of
Scotland, for that's what he said he was going to be. And why not?
He could beat them all in his class at school. He could take anyone on
in Florence Street, and that was saying something for just four closes
could produce enough boxers for an Olympic Games. And they said
there were some fearsome boys in the neighbouring streets; Sammy
wasn't frightened of them either. Of course, they didn't know the
rules of boxing like he did. They were street fighters. But he could
keep up with them as well.

But before setting out to be Champion . . . of whatever . . . Sammy
had to tackle his first battle. Finding a wage. Despite her turnover,
Fish Jean just got by with the meagre profits from her business.
Everyone in the household who reached working age had to work to
bring in some earnings, no matter how little. And when Fish Jean
realised young Sammy had cheated his way out of school she told
him in no uncertain terms that thirteen years of age or no, he would
have to work for his living.

There was always work to be had at the Yards. Apprentice or
labourer, skilled or unskilled, the Yards were the backstop for work.
Everyone wanted ships that had that magic stamp about them . . .
Clyde built. Such was their expertise that the Yards which flanked the
north and south shores of this single Scottish river had cornered
about twenty per cent of the world's market for ships. "Aye, she's
Clyde built, son," fathers would tell their children. And that meant it

was good. So good they gave the name to a whole variety of other products. Clyde built. Even model yachts for park boating ponds had the word put on them in order to make them sell. Clyde built. The bristle of scaffolding and supports and the skeletal frameworks of vessels of all shapes and sizes, angled to plunge into the river when they were complete, lined the river bank to the city's boundary and beyond.

Barclay Curle's and Blythswood Shipbuilding, John Brown's and Charles Connell's, Harland and Wolff and A. and J. Inglis, Lobnitz and Alexander Stephen's, Yarrow's and Fairfields. Every schoolchild knew the names. For their fathers, or brothers, or uncles or cousins of someone they knew worked in one of them. The Yards had the biggest and most concentrated workforce in Scotland. Half of Glasgow's young artisans got their bread and butter from them, either directly or indirectly . . . shipwrights and platers, riveters and carpenters, plumbers and caulkers, blacksmiths and painters.

Ulstermen from Belfast flooded over to swell that workforce when their own big yard, Harland and Wolff, opened an extension to their own site on the Clyde. They were Protestants to a man and Glasgow and Scotland was like an ould country to them. And besides wasn't there a grand football team that played just over the river from their yard and which they adopted as their very own . . . the Glasgow Rangers.

They travelled from all the old villages which had become suburbs to the yards every day . . . from Govan and Anderston, Bridgeton and Clydebank, Partick, Gorbals and Townhead. The Yard men were hard men. They had to be. Clambering around more than 100 feet up on frail body-width scaffolding clinging to the framework foetus of an iron monster in the making and exposed to the vagaries of the gaping mouth of the Clyde which sucked in the harsh furies of the Atlantic was no place for anyone who was less than hard.

Sammy Wilson enjoyed the hard physical contact of the work at Fairfields of Govan. Despite his size and slender build—five feet six inches and just over eight stones—Sammy was soon regarded as hard as any of the hard men in the Yards. He was one of the élite riveters. Together with the hauders-oan, or what the English would have called holders-on, they were the frontline troops of the Yards; they were the battalion which spent their lives battering at big plates of metal so that they were formed, fastened, made watertight and shaped into beautiful ships which sailed down the Clyde and predominated the Seven Seas. It needed a score and more of different tradesmen to make the ships, but none did it with more muscle than the riveters and the men who worked close with them, the hauders-oan.

✦

They worked in squads, usually of five men. Their operation began with the rivet heater, who was known to them as the rivet boy, even though he was often a man in his fifties. He would collect the rivets from the store, 200 panheads to the hundredweight bag, a rough hessian sack like an oversized Gladstone. He would take them to the site where they were working and heat them on his shallow-panned charcoal fire, bellowing them till they were white hot and sparking. He had to rotate his cooking of the rivets so that when he extracted them from the fire for the next part of the operation, they would be at the precisé temperature and that the others following on would be that way too when they were needed. The rivet heater was the first wheel in their clockwork operation; if he was a bad one the working of the squad could be thrown out of gear. And the hard men at the hard end of the operation didn't like that for they were on piece work and the more they produced, the more they were paid.

The rivet heater's job was more complicated than that, though. For there were times when they would be working with mixed sizes and shapes of rivets for the varying joints in which they were used . . . frame and seam, butt and scarf all needed their own particular rivet. On parts of the butt, succeeding sets of rivets would be required in varying diameters and had to be delivered in the correct sequence. Vulcan had to have his skills.

From the rivet heater the rivet was tonged to the catch boy. In America they caught them spectacularly in a pouch with the flair and show of a baseball catcher. On the Clyde they did it their own way, with less flair but no less effect. The boys didn't, in fact, actually catch them. They would position themselves near to the hauders-oan and the rivet, fuming on the tongs, was thrown so that it would land as close to them as possible. The catch boy, with a smaller pair of tongs, would then lift it and ram the fuming plug into the appropriate aperture in the holed plate, quickly cooling as he did so from a sunrise yellow to sunset red. For that reason the catch boy was often called the pitter-in, or as the English might have said . . . a putter-in.

The hauder-oan then took over. With marksman precision he swung his long sixteen-pound sledgehammer at the centre of the round face of the steel rivet, cooling from red to black, the tail remaining hottest, to punch it through till the thickening neck held firm in the hole. When the head of the rivet was flush with the plate and would go no further, the hauder-oan would press on it with the head of his hammer to allow the next stage of the operation to be carried out.

The hauders-oan and the catch boys worked on the inside of the forming ship. On the outside, in all elements, on scaffolding they called staging, were the riveters, one right-handed, one left-handed, two to every hauder-oan. They carried smaller mallet-like hammers, but with long thin heads which had to be used with uncanny precision to complete the riveting process, converting the shank of the hot bolt into a round head, a succession of which married metal plate to metal plate like a continuous weld. The entire operation went without words, such was the expertise and knowledge of their own and the other men's jobs.

Twenty-five such squads could all be working in close proximity, rivets flying from heater to catch boy, sometimes three storeys up on staging, molten meteors shooting across decks, clattering on platforms, rattling off bulkheads; hauders-oan with bass hammers, riveters with baritone ones, beating out the symphony of the ships.

Sammy had made a name for himself as an amateur and booth boxer. He knew what it was like to take on all-comers at Bill Strelley's Booth, Jimmy McOnie's "Ring" in the Gallowgate, and Watson's in Greendyke Street, facing the Glasgow Green and just a few yards along from the little St Andrew's by the Green Church, nicknamed the "Whistling Kirk" because the first organ-accompanied praise service in Scotland since the Reformation had been there. "An awfie nice wee church," Fish Jean used to say. For she and Auld Jock had been married there.

Jimmy Gilmour was from Bridgeton. They called it Brigton. Bridgeton got its name because it was the town of the bridge that went across the river in the east end of Glasgow to the town next to Glasgow, Rutherglen. Brigton people were different from South Side people. They didn't have the immigrant mix and were either descended from native Glasgow stock, or from incomers from other parts of Scotland. They were also mainly Protestant. Like Jim Gilmour, Sammy Wilson was Protestant; but that wasn't why they became the best of mates at Fairfields. Both young athletic men, they had a much stronger bond than that . . . they were boxers. As an amateur Gilmour was the only man to defeat Alec Ireland who later won the British Middleweight Championship from Tommy Milligan. And, as they learned to become tradesmen as hauders-oan they shared their boxing experiences together.

Lunchtime at Fairfields, as for lunch for the tradesmen at any of the yards, was strong black tea boiled up on the rivet fires with their dry tea and sugar carefully measured out and mixed together in an old mustard tin or a screw of newspaper. Not for them the posh oval tins specially made for the purpose, one end for the tea, the other for the sugar. Not for them either the specially made tea cans, copper wire handles and all. Hard men didn't use aids like that. And anyway, tea tasted better when it was made in an old peach tin, so they said. With their tea they would have their chits, their pieces, their sandwiches, man-sized and cut from the plain loaves bought by their wives, black-crusted and tasty at one end, dun-coloured and tough crusted at the other, and bought as a "cuttin' loaf" which meant they were a day old and sliced better.

The rivet fires became their camp fires, around which they would muster for the mid-day meal. Some would toast their bread with the catcher's or heater's tongs, others would put a piece of tin across the fire and use it as a hot plate to fry eggs or heat pies, the grease flooding from them and dripping into the fire to rise in hot plumes of appetising blue smoke. Others would spread their chits, or whatever food they had, on a cleaned baton of wood and the rivet heater would prepare a heavy metal plate on the fire till it was molten hot, then with his tongs he would pass the plate over the top of the assembled food and such was the heat and the effect of the glowing hot plate on the food that everything would be cooked, topside and bottomside, in an instant.

Chit time was chat time and they would talk about everything from the tricks and the tricksters of their trade, to world politics, to sport, to sex.

"Did ye dae the counter when he was round?" they might say. The counter was a collar-and-tie man and, as his name suggested, he counted the rivets the squads had worked for their piece-money payments. Sometimes he would dab them with white paint, and if he did a boy would walk behind him carrying the two-pint pot that he used to splash the rivet heads. At other times he would carry a piece of thick yellow chalk, no carrying boy this time, for marking off the rivets. A piece of hot charcoal from the heater's fire could rub out these marks and the rivets would be counted twice . . . doubling their payment. But they had to be fly not to push it when they did this for counters, often former riveters themselves, knew all the tricks. "Didnae score one the day for it was Charlie Boyle that was counting. Bastard was one of the best riveters in the yards and one of the flyest an' a'. He could rub out the chalk marks and naebody could tell, but see when you do it to him, he'll dob it aff yer pay. Swine, so he is."

They would speak about the great men of their trade. "Bet you Boyle wouldnae dob anything from Big Ginger Burns's chalkmarks. Any of youse ever work wi' him? What a grafter. I knew him at Harland & Wolff's . . . big ginger-headed fellah from Ulster. He could put in 1600 rivets in a day . . . worked that fast he needed two rivet heaters in the one day. And d'ye know what made him work so hard? . . to get money for his whisky. I've seen him knock back two bottles

in a day . . . and he could still walk hame straight." But somebody
always knew somebody better. "Two bob says he couldnae have kept
up wi' Baggy Davies. Naebody in the yards has ever moved like wee
Baggy. Came from Neptune Street and weighed only seven stone and
used to say he was the second best man in the Yards . . . aye, second
best, he would say, for every other bastard was saying they were the
best. He could have beat your Burns any day."

Others would hurry their lunch so that they could get a quick game
of cards—the favourite was pontoons—or hurry to one of the pitch-
and-toss schools. Sammy Wilson and Jimmy Gilmour were often at
the latter. These gambling schools weren't for the faint-hearted. Often
they would end in dissension of one kind or another and you had
always to be on guard. The two boxers loved the excitement of a
gamble at the pitch-and-toss, the coins spinning high, every eye on
them anticipating their clinking bounce as they landed and the cry
which would mean you either won . . . or lost.

A small, sharp-eyed elderly man with a big cloth cap which had
once been check, tugged at Sammy's sleeve near the end of one
lunchtime pitch-and-toss session. "Hey, Sammy, Sammy; d'ye see
what they've done; they've slipped in a double-header." Sammy's
nod was barely perceptible. Jimmy Gilmour was standing beside him
as they played and he whispered the word to him adding, "Get ready
to hop it when I move."

The loud blast of the work's whistle, shrilling a long tube of steam
skywards, was their signal. Sammy jumped into the middle of the
ring, grabbed all the banker's money and shouted "Cheating
bastards". Then he and Jimmy Gilmour were off their marks as the
last toss was still spinning upwards. The school broke up in total
confusion. Some shouted "Get them." Others demanded their names.
But, fearful of having their wages docked, they returned to their
worksites around the yard. Later in the day the word got to Sammy
and Jimmy that the men who had been running the school were
connected with one of the Govan gangs and that they would be
waiting for them that night when they went for the yellow tramcar.
(The double-deck electric tramcars had their upper decks painted in a
coloured band . . . easy for the short-sighted—and the illiterate—to
quickly recognise they were on the right tram for their destination.
From Govan to the Gorbals and beyond to Bridgeton, it was the
yellow tram.)

Govan Cross was only a short distance from Fairfields. The ornate
post which indicated a tramstop was at the Pearce Institute, on the
doorstep of Govan Cross. And standing across the pavement in front
of it as Sammy and Jim Gilmour approached were the men from

Govan, about eight of them. They made it obvious from the way they stood across the pavement, feet apart and face on towards the heavy traffic of workers pouring from Fairfields, that no one was going to pass without their consent.

The two boxers were only a few feet from them when Sammy turned to his mate and said, "Right . . . now, Jimmy; let's show them our wee friends." And from down their sleeves, each dropped their riveter's sledge hammer, the tool that provided the day-long metallic tympany which echoed from one yard to another, one bank to the opposite bank, bass pitch to alto, the real song of the Clyde. The Govan men got the message as Sammy and Jim grabbed the shafts of the hammers at their heavy heads, ready for action. No words were exchanged as the men drew abreast, but a parting in their ranks suddenly appeared. Their eyes met, nods were exchanged, and the pair went for their tram. Nothing more was ever said about the incident.

*   *   *

Pitch-and-toss was to figure even more in Sammy Wilson's life. Neither he nor Gilmour were content with making a career out of the gruelling tedium of life in the Yards. It had been all right as a job, but they had other ideas about their futures. Both wanted an involvement in boxing, but there was bread and butter to be earned as well. Sammy's father, Auld Jock, had run the bookmaker's pitch in Florence Street and Sammy had learned the tricks of the trade from him. His experience of handling the rough and wilder elements of the men at the pitch-and-toss schools at Fairfields gave him the confidence to freelance as a tossing school organiser on his own and with his brother John he initiated regular schools at the Mallsmyre, where Dixon's ironworks had moonscaped the shrinking vestige of countryside with manmade lava; where a once idyllic stream called Jenny's Burn had become a putrid green and yellow flow of industrial effluent and where not even the tadpoles lived any more.

The coin gamblers had to go to such out of the way places as the Mallsmyre because their game, like any other form of public betting, was illegal. The Gaming Statutes of 1869—The Prevention of Gaming (Scotland) Act—had listed all forms of the simple deed whereby one man staked his wits, or skill, or chance, plus money against another . . . and made them illegal: "All chain droppers, thimblers, loaded dice players, card sharpers and other persons of similar description who shall be found in any public place open to the public and who are there for other unlawful gaming shall be liable to up to 60 days' imprisonment and any money made at the gaming restored." The pitch-and-toss men were well within the grasp of the law, by statute, if they were caught.

Alex McGlynn and Georgie Welsh, two other Florence Street men, helped the Wilson brothers to run their school, getting their earnings from a split in the percentage money, known to them as tober money, which was taken from bets for . . . "organisational costs".

McGlynn and Welsh, like the best of pitch-and-toss school men, could handle most situations; their presence was usually sufficient to deter any they knew as "fly men" getting up to their tricks. And if anyone had a really big win, they would provide an escort service for them to the trams at Polmadie Road or Rutherglen Road. But it was Sammy himself who was the ultimate sanction. It was he they called for on the day that two men came to the vicinity of the school with a revolver . . . and started firing.

"Hey smartalec . . . what are you fuckin playing at?" The men recognised Wilson and made excuses that they were only using an old railway carriage for some target practice. Sammy faced up to the men with the gun. He addressed the one who was holding the weapon. "If you and your china don't get tae fuck you'll get your teeth in the back of your throat." Meekly the men turned away from him and walked off.

Between the money he made from the tober at these schools and the growing book he was running for the punters in Florence Street, Sammy was able to achieve the first of his big ambitions; to be independent of the need of a regular wage from an employer. Jimmy Gilmour too had become independent and, likewise, was running a book in Bridgeton and had established his own boxing club, in Barrack Street. He was one of the star boxers there himself, becoming the Scottish lightweight champion.

Having a club and being a champion boxer had always been Sammy's aim. He now had the chance of one day getting his club, but fate decreed he would never be a champion boxer. It happened one night when he was walking through the Gorbals on his way home from a late shift at Fairfields. There were few people about, the blue light of the street gas lamps casting dancing shadows on the black tenement walls as he hurried along Cumberland Street. It was the scuffle of feet on the wide pavement slabs and the dull thuds he knew only too well were fists hitting a body that made him look around with a startle. Across the road, just at the corner of Camden Street, and barely just visible through the dim light were two men assailing another. The third man was offering no resistance.

Sammy Wilson homed in on them almost by instinct and when he got closer he gasped . . . "Bastards!" The two men were beating up

Old Harry, a crippled newsvendor. They were trying to part him from his night's takings, bulging pockets of coppers, the odd piece of silver in a long tweed overcoat he had got second-hand at the Barrows, the market place. Had it been a ring contest, one of the footpads would have been classified a lightweight; the other a welter. Sammy would have been lucky to make the eight stone six pounds of bantamweight. Nevertheless, he set about them with a ferocity that even he had rarely used before. There was nothing Queensberry about this bout; it was entirely street corner; bare-knuckle, feet, head, knee. Points weren't for the scoring. Wounding was.

The lightweight of the pair staggered back, winded and with a badly gashed eye. Sammy Wilson's punches kept coming, this time aimed at the welter whose back was to the smooth, soot-black wall of the tenement. A flurry of vicious punches exploded from either direction. Then there was a shout from the wounded lightweight and, in a flash, the pair of them were off, disappearing in the safety of the black night.

It was more than ten minutes before the adrenalin stopped pumping and after Sammy Wilson had helped his old vendor friend to his feet and on his way home before he felt the pain. It came like a sharp stab to one of his knuckles first of all. Then the others began to throb, painfully so, and when he looked at them he understood why the pain was so excruciating. He could see the blood pumping from the middle two knuckles of his right hand, messy and sticky, the gristle of one of them bared beneath an ugly raw opening.

The last few moments of the fight came back to him. He had held the bigger of the men firmly upright, left hand on his jacket lapels holding him firmly against the tenement wall so that every punch counted for two. Then there was a miss. It didn't seem important at the time that his hand crashed straight into that stone wall for it didn't hurt. He felt the chill air on it shortly afterwards as the blood spilled and the sinews exposed; but no great pain, not like there was now. He had never quite known pain like it. Worse even than the time when he had got near-frostbite on a high site in the yards in the worst January for years. Then, when the circulation had returned to his hands it was like a thousand red hot pins all stabbing into them at once, and not even plunging them into a bucket of icy water cooled them. It was that same feeling now. He felt queasy as he looked at the mess of his best hand; his right; his boxer's right; the right that could have won him titles, made him a champion. Now it was a pathetic crumple.

"The bones will set all right," said the doctor. "But the joints have had it. They'll no' give you all that much trouble. Maybe a touch of the rheumatics when you're older. What kind of work do you do anyway?"

"Boxer."

"What?" said the doctor.

"S'all right doctor," said Sammy. "I was just joking."

Sammy Wilson accepted that he could now never be the top boxer he had dreamt of. Just one blow which hit a wrong target and a career was over; over, really, before it had started. He would need to think about something else.

Immediately there was his business as a bookie and between that and the regular pitch-and-toss schools on Sundays, holidays and long summer nights on the wastes behind Shawfield or the Mallsmyre, he was making a good living; much more than anyone roundabout— except other bookies, that is.

Sammy was one of the first full-time bookies in the Gorbals. He made his pitch at 85 Florence Street, just next to Elliott's dairy whose counter was always piled with rolls fresh from Willie Marks, the Ballater Street bakers who made the best breadrolls in the Gorbals. Ned and Mary Scanlon, an old Irish couple who Sammy said were as "dirty as the pigs of Drogheda" lived in the close and they got a weekly "bung" of a few shillings from Sammy as "inconvenience money." Most of the bookies did that. Some tenants would provide an extra service for it. They would allow their groundfloor room window to be used for handing in lines, collecting cash and paying out stake dividends. And they could always be relied on as a "hide" if there was a police raid. The Scanlons, despite their appearance, were a kindly old couple and would hand out morning and afternoon tea in big mugs with squashy leaves floating in it and so strong that the tang of the tanine would make certain refusal of all offers of a second cup. Old Ned would sometimes tender Sammy and his workers a "piece" or a roll with dubious contents and from hands that were calloused and unwashed. "Aye, thanks Ned," they would say . . . and when he shambled off to his single-end in the close they would look at each other and laugh. "Dirty auld bastard . . . his missus hides her money beneath the soap." And the intrepid pigeons would swoop down for another good feed.

If there was dog racing on somewhere, Sammy Wilson's betting operation was in business throughout the day and night.

But if you didn't live in Florence Street you hadn't far to go to find another bookie. There was Abie Grossman in Hospital Street who traded under the name of A. Titch and operated from the first close past the Turf Bar and Fogels the bakers. Lawmoor Street was served by old Willie Scott and Matt Miller was in Commercial Road. Mick

Foley lifted at 54, 44 and 34 Portugal Street and Mick Donaghue was in Coburg Street. The police knew all of them . . . and their illegal activities. But, like the runners, the police were on the bookies' payrolls. Sammy Wilson paid the regular constables who patrolled Florence Street ten shillings a week. If they added half a crown on to that they had enough for a bottle of Johnnie Walker. The beat sergeant got £1. That was enough to give them security from harassment. When there were orders from the Inspector that there was to be a raid, word would be passed on to them. But from time to time, more . senior officers at St Andrew's Square, the Police Headquarters, would send in men from other areas to make raids. They knew that was the only way they could make a raid "stick". But it wasn't easy for them to make these unannounced raids. For the corner boys, protectors of their own street clan, kept an experienced eye on all movements in their area; friend or foe, the police being unqualified constituents of the latter, had great difficulty in moving without their notice; nothing was faster than their street telegraph.

If there was a real raid, the cry would go out . . . "Edge up!" And everyone moved at the double from the pitch, scattering in all directions, some through the back close and into the warren of courts that led to a variety of other closes; some into houses and under beds; some running up the stairs and into houses on the first and second storeys; some even "dreeping" or shinnying down rone pipes from the first and second landings.

If there was an "Edge Up" call, they would first of all get rid of any kind of evidence which could be used to prosecute them . . . betting slips, results and runners boards, chalk, notepads. The police would even show the faded pink newspaper, the *Noon Record*, as evidence that these men were engaged in the nefarious activity of illegal gambling. But the people of the houses roundabout the pitches were on the side of the men and would willingly hide anything they were asked from the police. Mrs McKay at 91 Florence Street often helped Sammy Wilson's men on such occasions. Once she was thrust a bulging handkerchief, packed with betting slips. She hid it . . . in her wash. Another woman up the same close lifted the lid of the big soup pot bubbling on her range . . . and in went the "lines". And houseproud Mrs Boyd nearly fainted when one of Sammy's men ran into her second storey house, lifted the window and started walking along the six inch ledge to the first house in the next close, tapped on a window, and was taken in and made his escape.

The bookies themselves were rarely caught, for they never carried any evidence and tried as best as they could not to physically take part in their pitch's proceedings; they were the banker; the money back-up who paid out if the punters were winning; and collected if they were losing. They did more of the latter than the former. The runners and other regular workers at the pitch had their fines paid by the bookie. If it was a "fixed" raid by the local police the bookie, in connivance with them, would "permit" his stance to be raided in order to impress police HQ the branch men were being vigilant. On such occasions substitute runners would stand in for the regular men. This was because fines were based on a previous convictions basis. If any of his regular men had too many convictions they could become a financial liability should there be a genuine raid. But there were always willing surrogates on duty when the police raided, ready for a subsequent first-offender's fine at the Central Police Court. For that they would get a good "bung" from the bookie.

To make genuine raids effective and in order to out-manoeuvre the corner boys, the police would often send in plain-clothes men dressed in a variety of disguises. The day they sent in Constable Watson on a spying mission to Florence Street was what they spoke of locally as "the talk of the steamie". The word that he was there went from corner to corner, from the men grasping their big dark pints in the Moy to the men squeezing out the last golden drops of their "halfs" into their beer in Cameron's, round the diners in Knotts Restaurant as they slid the long ham rib bones deftly along their mouths like harmonica virtuosos, round the shoppers in Cosgrove's, the licensed grocer who had his own name stamped on the little whisky muskins, and round Nicholl's spotless dairy.

"Aye . . . it's Busy Watson; dressed up like a navvy, tackety boots and a big bunnet, and he's digging up the road at the corner of Cumberland Street."

Sure as fate, there he was in his stage clothes playing his bit part with a team of genuine navvies digging for a water main. It was the first time they had ever seen him out of his constable's tunic, shiny silver buttons right up to the neck and his tall, chrome topped helmet. Everyone who passed gave him a stare as he went about his arduous task, totally unaware that the word was out about him.

But as the day wore on, it got too much for some of them, especially after the first of the early drinking session at the Moy came out of the bar. "How's it gaun' big Watson?" they started to shout. The other navvies looked puzzled at the ribbing. "Aye, yer man's a Busy," the corner boys began shouting and laughing. It was too much for him. The cover he had thought had been so successful was blown. Busy Watson handed the gaffer his pick and went back to the police station.

They put Davie Scott, another Busy, in disguise as well. But his worked. He dressed as an old woman, hunch-backed, carrying an old blanket packed with rags and smoking a clay pipe. People thought it unusual when she stopped to talk for a long while with the men outside the Model Lodging House in Portugal Street. Even the old rag wives rarely did that and anything that didn't comply with the normality of local behaviour was always considered suspicious. Nevertheless, no one thought the worst . . . that the ragwife was a Busy. And across the street from where she chatted with the Modellers, plumes of blue smoke coming from her clay pipe stuffed with thick black, one of bookie Mick Foley's men was lifting betting lines. Suddenly, and amidst screams of commotion, the ragwife dropped the big black bag slung on her back, spat out the pipe, her hunchback disappeared . . . and a runner was lifted.

*   *   *

Sammy Wilson envied Jim Gilmour's club in Barrack Street, off the Gallowgate, where they used to lodge cavalry troops. Boxing was one of the favourite topics of conversation between Sammy and his workers, Jim Todd, Jim Lamont, and the Holden brothers, Sunny, Jacky and Harry. "Definitely going to start a boxing club," Sammy would tell them. "My hand is all right now . . . well, for sparring like; no' fighting. And I could build up a good stable of young lads like my old mate Jim Gilmour has. Never know. Might even get ourselves a wee champ. There's a few good boys around." Then he'd laugh. "Christ they'd need to be tae survive some of the tykes they've got in these streets."

It was only an eight minute walk from Gorbals Cross to the start of the cargo quays and sheds of the Clyde . . . straight down Gorbals Street to the Victoria Bridge, turn left and along Carlton Place past the Suspension Bridge, built to take the workers from the Gorbals over to the numerous textile works on the other side of the river, past the Glasgow Bridge and under the wide railway bridges, then past the last thoroughfare over the Clyde, the King George V Bridge with its polished granite balustrades, and into Clyde Place. The quay at Clyde Place was the first in a long chain of busy quays which went all the way down the south bank of the river—Windmillcroft Quay, Mossbank Quay, Plantation Quay and the Govan docks. In Clyde Place opposite the quay and its cavernous cargo sheds which always had the heavy smell of hemp and bananas, was a row of dock ancillary buildings, warehouses, shipping agents, offices, and the occasional repair shed or smithy. It was the size of one of these which first attracted Sammy Wilson one day as he strolled down by the wharves. It had a big "To Let" sign outside it. Has potential, he thought. Near the Gorbals. Could be painted up. Big enough inside for a ring and space roundabout for sparring, skipping and other forms of training.

Number 49 Clyde Place was to achieve Sammy's great ambition. His own boxing club. He rented the premises, had them renovated and christened with the name of Glasgow's newest boxing club, the New Polytechnic Club. This could be the start of a great new adventure, he thought.

With the help of some of "his boys" from Florence Street, they set to in converting the former workshop. A team came to build a ring. "S'got to be fullsize," said Sammy. "If my boys are going to go for the big time, then they've got to get used to it right at the start. You work harder in a big ring; keeps your legs on the go the whole time. Gie them one of these wee fourteen by sixteen feet jobs and a' they need to do is take a couple of steps back and get a rest on the ropes. Make it twenty by twenty feet."

"How did you get the name, Sammy?" he was asked by Sunny Holden. "Made up my mind about that a long time ago. The best one they've got in London is the Polytechnic. So I thought, when I get mine it will be the New Polytechnic."

They didn't have to canvas for members for Sammy Wilson's New Polytechnic. The name Sammy Wilson and all that it meant in the Gorbals was sufficient to pull away some of the best young amateur boxers from a variety of small clubs, plus the scores who were always waiting to take up the sport; a sport that, if they were good enough, could provide them with the key to an escape from the hodden existence of a working man in the tenements. No other sport could do it for them, although the footballers were starting to get a good wage and they could occasionally hit the jackpot, like Rangers' James Marshall, a doctor no less, who had gone to Arsenal and got himself a transfer from there to West Ham for £5,000, a percentage of which would be his.

If you were good enough at the boxing, however, there were wages to be picked up around the booths, and there were plenty of them; permanent ones in Glasgow, Edinburgh, Falkirk and other towns, plus all the travelling ones to the fairs in the summertime. Sometimes you could get £2 to £3 a fight at the booths and if you were game enough, you could get a fight a day; some would be so game that at the big fairs they would often fight in one booth under one name, then go to another booth at the same fair and fight under another name. They had to pay their living and other expenses from their wages, but if it was a good week they could often make between £10 and £12 and with the average weekly wage £2 15s they were in the big time. Being a fighting man could offer these Followers of the Fancy a whole new way of life. And there was always the chance that they might be a real improver and hit the real big time just like Elky Clark and Tommy Milligan had done. They had been so good they could get hundreds of pounds, just for one fight; mind you, there were lots of hands in for a share; manager and promoter, trainer and seconds, sparring partners and living and training expenses. But it was better than the booths. And the booths were better than being an ordinary working man.

"Sammy Wilson's got a club." The word fire-flashed through the Gorbals, Florence Street to Cumberland Street, Rutherglen Road, Caledonian Road and Camden Street. The message was simple . . . "He calls it the Polly and it's at 49 Clyde Place and ye want tae see the size of the ring." They also said he was charging them 6d a week to be a member just to let them know that you got nothing for nothing.

Sammy was King. Getting the Polly was his Crown. Now he needed some Crown jewels.

*   *   *

The first time that Sammy saw him was at Tommy Watson's Boxing Booth in Greendyke Street. He smiled when he heard the crowd whistling in unison "Pop Goes The Weasel" at the bobbing dance of the young slender boxer in the ring. He had never seen anyone quite like him. His rival, like most boxers, had his feet firmly on the ground and advancing on the slim, almost frail, lad who kept jumping and bouncing from one foot to another, almost like one of the fancy dancers who were the rage around the town. The conventional boxer looked more than a match for him, but he had great difficulty in making contact with the young man because of his bob and bounce. Then every now and then he would give a series of jabs which would connect with the man whose feet stayed firm. The referee had no hesitation in raising the dancer's hand at the end of the fight and the verdict met with the approval of the appreciative audience. Sammy Wilson knew the young lad. He was a Florence Street boy. And he knew all the Florence Street boys.

The following day Sammy went to Jim Gilmour's club to talk to his old mate and see the lads in training there. There was one training by himself, shadow boxing. Sammy stood by himself and stared at him. He was wearing black tights and a heavy grey pullover, two sizes too big for him, and his dark hair hung over his forehead, coated in

sweat. It was the same lad the crowd had whistled accompaniment
for the day before. Sammy was mesmerised by his shadow boxing as
the lad southpawed forward on the attack, upper-cutting, jabbing,
counterpunching, then switching stance to the conventional without
losing balance or gait.

Boxing clubs are not beautiful places. The Barrack Street club was no
exception. The air hung heavy with the stale smell of sweat combined
with old cigarette smoke from Players, Capstan and Woodbine which
had stained the walls and ceiling a Virginian brown. It was grimy and
cold. But what Sammy Wilson was watching was beauty. An aura of
athletic grace overpowered the surroundings as the young lad
weaved and swayed, hooked and spun, checked and reached and
gave short fist flurries at an imaginary opponent who Sammy, in his
empathy, knew, was the champion of the world about to be stripped
of the title.

The long session of shadow boxing over, the young pugilist
dropped his hands to his side, did a light shuffle on the spot, shaking
his head from side to side for a few moments then stopped still, the
sweat steaming from under his jersey collar, drifting up the side of
his face and into his long black hair.

"Benny Lynch," Sammy said to him.

"Aye."

"Know your father Johnny. Knew your big brother as well afore he
died. Good lad. Could have done well at the boxing. Who are you
with Benny?"

The ambiguity of the question didn't occur to Benny. He knew that
in the lingo of his trade, that question meant only one thing. Who's
your manager?"

"Nobody, Mr Wilson."

"Right. Get your jacket."

And, as an afterthought he added . . . "The name is Sammy."

5

A Brother Dies

Gorbals, 1913. The new century, the 20th century, was just thirteen years old. But in the Gorbals there were conditions that were from centuries gone by: conditions that were the breeding ground of fevers and diseases not associated with such modern times. Such was the overcrowding and squalor of Britain's most congested slum quarter that just thirteen years previously the Gorbals had been visited by a scourge, the like of which the Western World hadn't known since the Middle Ages. The like of which civilised man thought he had rid himself for all time. The Plague . . . the Bubonic Plague. The very same Black Death that had constituted the pandemic in London in 1660 which consumed the lives of 68,000, the city only being saved by the Great Fire. The Filth Disease, transmitted by the fleas that infest the bodies of sick rats and leave them the moment they are about to die. And from the sick rats, the virus spreads by the fleas to lice and ants . . . and humans.

They used to tip household refuse in what the Sanitary Department called back court shelters. The tenants called them middens, that being one of the many descriptive words the Norse Invaders had brought and left. In the midden shelters were deep galvanised cans into which the spillage went from houses. But there was rarely room enough in them for the refuse of the sixteen or more families from the one tenement which they served. And the pans of ashes from the house fires which burned all day and much of the night, food waste and often lavatory slops, because there weren't sufficient water closets to cope with the crush of humanity packed into the tiny tenement homes, would all pile up and overflow over the midden cans. Often they would smoulder giving off the most evil smells as the combustible ashes cooked the rotting garbage around them.

The neighbourhood dogs would scour the middens for bones and scraps, and the bigger dogs knew that if they put their front paws on the edge of the tall cans they could unbalance them to scatter the contents and make their search easier. When they left, the cats had their share. And at night when the restless still of a Gorbals night settled on them, the mice and rats would scurry in the human jetsam.

Such middens weren't confined to the Gorbals. It was the standard system of waste disposal throughout Glasgow. But like everything else because of the gross overcrowding of the area, it was more of a problem there.

They say the plague never ever goes away. It's always there, a sleeping volcano of disease, waiting to erupt. There were ample conditions for its return after London had been cleansed by the Great Fire. But despite the squalor of the poor in more than a dozen cities of Britain through Dickensian times and after, it wasn't to reappear . . . until 1900. And then it chose Scotland. The community in Scotland was to be of its biggest city, Glasgow. And it was to be among the people of the Gorbals, the most deprived part of that city. And that part of the Gorbals where the deadly bacillus was to re-emerge after a hibernation of 220 years was to be . . . Florence Street, or, to be precise, the original part of the street, called Rose Street at the time. Before they could identify it—for the plague was the last of the fevers the doctors suspected—the seeds had been scattered and the virus was raging. From Rose Street to Thistle Street, then to Oxford Lane, back again to Thistle Street, to nearby Mathieson Street, down into South Coburg Street and South Wellington Street, then to Cook Street, back to Rose Street and its newer extension, Florence Street. Before the autumn of the year had cooled into the darkening days of winter, thirty-six had died and well over 100 were badly affected. And the shame of the plague that returned to the Gorbals was to linger for years.

Number 17 Florence Street was only two closes away from one of the houses where there had been the plague. John Lynch and his wife Lizzie had got their first home there. John, born in 1888, was one of the two sons and three daughters born to James and Rebecca Lynch who had come to the Gorbals from Carnamoyle in Donegal. John's brother in law was John Kilcoyne, whose parents also came from Ireland, and they were mates. John Kilcoyne helped him get a job in the railway as a line surfaceman and, when he married Lizzie Hunter, tipped him off that there was a house to let up the same close as him at No 17 Florence Street.

John Lynch was a man's man. He loved his family, but he loved the comradeship of the pub. When some of his mates told him there was another chance of mateship in what they did with their spare time—

volunteers in the Army Reserve—John joined the finest regiment in which any Glasgow man could belong, the Highland Light Infantry, Glasgow's Own, as a spare time soldier.

The Lynch's already had a son James, named after his Donegal grandfather, when a second son was pulled from his mother's womb in their little single-roomed house in Florence Street on April 2, 1913, a typical early-spring day, with the rainshowers falling warmer than the chilling ones they had known the month before. They called him Benjamin John, after his mother's father and own father's names.

April, 1913, and Western Europe was plunging towards the depravity to be known as The Great War. Mrs Pankhurst was fighting for female emancipation; an early urban terrorist, she was in court on April 1 for trying to blow up Lloyd George at Walton Heath. The Royal Navy desperately needed men and were appealing for recruits as stokers at a wage of forty shillings and ten pence per week . . . plus a free outfit. The colonies needed people too and there were fares to Australia at special rates, £3 for domestic servants, £7 if you were a "British lad" and £14 for artisans. The Donaldson Line, on the other hand, could take you to Canada "in great comfort" for £6 and five shillings. In Glasgow there was tremendous talk among the sporting community about the big contest in the Savoy Theatre between Keni Omaru, champion of Japan, and Tarro Miyake, in what was billed as the "sensational challenge for the ju-jitsu championship of the world"; Harland and Wolff of Belfast revealed their plans for their big new extension in Glasgow; That Coloured Five, "a quartette of delightful harmonions" were at the Alhambra and the incomparable Whit Cunliff "the premier light comedian" was packing them in at the Pavilion. And Benny Lynch, neatly in position, emerged from his very first battle.

Despite the number of children already up the close and in the other closes nearby, it was always a great occasion when another arrived. They would wet its head, as they would say, with a stone jar of whisky and bring jugs of beer, frothing and jawping, from the pub at the corner.

The fourteen tenants at number 17 Florence Street who celebrated the birth were the average Irish-Scots mix for the Gorbals, as their names told . . . Muir, Donnelly, McGinty, Watson, Currie, Gow, McGrath, Carolan, Rodgers, McArdle, McLellan, Kilcoyne and Lynch.

But the long years of the war and John's absence in the H.L.I. was the beginning of the end of the Lynch's as a complete family unit. On his return from active service John, like so many others, had great difficulty in becoming a good family man. The mates he had served with seemed better company that being at home. Lizzie, an attractive dark-haired woman, tired of her husband's neglect and his drinking, and heavily depressed after the accidental death through choking of their third child, a daughter, began to be seen with a merchant seaman called George Robertson.

John Lynch and his family were now living in Cumberland Lane, a warren of even poorer houses, built like several other similar rows in the Gorbals, behind rows of other houses. Their only outlook was the rear of the houses behind which they were hidden. They were a ghetto within a ghetto. Being a member of the Lane community was like being in a very special clan. For they were apart from everyone else. To get access to them you had to enter what they called a "thru-gaun" close, a close which had direct access from Cumberland Street through to the lane houses at the rear. There were also small pends which led to the lane from Wellcroft Place and Eglinton Street.

Although John Lynch had been drinking heavily and neglecting his family, that was his business, thought the people of the Lane; many of the other men did likewise and it was accepted. Anyway, wasn't it as good an escape route as any from the miseries that life could bring in the Lane and the Gorbals? Drinking they understood. And tolerated. But infidelity was sin. And they had already shown their feelings on that subject when Johnny Lynch's drinking mate George Robertson had begun paying more attention to Lizzie than to Johnny Lynch. George was serving with the Clan boats at the time, mainly on their short runs to America and back and, like most seamen, when he returned there were a few weeks wages to be spent before signing on for another trip. His attentions on young Lizzie Lynch were sacrilege to those who lived in the Lane. And, on one of his visits, when John Lynch was at work, their ire overflowed. Matters like this were for the women to sort out. There was an impromptu gathering of them when Robertson was in the house and their concern for the propriety of family agitated them so that they were transformed in to a pack of screaming Celtic warrior women. They were going to kill Robertson, they yelled. They were shouting it not as a threat or as a measure of their anger . . . but because they really were going to kill him.

The unfortunate man had answered the door to them after they had charged up the stairs to the Lynch house. He was bleeding badly about the head as they pulled him down the stairs for a lynching. Two men from the Lane, Daddy Hynes and Joe Shields, heard the screams of the women and, quickly assessing the position, went to the aid of the bewildered and battered suitor. They had understood the feelings of the women, but killing Robertson wasn't the way to help Lizzie Lynch. Hynes and Shields were successful in their rescue attempt, and Robertson escaped never to return to the Lane again.

Young Jimmy and Benny Lynch liked living in the Lane. Children don't notice things like decay and squalor; their world is play. In a corner of the big yard where they played was a horse dung heap, the overnight emptyings from the bowels of the seventeen horses in P.L. Robertson's stables being added to it every morning, releasing big clouds of stinking steam when they up-ended the wheelbarrow that brought the loads from the stables. The dung heap, and the various activities surrounding it, were just one of the fascinations of the Lane for the children. So too were the sparks that used to jump and bounce when the men were hammering out the long lassoes of molten steel as they forged chains in the smiddy's shop; and the bustling chores of the white-aproned workers who were employed in A.W. Robertson's, the cabinetmakers; and old Dodd the Englishman who would line up the products of his special trade . . . coffins. And besides all that, there were plenty of games to be played, one of the best of them being to get an old rope and put it round the four poles, set in a square which the wives used as a drying green. With a rope round it like that, it looked for all the world to them like a real boxing ring and they could have their very own champion of Scotland fights . . . Benny and Jimmy, Tony and Jack Kilcoyne, Josie Tohill, some of the Kelter boys, and lots of others.

It wasn't long after the incident with the women and Robertson that Lizzie left home. She went to live with him in Blackburn Street, one of several long streets of uniform tenements behind the deep basins and quays of the Prince's Docks in Govan. Johnny had to get someone to look after the boys. There were never any shortage of helpers for things like that in the Gorbals. It was common among the over-crowded for the older children to go and live with a granny or aunt or someone they called granny or aunt. Hard times nurtured a special compassion for children and they would be willingly taken in if there was a time of need by relatives or friends. Brother-in-law John Kilcoyne, who had moved from Florence Street to live at 117 Hospital Street, two flights up in a room-and-kitchen which they shared with their seven children, Rebecca, Helen, Tony, Jackie, John, Peggy and James came to the rescue.

Despite their numbers they didn't flinch at taking in another two. The boys in the family thought it a great scheme. It made their gang all the bigger. In the summer months when they were off school they could go on long jaunts together. For just three pence, a penny there a penny back and a penny to spend, they could take the long tram ride on the blue tram which went all the way to Renfrew, the furthest place they knew from the Gorbals, so far that they passed real fields with real cows in them and others with haystacks. And when they got to Renfrew they could play on the broad slipway of the chain ferry which clanked to and forth across the river to Yoker. Getting a few pennies together for such trips was no great problem for the enterprising. There was a penny back on the brown screwtop beer bottles, but you had to take them to the right pub, particularly if they had their name stamped on the label which most of them did. There was money back on ginger bottles too. They knew the houses where the women would make use of them for running errands. And if you were up early on a Saturday morning and were first to call at the Jews' houses you could light their housefires. It was against their religious laws to use any form of labour on their Saturday Sabbath and even though that same law decreed that "neither shall your man-servant labour" they could always make some compromises. "Well," they could argue, "we don't seek them out and hire them. They come to our doors and they come in voluntarily to light our fires. Are we to refuse a nice gesture like that?" And in their hearths, a penny would always be placed for the firelighter. The Lynchs and Kilcoynes knew most of the Jewish families, particularly the ones where they could light a Sabbath fire.

The Jews were easy to spot. For their names were nothing like an Irish or Scottish name. There were the Kilbronskies and Yedds, Boxenbauns and Myers, Yonaces and Nathans, Rosenheims and Ranusys; Shears, Saffers and Shoskeys; Greenblats, Gelfers, Geneens, Gancheroffs, Gruebergs and Goodmans. And at number 3 Abbotsford Place it seemed that everyone was Jewish . . . Yankal Chitkin, Joseph Sherman, Isaac Goldberg, Leon Simons, Joseph Rubinstein, Millicent Blint and Sarah Kersh. But you never knocked on the door of David Jacobs. For he was the rabbi and he would wait till sunset when their laws said the Sabbath was over.

Number 117 Hospital Street was one of the best closes in the whole street for children. Any of them would have told you that. For at the mouth of the close there was Gallacher's sweet shop, full of all the wonders of the sweety world, a multi-coloured panorama of big glass jars with every conceivable sugared delicacy. The mono-chromatic life of the Gorbals stopped at the door of Gallacher's little shop. Inside, it seemed, they were immediately transported to another world, an Aladdin's Cave of coloured treasures which they could chew, crunch, suck, lick, hold on sticks, draw through straws, mix with water and drink, or allow to remain motionless on their tongues until they melted in a sugary swallow.

There were wagon wheels, white with coloured spokes and in varying flavours, fishes in ice, mint oblongs embedded with a tiny confectionary fish; ogo-pogo eyes, hard and highly flavoured and if you took them out of your mouth once a minute they had changed colour and so had your tongue; rhubarb rock, red and green, great for sucking, but if you let any of the juice drip on your dress they said it was stained forever; conversation lozenges, fun for the couplets and good, mammy said, if you had a cold; there were bullseyes and yellowmen, gobstoppers and soor plooms, so soor they would clap your jaws together, tiger nuts and cherry lips, sojers buttons and rosebuds, clove rock and cheugh jean candy, sugarolly pipes and paradise fruits . . . and jelly babies, black being best, red next and the green were horrible. There were sweets that they could do things with, like sherbet in a tube which they sucked through a liquorice straw, liquorice straps they played teacher with until they had eaten them too short to be played with, and cinammon sticks which the girls chewed and the boys smoked in the back close. And some even offered them a game of chance, like lucky bags from which the girls might get a real ring made of polished wire, but if they didn't there were always some dolly mixtures, and gold mines, a macaroon bar which you broke in two before the shopkeeper and if it was pink instead of the usual white you got another one free and they said that one wee boy in the street once got three pink ones in a row, but no one ever knew his name.

Aunty Kilcoyne was a great cook. She made big plates of tripe, but didn't buy her tripe from the man who came round every week with his pony and cart on which there were two cavernous casks filled with white, honeycombed tripe bags swimming in gallons of water like half a street's wash. Among them were the darker reeds, the sweetmeat delicacy cooked with the tripe to give extra flavour. She preferred to buy what she called "dirty bags" . . . unwashed tripe; it was cheaper and when washed at home she swore it tasted much better than the tripe man's. To get the "dirty bags" she had to go to one of the butcher's they called a Benefit Shop, run by retired butchers who were given the right, as a form of pension to be able to collect unwanted offals and cuts at the the slaughterhouse up in Duke Street.

When she made stew, she would eke out a small cut of meat by putting doughballs in the pot and in the middle of each ball she would stick a link sausage and everyone voted that was the best dinner of all . . . and not one of them would dare touch a bit of it till Father Kilcoyne came home from work.

Maw Kelter was something of an institution around her area in the Gorbals. The Kelters, Maw and her fourteen children, lived in Wellcroft Place, on the other side of Cumberland Lane from Cumberland Street. They had come to Glasgow from Johnstone in

Renfrewshire. Unlike the old woman who lived in a shoe, Maw Kelter knew what to do with so many children. Her house was alive with the sound of laughter and happiness and with some of them left to be married, taking on another two mouths was no problem to her. So the Lynch boys moved from the aunt and uncle's in Hospital Street to Wellcroft Place, back to the vicinity of the Lane. It was like being home again.

During the day they played all the old games. Jimmy and Benny showed the Wellcroft boys how to play bangers, better bangers than they had ever played before, better even than getting together ten of the little red percussion caps and exploding them under a cobblestone. "What you do," Jimmy and Benny told them, "is to buy sulphur tablets at your chemist's, you get a fair bag of them for a penny. If the chemist asks what they were for just say they're for your maw to make treacle and sulphur to get rid of your pimples." The trick with the sulphur tablets was to put them on a flat slate two at a time, then from a dyke drop a brick, or better still a causey, on them and you got a bang and smoke just like a real shell in the war.

They chased girls and if boys from other streets came to their place they would chase them as well, unless they were much bigger. Sometimes they would wander to far away streets in the Gorbals, like Raeburn and Mathieson Streets, where they said there were some real bad boys; or on big adventures they would wander all the way along Caledonia Road, past the big graveyard that was behind the high wall, and into Rutherglen Road by which time they were out of the Gorbals and into Oatlands and a few hundred yards up the road on the left was the Richmond Park, on the banks of the Clyde, where there were swings and roundabouts and a big pond into which you could throw stones, till the Parkie chased you. Other boys would come to the Richmond Park to play from the other side of the Clyde, from Dalmarnock and Bridgeton and some of the boys who came from there were real bad boys too for they used to shout "Hey whit religion are you . . . Proddie or a Pape?" They would shout that if they knew you were from the Gorbals and if Pape was the answer you gave them then you had to make sure you had a good start or else you would get a "doing". The boys would often return to Wellcroft Place with their pals showing the scrapes of their infant conflicts.

"Hey, daeye know," said one of their gang one day. "Ah know where ye can get real fights in a real boxing ring and they gie ye real boxing gloves . . . an' lessons an' a'." The magic place he told them was St John's Boys' Guild. St John's R.C. church was one of the three parish chapels in the Gorbals which tended the spiritual and other needs of the 30,000 of the faith, mainly of Irish origin, who lived in the area. The chapel was in Portugal Street but the nearest it could get premises for the boys' guild was in Dale Street, in neighbouring Tradeston and given to them by James Henderson, horse hirer and funeral undertaker.

The priest in charge of St John's was Canon Ryan, a Limerick man. It was whispered and, at that, only to those you could trust, that just a few years before, the greatest of all the Irish rebels, Eamonn de Valera, had come to Glasgow when he was on the run after his sensational escape from Lincoln Jail. Stole the wax from old candles in the jail's sacristy, so he did, and made an impression of the chaplain's key from which a copy was made to free him. And when he came to Glasgow, said the whisperers who said they knew, he was looked after at St John's and by members of the Major John McBride Sinn Fein Club.

Working with Canon Ryan at St John's were four young curates. One of them was a Father James Fletcher, a tall, fair-haired and fresh-complexioned man from Flemington, Motherwell. The young boys of the district were his concern; the streets were virtually their only outlet for sport and recreation. Their great loves were football and boxing. If they played football in the streets they would be chased by the police and it was a five or ten shilling fine if you were caught. Whatever pastimes they had in the street had to be of their own creation. Father Fletcher argued that they had to have an outlet, something that would appeal to their outgoing nature, to satisfy their inherent aggression, a sport that they loved. There was no difficulty in choosing that pursuit for it was the one he loved himself and had demonstrated that amply at college where they told him he looked like becoming a better pugilist than priest.

After they got the premises in Dale Street, they converted it into a hall for the League of the Cross, their temperance movement. After morning mass the men would walk to the League Hall for their card schools, solo and pontoons, where they would play until four o'clock sharp. The wives had the Sunday dinner ready then, thick broth with barley and dried peas, and an ashet steak pie on top of which sat two inches of flaky pastry, if they were lucky that was and mistress was a good housekeeper, a piece of boiled mutton with bottle sauce and bread and butter if she wasn't.

St John's had no funds to buy equipment for the Guild's new boxing club. But that didn't daunt the easygoing young priest. He toured the police barracks and police stations and told them about his great plan to help the boys which not only would get them off the street but would save the police a lot of harassment. They responded

and vans turned up with surplus gear from the constabulary . . .
bucks and horses, straw mats, punch bags, skipping ropes. A
sawmiller helped with some wood and he enrolled the top joiners
from the parish. When they were finished Father Fletcher could boast
that they had one of the best boxing rings in the whole of Glasgow.
Champions like Tommy Milligan and Johnny McMillan plus a string
of old-timers came along to show the boys what real boxing was like.

"That's a good boy," they would often say. "Good sized boy. Well
proportioned. Has the makings of a lightweight one day. Look at his
natural style. That'll help keep him out of trouble. What did you say
his name was?"

"He's Lynch," would be the reply. "James Lynch. From Wellcroft
Place. Has a brother that comes too, as well as cousins . . . the
Kilcoyne boys. Tony's very good."

Young Johnny McGrory was another of the boys that they said
would be good one day. But he had terrible problems with his nose.

"Hey Father, that's my nose bleeding again," he would appeal to
Father Fletcher.

"Don't worry, son. I'll bet you that after it bleeds another dozen
times it'll be as hard as that ring post there and won't bleed again."

History was to show the wisdom of the advice.

Father Fletcher would join them regularly in the ring and
encourage them to try and break through his long arm defence and it
was a great victory for anyone who could score with a connection.

Two of the eleven-year-olds were so small and skinny they looked
comical with their big gloves on, even though it was the smallest pair
they could find. But they would provide tremendous scraps. They
fought regularly together and a crowd would always gather to watch
them, particularly when someone nicknamed them the Mighty
Midgets. One was Tony Kilcoyne. The other was his cousin from
Wellcroft Place, Benny Lynch, brother of the bigger boy James who
they said had a good future in the sport.

Some of the men at the Guild told the boys that they would be a
great turn at the booths . . . and they would even get paid for
scrapping the way they did over a couple of rounds. Tom Berry, the
old cruiserweight champion, had a booth in a tent in the same street as
the club and he invited them to put on a match there one night.
Unlike at the club, they wore no vests for this was a paid match . . .
they were professionals. People laughed at the Mighty Midgets when
they took to the ring before the programmed bouts but at the end of
their two-round exhibition there were cries of appreciation as they
demonstrated that not only had they courage but they had skills
enough to feint and weave. Even their footwork was accomplished.

Meanwhile James Lynch progressed with the amateurs at St John's Boys' Guild so much that one of the instructors suggested he go on to another club nearby, one which had a reputation of being among the finest of its kind in Scotland, the L.M.S. Rovers Boxing Club, an affiliate of one of Britain's biggest private railway companies, the London, Midland and Scottish. It was a thriving club and was well used by the railwaymen, the steam engine stokers who were called firemen, trainee drivers and the locomotive tradesmen who worked at the huge depot known as the Polmadie Sheds. The competition at the Rovers was fierce by comparison to St John's but James Lynch's style, cool and poised and his excellent balance showed them that he had the makings of a fine boxer. Guy Adams, a former British amateur lightweight champion and a platform cleaner at the Central Station, was one of the leading trainers at the Rovers, and he gave James special coaching, particularly after one fight he had. His opponent was an engine driver called Alex Lyons, an experienced battler and, on form, he should have dispensed with his younger rival. But because of his deft foot work, Lyons struggled and punch after punch missed its target. But the older man knew other tricks. After the fight, Guy Adams told the young Lynch, "Don't worry about it, son. He took liberties with you . . . that's why he was grabbing you. It was to keep you still so that he could get a swipe at you. He knew you were the better boxer."

At home and at the Boys' Guild, James would pass on all his lessons to wee brother Benny. "Listen, Benny," he would tell him. "Just mind, when you're in the ring, you're no' having a scrap like you do in the street. Don't worry, I know what you're like. I've heard about you having a go in the street. But that's not the kind of fighting you do when you're a boxer. You've got to take it easier. Study your opponent. You've got to pick every punch so that when you send it on the way it connects. You've got to develop your timing. You've got to get your accuracy dead on. And you've got to get a right good defence. Right . . . now watch me again. That's it wee man, you're learning fast. Maybe you'll be as good as your big brother one day. Aye, that'll be right." They laughed together as they sparred and James made feints which would make Benny miss wildly and that would be another joke between them.

Benny had never known real sadness till the day they told him that his brother James was ill in hospital. He didn't understand the long word they told him that was the trouble with James. All he knew was everyone's faces were all sad, especially Maw Kelter; for she had become their very own Maw. The older ones knew the meaning of that word. They knew that when the doctors said that about anyone, particularly a younger person, they rarely came back from the hospital. It was . . . meningitis; inflammation of the membranes which envelop the brain. It had developed in James after he had suffered a head injury in a fall at his work, Babcock and Wilcox in Renfrew where he was an apprentice boilermaker. Benny hadn't even been this sad when his mother had left home for he had been too young then to realise what that meant, although James realised what she had done and it had made him resentful to the point of bitterness.

It was Benny's first experience of a death in the family. He had heard about death a lot; schoolpals had taken fevers with strange names and never come back to school again. And playpals in the street would often suddenly disappear from their daily activities, victims of one of the dreaded diseases which were rife over the city in which more children died than any other community in Britain. But never had anyone he loved died. This was a new experience, an experience his young mind had difficulty in fully appreciating. How could it be that James would not return? He had been there only yesterday and they played together; now they were telling him he would never be back; never.

The world just wasn't the same without his best pal and brother. Even the boxing was different; it wasn't fun any more. So he didn't go back. His days as an amateur boxer were over. Who needed silly old boxing anyway? Why should he have to obey all their rules and regulations and do all that training just to have a fight? If he wanted a fight he could always get one in the street. You didn't need any rules or regulations there. Neither did you have to train. And there was never any shortage of challenges in the long black gorges of the Gorbals.

They called it a "claim" if a feud, whether individual or collective, was to merit physical violence. Anything could lead to a "claim" and often did . . . petty rivalries or jealousies over a girl or their ability as a ballroom dancer; the territorial rights of one group over another or tit-for-tat warfare between certain groups, the origins of which had been obscured by time. Religious bigotry was always a reason for a "claim." If you were Catholic then that was as good a reason as any to many young Protestants to give a man a kicking . . . or worse. And it was the same in reverse. The folly of religion was its division of mankind, and they were wont to keep it that way.

It was in Surrey Lane, a narrow and rough-cobbled alley between Surrey and Nicholson Streets, that the cry went up one evening as Benny and some chums were walking home. It was a "claim" and the one word that the others called let them know what kind of claim it was going to be.

"PAPES."

The gang came in on them from all directions and they were outnumbered. The scuffles between them were short and furious; bare-knuckle and in with the boot if you fell to the screams of "Papish Bastards". They fought from one side of the lane to the other, some with their backs to the wall, others rolling on the uneven cobbles. They punched and butted and booted and a knife was flashed. Two were pummelling at one against the door of a storeroom. Three surrounded another, flailing at him with fist and feet. The speed and ferocity of it had never been seen in any boxing ring. The occasional word erupted from them as they scrambled and fought. "Bastard! . . . Frank! . . . Fucker! . . . Get him! . . . He's a chib! . . . Benny!"

Windows went up from the rear of the tenements which looked down on the lane and there were screams from the women in them.

"Messins." "Messin bastarts." "Polis."

Some men ran from the houses towards the mêlée but as suddenly as it had started, it was over, the attackers melting into the dimness of the approaching night.

Benny and his friends checked with each other to see if any of them had been seriously hurt. None were. Two had nosebleeds, others had cuts and bruises, but nothing really serious. "What's up with your face?" one of them asked Benny. "Your cheek . . . your right cheek." He put his hand to it and only then did he feel the stinging pain and the sticky wetness that stained his hand red. "You've been chibbed, Benny. Christ, looks bad an' a'. You better get it fixed."

It was just superficial, however, and didn't need the grotesque patchwork of the gut sutures and the ugly scars they left. "That's terrible," said Maw Kelter when she bathed his face with a big piece of pink lint then dabbed the long gash with iodine which made him jerk with pain. "My God, boy, you're gonnie be scarred for life. Terrible, so it is, a' this fightin'."

There were other fights. Sometimes he was as innocent as that night in Surrey Lane. Other times he wasn't so innocent. There was one in a picture house. Another in a Lane outside a picture house. And the Busies caught him for that one. It was Paddy Docherty and some of the other friends he had met at the Boys' Guild and the LMS Rovers that prevailed on him after he was fined ten shillings in court for street fighting. It hurt when someone asked what Jimmy would have said had he known about him. The more he thought about that, the more it hurt for he knew big brother would have been angry. The memory of the good times they had in the clubs and the various venues where they had boxed flooded back.

"Study your opponent, Benny . . . get your accuracy right . . . you've got to have a good defence as well." It seemed like it was just yesterday when James was saying those words to him. He fought back the tears as he thought of the old days, but no one was allowed to see the emotion; a man didn't do that.

"Tell you what," Benny told his friends. "You can keep your amateur boxing. If I'm gonnie fight, it's for money. Right . . . I'll meet you for training."

6

Tash the Sage

Tash Conlin was one of the sages of the Gorbals. The jokesters, pranksters, patter-merchants, idlers and victims of the depression may have prevailed, but amidst them, like diamonds in the coalheap, were the thinkers and the philosophers. Tash Conlin was one of the best of them.

Tash was from Florence Street . . . Florence Street when it was called Rose Street. His parents had come from there too and before that they had come from Ireland, he knew not where except it had been in the south because he was only an infant when they died. Tash's close was number 188 Florence Street, just two closes down from the Moy Bar at the corner of Cumberland Street. Across the road, and up to the right in the part they called "higher Florence Street" lived one of his contemporaries, Johnny Lynch. Few remembered how Tash got his name. His real name was Henry. But as a teenager in the height of the Edwardian fashion for moustaches, he had appeared at the corner, after hiding himself away for three weeks in order to cultivate it, sporting a heavy shadow of the stylish shape on his upper lip. "Christ, look at the 'tash," said one of the corner boys. Henry shaved it off within the week. But the name stuck. And he was Tash for evermore. Even his wife Mary called him Tash. And when her brothers and sisters got husbands and wives they called him Tash and when they had children they called him Uncle Tash.

Tash knew everyone in Florence Street, particularly the Lynch's because Johnny Lynch and he had served out of the same depot of the Highland Light Infantry at Greendyke Street, by the Green. They were in different battalions, however, Johnny being in the 7th, Tash in the 3/9th (Glasgow Highlanders). And when he returned from the war he had but one simple ambition which was to be his destiny, and one which he found relatively easy to fulfil . . . never to work again.

Tash and his family lived in a big house for the street . . . three apartments. Nine of them lived in it. There was Tash's wife Mary, a petite and attractive brunette who had lost her figure after the birth of her third son Joseph. Mary rolled cigars in Mitchells, the big tobacco factory up in the Alexandra Parade and, like the majority of working women at the time, dressed sombrely, usually in black, over which she would wrap a dark brown plaid shawl, the same one she had used to carry her three sons, and she read tea cups. "Don't drink it a'," she would say if you asked her to read your cup. "Leave a wee tate in it." Then she would swirl the contents round, place a saucer on top till the leaves settled and then slowly drain off the last of the liquid. She would then gaze into the cup with a long, unblinking stare until she found what she called her "shapes". She could see all kinds of shapes from the formations of the little leaves, An anchor told her all sorts of things. If it was at the bottom of the cup then you were going to have a good sea voyage. If it was at the top of the cup then you would be constant in love and affection. But if there were little specks around it, the opposite would be the case. And if she saw the cross she would mutter only to herself for the cross was the sign of suffering and if it was in a certain place in the cup then woe betide you.

Although her figure had gone, Mary was still proud of her appearance and every Friday night she would wash and wave her black, greying hair. "Friday night is Amami night," said the advertisments. Amami, however, was a luxury she couldn't afford. But she did have her genuine Marcel irons—"made only by the Maison Pelleray, Paris"—which she had saved for and bought herself when the overtime had been good. She called them her tongs and heated them on the big gas ring which sat on the range in her kitchen. She was an expert with her tongs and could tell by sniffing them if they were at the right temperature; lesser experts used the torn corner of a newspaper and if the paper singed too quickly they were too hot and that could frizzle your hair and cause split ends. Mary had kept the same hair style since she had met Tash, a flat bandeau with oblique waves either side of a ruler-straight centre parting. And she would carefully tong each succeeding wave, pressing them finally into place with her fingers.

Mary and Tash and their three sons lived in a single kitchen room with a recess bed at one end of the house. At the other end of the house in a similar kitchen room with recess bed lived Mary's mother and father. Mother was called Maw and she dressed in the same late nineteenth century style as all the older women did, a long black dress, which covered the laced bootees she wore.

Maw's pride was her stove. Every house in Florence Street and the Gorbals had its stove which was known as a range. Maw's range was typical . . . about four feet long with hotplates, ashcan and draught flue. Maw's range breathed and lived. There was always a kettle on it at near boil and she only had to move it an inch nearer one of the hotplates and its long spout would shoot out a long trail of steam; at the other side, on a cooler part, was her ever-present soup pot; and ashes, white and powdery, would regularly drift down together with the occasional red-hot piece to clank in the oblong pan beneath the grate. Maw polished her range every morning with zebo from its orange-striped can kept with the polishing cloths in an old shoebox beneath the jawbox by the window. She would rub the various lettering on it so that the stainless steel glistened. The boys had learned their alphabet on these letters, first the big ones on the top of the stove which said "The Improvement Range" and the other ones at the foot of the oven door, its polished hinges picked out likewise from the zebo-ed black, and which were the names of the maker . . . Smith and Wellswood, Dixon Street, Glasgow.

Father was Auld Jake. Jake McNulty, white moustached and tattooed, an anchor on one arm, a dagger on the other, had finished his seagoing days on the last of the wool clippers on their fast and arduous runs to Geelong and back. After that he had worked in the docks but had been involved in whisky stealing and was sacked after being jailed for reset. Except for a twice a week visit to the Moy, Jake just sat by the fire, spending much of his time fussing with his clay pipe, cutting and rubbing the treacly thick black tobacco from a plug and mothering it lit with long wax tapers he kept in a wooden box nailed to the wall by the side of the range. Auld Jake was King. No one spoke to him, not even Maw, unless he spoke first. He was Chief Sitting Bull and from him, chairbound in old age, there emitted an awesome image of fearsome authority.

Mary's three sons would often play through in Maw's but would scurry back again to their own kitchen when Auld Jake's pipe made him cough and splutter and finally retch into the spitoon which sat on the floor by the right side of his chair and which Maw, placid, uncomplaining Maw, washed out for him twice a day; and if anyone had the temerity to ask Jake why she did a chore like that he would have bristled . . . "that's a wumman's job."

Maw and Jake had another son and daughter, Hughie and Nellie, both in their late thirties. Hughie was mentally handicapped but if anyone asked what was wrong with him they were told, simply . . . "He's daft." Hughie loved to be asked the time and no matter when he was asked it he would give the one reply, "Ten by six." And Mary's boys would tease him when the big brass-pendulum wall clock above Auld Jake's chair got to ten past six. They would shout, "Hey, Hughie, c'mon 'n tell us the time" and he would grin and chortle and drivel at the mouth as he repeated over and over to them "Ten by six . . . ten by six . . . ten by six . . ."

Hughie slept in a recess bed in the passageway between the two kitchens. His sister, Nellie, slept in the little room facing on to the street and called "the front room". Nellie was physically handicapped, but they called her "crippled". Nellie never left the house. She had been the victim of one of the fevers which had regularly flushed through the Gorbals leaving scores of dead and maimed in their wake.

The war had devastated Tash Conlin. He had been one of the first volunteers during the heady rash of patriotism in the early months of the war and prior to the National Registration Act of 1915 which meant that the men no longer had a choice of regiment. He had read the block advertisements in the *Daily Record* about recruitment and they had appealled to him.

They had read: "The surest way to see service is to join the Glasgow Highlanders . . . at once." They had a sense of urgency about them and didn't lecture the point. Seeing service, as they said, could be a great adventure. Besides, Tash was a conscientious man. He regularly read the newspapers in the library and his conclusion had been that this was a just war and the more men like him who flocked to it the more it would help preserve the great democracy in which they lived. The newspapers had said that too.

Lord Rosebery's recruiting speech, which he had also read in the *Record*, was another inspiration. "In a few weeks, if you enrol you may all be heroes . . . and you will be a hero for the rest of your lives." Tash was no fighting man and being a hero was the furthest thing from his mind. Tash liked the quiet life; to talk and philosophise. He took great pride in his work as a boilermaker in Dubb's at Polmadie, locomotive makers to the world and whose products caused generations of South Side children to gape in wonderment when, after their final polish, and atop countless wheeled bogies, they were rolled out, like the Great Horse of Troy, through the massive gateway of the works at Aikenhead Road on their way to the docks for shipment. Days like that made Tash feel really proud, having helped make such a beautiful monster. But Tash was also a patriot and he believed his country really did need him. He had obeyed Rosebery's call and become a volunteer in the Glasgow Highlanders. And when he marched with the other men from the Gorbals and from throughout the city, thousands of them, on the big recruiting parade which went all the way from Kelvingrove Park through crowds cheering all the way to the saluting base in George Square, it had been one of the proudest days of his life. Maybe he really would be a hero for the rest of his life. He didn't have to wait long to find out.

It was Fair Friday, 1916, at a place near Fricourt in France that Tash Conlin and the men of the 3/9th went into their first major offensive. They marched past Crucifix Corner, through the Valley of Death to a place called the High Wood and the order was to wrest it from the Germans.

Other regiments had been trying to get control of the High Wood and their dead and injured lay all about. The Glasgow Highlanders were marched so close to their target they could hear the Germans shouting taunts at them . . . "Come and get us boys." Then the order was given as they stood on the duckboards of their long dusty trenches . . . "Fix bayonets". Suddenly they were up and over and running towards the High Wood.

The Glasgow Highlanders lost more than 400 men and twenty-one officers in the first thirty hours of that attack on High Wood and trainloads of them, muddied and bloodied, were taken straight back to Glasgow where they arrived before the end of the Fair holiday, all of them destined for the city's hospitals and infirmaries, unfit ever to be heroes again.

Tash was lucky not to be one of them. His luck was that he was to survive the war with only superficial wounds, none of them warranting his withdrawal from action. He went right through the Somme offensive with the 3/9th and spent almost two years in the trenches. Two years of a kind of torture he never thought existed. Their kilts froze in the winter and cut weals into their legs. They lost comrades who drowned in the fertile loam that had been churned into bottomless battlefield quagmires. And when the fighting was at its pitch and the graves squads weren't operating they had watched the packs of rats gnawing at the bodies of dead comrades. He had seen men go berserk with what they called shellshock; he had watched the others who hadn't gone berserk but became mumbling cretins, driven out of their minds by a daily routine that had no variation, just death and dying, carnage and horror.

When the final shot had been fired, Tash and the men of the 3/9th dressed in their Full Service Marching Order for the last time and were taken back to Greendyke Street from the station where they got the command "Square turn to the right" for the ultimate dismiss.

"I'm back," he said to Mary and Maw and Jake when he returned to Florence Street that day. "Aye, I'm back. And yer Lord whit's-his-name said I'd be a hero for the rest of my life when I came back. Well that's just what I'm gonnie be. A hero. Aye, a right hero. I'm gonnie

hing oot o' that window there for the rest of my days. That's the way
I'm gonnie be a hero."

Hinging was a Glasgow custom. In France a man could watch the
world go by from a seat at the corner cafe. In other places they could
loaf on sidewalks or on the verandah. But in Glasgow they had a
window on the world; a tenement window which looked on to the
street. They would raise the window, put an uncased pillow or a
velour cushion on the sill on which to rest their elbows and pass the
time of day with a "hing". Some only did their "hing" at week-ends,
or on long summer nights. Some did it in pairs, arms folded as they
were neat for space at a single window and so tightly crammed
together that they appeared Siamese-like; if they had a double
window, they would be at either side of the dividing pillar, but as
close to each other as possible so that they could converse; some
would knit and hing; read and hing; peel the potatoes and pod the
peas and hing; do crosswords and study Gary Owen and hing; some
would have a hing so regularly that if they weren't at their window,
the street would take on another appearance, as though some vital
part had been obliterated.

True to his vow, Tash Conlin spent some part of every day of the
rest of his life having a hing. The remainder of his time he spent
either with the boys at the corner, at the libraries in Norfolk and
McNeil Streets, and occasionally up town at the Mitchell, or, if he had
the money, in the Moy Bar.

No one, not even Mary, ever questioned the fact that he had
decided never to work again, except for a few weeks in December
when he got a job as a temporary postman to get some extra money
for the Ne'erday drink. He never once spoke about his time as a
Glasgow Highlander or about the war, except when he debated
religion—a subject he relished. Tash had gone to the war a Catholic
and returned an atheist. "The chaplains and padres came round a'
pious telling us God was on our side, an' a few yards away the
Gerries had their ministers telling them the same thing and there's
the pair o' us exterminating one another. What kind of God is that?"
His other favourite subjects were politics, world, social and local
history, all of which he studied when he went to the libraries. The
corner boys would listen intently when Tash spoke for they knew he
had read books and had knowledge about things and events which
were way beyond their ken. Tash knew everything there was to know
about the Gorbals. If he was asked about any family, he could relate
their history and genealogy. Like he would if he was asked about the
Lynch's.

"I remember the day they moved into the street, Johnny and his wee wife Lizzie. It was afore the war. No' all that many years after we had the plague. Aye, no' many of you will know that we had the plague, the bubonic plague they call it, here in the South Side and, Christ, where does it have to start . . . right here in our street. I was only ten when it started but I remember enough about it. You know, they say once the plague has been to a place it's always there, just waiting to break out again, the vilest of a' diseases. Well they had it here centuries ago and it must have been lurking about just waiting to erupt given the right conditions. Well, it got these conditions right here, and Christ nae wonder the state some of them kept their middens."

"It started down in the Bogie's house at number 71. The auld Maw was a fish hawker and her man a docker and they had a grandwean lived with them. The wean took it first and the grannie died two days later. They had a wake for the woman and a hundred turned up for it; aye a hundred in their single-end. Christ, ye know what wakes are like. A' the scroungers turn up for they think they'll get a drink . . . 'Oh, ah knew auld Mrs Bogie; awfie fine wumman; awfie sad her dyin' an' a' an' the grandwean as well; aye I'll hae a wee drink if ye insist.' I was at one wake and d'ye know they ended up playing pontoons on the coffin lid and the weans were playing hide-the-shirt-button and putting it in the corpse's hand. Anyway, there they are a' crowded into the Bogie's house looking at the auld Maw and her lying there wi' the plague. Next thing ye know they're a' dropping wi' it. From our street it went to the Molloy family in Thistle Street. They all got it. And more went to their wakes and took it hame to other streets. The Tierneys and McMahons in Oxford Lane got it. There's no a disease like it, I'm telling you. Starts off with a simple fever, then they get the bile . . . no' the green bile or the grey one ye get wi' booze but a pink bile, can ye imagine that, and then they get swellings in their groin and they spread right up your body. They're the swellings that lets them know it's the plague . . . aye, right in there where you get hernia. They call them the buboes."

Tash was proud that he knew such words and would emphasize them by enunciating them slowly and deliberately like "bew-bows" for he knew no one had heard it said before and it made him sound really learned and well read which, comparatively, he was. He would relish going into the horrific details of the disease for they would stand, enraptured at the specifics he would relate, mouths gaping in incredulity that such tortures existed. "D'ye see these bew-bows, well what happens is that the spleen swells up to four times its size in just three days and the glands round about blow up till they're as big as one of they South African oranges and inside there's a pus that eventually comes out and it looks like cauld runny porridge. Then they start rambling like loonies wi' tongues coated in a grey fur gasping for air for they think their bodies are on fire and that's when the fever is at its worst. After that they just snuff it. They go that quick it's just like somebody switching off the electric light. Moaning and groaning and screaming one minute, the next deid as a doornail." As he said this he would snap his fingers to describe the suddenness of that last tortuous moment in the plague victim's life.

"It was auld Doctor Colvin, him from Crown Street next to the toff's school, that first noticed it, they say. Aye, they say if it wasn't for him, there wouldn't be anybody left in the Gorbals. They made him a Knight of St Gregory for his work, so they did."

"My Maw said it was a' the warm weather we had that summer that did it. Too much sunshine, she said. It was bad for you. That's how a' the darkies were aye sick. She also said you would end up in hell if you ate meat on a Friday. What she didnae realise was that we haven't improved our conditions here all that much in the last two hundred years. Christ, they talk about the darkies in the jungle. We get a' the jungle diseases here and don't realise it. We just say 'it's the fever' and that's it. I think it was the same year that Johnny and Lizzie Lynch moved into their house that we had the spotted fever. It started over in Main Street and although the plague was bad, this was ten times worse. Weans died within a day of getting it and before it went away 900 had died. We've had everything in this street . . . sleeping sickness, the scarlet fever, fevers wi' names you couldn't pronounce and typhus, stinking typhus; you know it's in a house when you get the smell of rotten straw. See if a wean survives in'this street to the age of ten without getting any of they fevers and diseases it's got something special about it. Like they Lynch boys. They're a bit special. I know all the weans in this street. When you hing out of a window every day of your life you get to know people like nobody else does, especially the weans. You see them getting put out on the street to play for the first time on their own, some of them can barely walk they're that young."

"And if you study them you can tell what they're going to be like for the rest of their lives. See the greetin' faced ones? Greetin' faced a' their lives, so they are. The wee timid and feart ones are the same. The bullies an' a' . . . plenty of them among the boys, especially the bigger ones. Some tuaregs among the lassies as well, mind you. It's like being a dug breeder watching a litter of pups. He knows the ones he's going to sell . . . and the ones he's going to keep. He studies them for hours when they're at their first play and he spots all the same things. That's how I know the Lynchs. Saw them on their first days out. You could tell Jimmy was going to be a good boy, played well wi' the others and was a good mixer. And wee Benny . . . feart frae nothing. He was wee for his age and some of the bigger boys tried to take a lend of him. He put them right, quick and smart. I saw two boys one day, Danny McAulay and Willie McDougall, both bigger than him, and they tried to do him out of some cigarette cards. They were playing face-or-bluff and ran away with some of Benny's cards. But he caught the pair of them in that shop doorway over there and gave them a wee doing each. Size o' him as well! You would think a boy that could fight like that would be a bully, but he wasn't. But, Christ, was he game! I knew then he would make something. And there he is. Benny Lynch, our first real hero. Aye, *real* hero. Rosebery said we would a' be heroes for the rest of our lives. Who knows us? Naebody. But everybody knows wee Benny. The only thing they knew about the Gorbals or Florence Street before Benny was that we were the arsehole of the country."

"Before Benny, nobody from the Gorbals became world champion of anything. Tommy Lipton and a' the others that became millionaires a' went away and sailed their fancy yachts and nobody knew where they had come from. But everybody knows where the wee man is from. And so what if he does go off the rails now and then? That's between him and his conscience . . . nothing to do wi' anybody. I've heard some of them talk, you know how they talk, that he'll no' do this and he'll no' do that and that he'll end up this way and end up that way. What's that got to do with them? The wee man *has* done it for us . . . gave us more pride than a' the H.L.I. put thegither. and we don't want to forget it."

7

This is the Plan

Sammy Wilson held the long open razor with the yellowing ivory handle that had belonged to his Dad and stared hard at the mirror as he stroked it down his cheeks. "The plan of campaign," he said, staring intently into the mirror, "is this."

Behind him in the new £2.10 shilling suit his new manager had got him the day before in Louis Bloomingfields in the Saltmarket—"Only takes a day to make up a suit, sir, but we've got lots of lovely ones ready made"—stood Benny Lynch. His strong dark hair had the fashionable middle-shed and was combed straight back and cut in a straight bob at his neck. He listened intently as Sammy spoke, his face serious, although even when he was solemn there was still a trace of the impish grin, revealing the boy at heart he always was. His dark Irish brown eyes were fixed on the man in front of him, who had the neckband of his collarless shirt inverted, the top two buttons loosened, as he shaved the night's growth from his long lean face. Although his mother had left him when he was young, Benny had always loved her, unlike Jimmy who, being older and more sensitive had taken her desertion much more to heart; he had loved and respected his father too, but neither mother or father had shown him the attention of the man before him. He never in his wildest dreams imagined he would be here in the house of the man who, to him, was a legend in Florence Street. And wasn't Florence Street just about the most important place in the world?

"Imagine him, the great Sammy Wilson, taking an interest in me, wee Benny Lynch, cabinetmaker's tea boy, butcher shop's message boy, Mally Corner *Times-News*-and-*Citizen* boy, and Yarrow's can boy; I'll need to listen to every word he tells me and do what he says."

"Well, the plan of campaign, Benny is . . . you're going to have to get fit. Oh, I know you've done a' the skipping bit and punchbag work that you needed to do for the amateurs and the booths. And I saw you training at Gilmour's. But what I'm speaking about is another kind of fitness. The kind of fitness that could make you world champ.

Aye, that's right. Champion of all the world," he said, repeating the sentence again with more emphasis as he noted the impact of what he was saying on the face of the young man. There were no raised eyebrows or signs of visible disbelief, however; the face remaining impassive, receptive.

"Ever been up the Cathkin Braes? Well, that's where we're going every morning. Get the miles into the legs. The hard miles; they're the ones that count. Hard miles. Uphill miles. None of your flat, easy roadwork stuff. It's on wi' the boots and up that rough track that goes up from Stonelaw Street, Rutherglen. Six, maybe more, miles.Then back to the house, get a break, and in the afternoon down to the club. You need lots of sparring. Up to twenty rounds a day you'll be doing before you're finished. That's a lot. It'll help build up the top part of your body as well. Thicken your neck to absorb jaw punches. Square up your shoulders a bit. It's gonnie be a helluva amount of work. It's gonnie get real tough. But you'll do it; you've got it."

Benny stood transfixed. Nothing that Sammy Wilson had said so far had daunted him. Not even the bit about becoming champion of the world. He had never thought about it before. But if Sammy Wilson was saying he could do it, then probably he could. The rest would be little problem to him. He could do the running and the sparring. Even twenty rounds a day.

The Cathkin Braes were the back garden of the Gorbals. Urban Glasgow is a saucer, the city and its cluster of dwellings is where you put the cup, the rim a circle of pleasant hills, broken only by the estuary of the Clyde, due west of the city. To the north there are the Campsies, steep and dominating, the Ochils to the north east, the Kilpatricks to the north west, the Gryfe Moors, the Gleniffers and the high and lonely Fenwick Moors sweeping round from west to south, the Cathkin Braes, hugging in closest of all on the southern lip of the saucer. James Dick, the local man who exploited the sapodilla trees of Malaya to become the gutta percha king, donated the Braes as parkland to the City of Glasgow, to be kept unspoiled in perpetuity. In the summer months they were a great adventure playground for the children of the South Side, Gorbals and Hutchesontown, Tradeston and Oatlands, Govanhill and Polmadie. Round the Braes they could see real cows and sheep and horses too, horses that didn't pull carts like they did in the Gorbals, but idly wandered in meadows and ate grass. And there were trees for climbing—a place they called the bluebell woods—and there really were bluebells in them in the Springtime. But by the time they got them home to Mammy, the shiny green stalks had gone limp and the heads of the happy flower drooped sadly. Mammy always said they were lovely anyway.

There were streams to splash in, lots of little streams they knew as burns, Bourtree and Cityford, Croftfoot and Eastfield, Jenny's and Mallsmyre, Springhall, Stonelaw, Trinity, West and Whitlaw. They rolled their first Easter eggs gaily coloured and painted the night before on the higher and steeper parts of the Braes and they had their first disappointments too when they had to eat the cold egg and discover it wasn't nearly as nice as a warm one.

And when they scrambled to the very top of the Braes, 650 feet up by the place known as Queen Mary's Seat it was like climbing the highest mountain. Beneath them was their sepia world of soot-encrusted tenements, a black Cairo with half a million yellow clay chimney pots exhaling a range of hues from beige to brown, into a cloudless sky, forming a blanket to prevent the healthy rays of the summer sun ever reaching the playstreets around their houses.

They would drive out together, Sammy and Benny, in the bookie's new four door Morris Cowley, park it at the top of Stonelaw Street, then start running towards the Braes. Sammy, in his mid-thirties, had retained his old boxing fitness, and ran with a long, loping stride. Despite the permanent John Player which adorned his lips when he stood in the street with his men and punters, his lungs seemed unaffected and he said he had styled himself on the great runner he had once seen, the Blue Flash who, like him, had a peculiar running gait. Sammy saw himself as the Blue Flash as they ran, Scouts fashion like Kim had; run 100 yards, walk 100 yards. Kipling's man had done it that way to cover great distances. Sammy Wilson and his man did it that way for another purpose . . . fitness. They varied the running, sometimes from one telegraph pole to the next, walking between the next two. Then they would run two and walk two. Run three, walk three. They would jump the burns on the Brae, pick up heavy logs and heave them together from one shoulder to the other and back again until biceps and triceps and deltoids screamed for relief. Then they would run through the woods and pick up smaller pieces of wood to use like Indian clubs, throwing them to each other.

Their rough Indian club work was good for balance, timing and reflexes, the three sometimes all being used at once, at other times consecutively. More running again, this time up the steeper slopes, arms pumping hard, legs jarring on the scree of the steep paths. No resting to look at the view from the summit—that was the place for deep breathing exercises. "Fill them, fill them, fill them right up wi' air till you think they're gonnie burst, then take in another big breath," Sammy would say. "Right . . . c'mon I'll race you to the car." And down the Braes they would slalom-scramble, miss this tree to the right, that one to the left, jump the bushes, leap the fences—styles are for old men—and soar over the burns. This boxing business had its moments and on the good days on the Braes, with their idyllic contrast from the Gorbals, these were the best of moments. On other days, they would be wet and cold and they would sink into the mud on the soft and undrained slopes. "Got to get the miles into the legs, Benny," Sammy would urge. "These are the ones that get you jumping out of your stool in the fifteenth round when the other guy is dying for the final bell. That's when you can tell who has done his training or not."

They would vary the routine at the Polytechnic in the afternoon to avoid boredom. Sammy would scatter a box of Vulcan matches on a table. "Right, see how quickly you can pick them up . . . one by one. C'mon, Benny, that's no' quick. Look, like this," and the fingers of one hand would dart to the table and snatch the matches, one by one, so quickly his hand almost became a blur of movement. Benny was a good pupil and would do the match pecking with enthusiasm; although he was left-handed, Sammy noted his right hand was just as fast, the basis of the superb two-fisted balance he had noticed that first day he had seen him shadow box in Gilmour's club.

Sammy taught him a routine for shadow boxing. It was based on a sequence of eight, slow-motion movements in front of the big mirror in the club, a choreography which encompassed all the essential movements of ringcraft.

First a left to the body, then the right over to the opponent's chin, another left, this time to the chin; a right to the rival's left ear to get him off balance; a straight left, then a right hook, a left hook and finishing with a right upper cut.

"It's not how many punches you can take, it's how many you make him miss," Sammy would preach. "Right now, your eight movements again." He would go over them in sequence so often he lost count; left, right, left, right, straight left, right hook, left hook, uppercut, until eventually he did them by rote at speeds which ranged from a graceful ballet to a wicked whirlwind.

Despite the number of other unknown lads like Benny who acted as sparring partners for each other, Sammy would take his turn in the ring. "Bet I'm the only manager in the world that's as fit as his boy," he would laugh . . . "Aye, an' I'll tell you what," he would say as an aftermath, "If it wasn't for this right hand and its rattling knuckles, it would be me that's in there for the title."

Few were more wily than Sammy Wilson. His ringcraft was that of the fox, never the bear. He would mesmerise with his feints and weaves. And his psychology was never to let the protégé think he was getting too good, too quick; that could be fatal. "Chrissakes Benny, you're sparring like a daft boy. Honestly, ye havenae a clue at

times. C'mon you'll need to dae better than that." And when he got
the chance he would catch him off balance, slip a glove under one of
his elbows and flip his hand up quickly to make him whirl round in
the opposite direction to his rival. Then Sammy would kick him in
the pants.

"Ye auld bastard Sammy . . . how'd ye do that?"

"Cos I can catch ye off balance when I want. Now see how
important it is not to be caught. There's nae going to sleep in the ring;
that mind of yours has got to be working harder than your arms and
legs. It cannae even stop for a blink."

Sammy laboured home that point the day Jimmy Hogg, one of the
regulars at the club, came in when Benny was sparring. "Hiya Benny,"
shouted Jimmy and back came a similar greeting from the middle of
the ring. "Jeeesus Christ," stormed Sammy. "Whit's this 'Hiya
Jimmy?' Christ, Benny you're in training. You're supposed to be
concentrating. God Almighty, see if that mind of yours ever thinks
'Jimmy' in a fight, then you'll get clobbered good an' proper. Now, if
the bloody King comes through that door, you're the last one that'll
see him if you're in the ring. You'll never be a bloody champ wi' a
mind that farts about like that. Right . . . a shower and pack it up for
the day."

Benny and the other young apprentices would scream with the
initial shock of their cold water showers, the freezing water immediately dousing the fire and sweat of their belaboured bodies. One
new lad complained and shouted at Sammy for warm water. Sammy
had just finished sparring himself and his response was to disrobe
and jôin them in the chilly water. He threw a scrubbing brush at the
complainer. "That'll make ye warm son. But listen to me. It's
champions I'm out to make . . . and ye don't make them under a
warm shower."

As well as his new training régime, there were a series of fights
around the well-attended venues of Glasgow—McOnie's "Ring" in the
Gallowgate, Watson's Booth, Premierland, and visits to similar boxing
venues in other towns. Each was a stepping stone to the big-time that
Sammy knew and kept telling him was there and would be his one
day . . . "if you do as you're told." Fighters like Jim Maharg, Jim
Campbell, Johnny McMillan and Alex Farries were getting the big
print on the fight bills at the time. Benny Lynch and his string of
opponents, sometimes one a week, got the small print and a two-line
report in the morning *Record* if they were lucky. They included Young
McColl, Billy Leggatt, Young Donnelly, Jim Devanney, Young
O'Brien, Jim McKenzie, Joe Boag, his old St John's pal Paddy
Docherty, who gave him what Sammy said was a "right good boxing

lesson", Young McAdam, Mick Cassidy, Peter Sherry and Pat Sweeney. Most of them he won on points decisions. If he lost he would try his damnedest to get a rematch which he made sure he would win. The thing was to keep fighting, to cram in the experience, know all the moves, suffer all the punishment and, just as important, try and earn enough to keep him as a fulltime pro. But his purse-rating didn't even match the average weekly wage of £2 10 shillings. He had fought Jim Easdale at the Star Palace in Dumbarton for £1, off which he had to pay the return bus fare of one shilling and five pence, and a few coppers to the man who acted as his second. At McOnie's "Ring" the prizemoney was £1 and 5 shillings for a six-rounder, off which you paid one shilling to the second; ten rounds (bottom of the bill) shared £5; £3 to the winner, £2 to the lower, and an equal split for a draw. Ten rounds (top of the bill) shared £7; £4 to the winner, £3 to the loser, £3 and 10 shillings per man for a draw.

But Sammy wasn't taking a percentage—"Keep it till we're in the big-time son." And he could always get a good feed at Maw Kelter's, the Kilcoynes, or when Sammy's sister Star brought in the big newspaper-wrapped parcels of fish suppers from the Tally's next to the Polytechnic in Clyde Place. He wasn't into the beer and whisky—yet—so there was always a shilling or two left for the dancing. And there was plenty of that to be done in Glasgow.

8

A Pro's Hard Times

The professionals and boothmen were a special breed of men. The most popular were the lighter weights and, of all of them, the flyweights were the most spectacular. They had terrier ferocity, whippet quickness, bulldog toughness. They varied between five feet and five feet four inches in height and, by the rules, had to be eight stones or under when they weighed in for a fight. For many that was a natural weight. For others it meant the cruelty of a diet and a fitness régime to keep them within the weight while not depriving them of the stamina they so vitally needed for their trade.

Alex Farries was only seven years older than Benny Lynch. But a boxer can live several lifetimes in seven years. Alex Farries had. By the time he met Benny Lynch he had lost count of the number of times he had ducked through the ropes to wipe his feet on the cape. "Hundreds . . . just hundreds," he would say if he was asked to put a figure to them. Alex's whole life had been boxing. His furthest memory was about fighting. He could even remember the old bare-knuckle grudge fights in the ring. And one of the best of them had been between two old-time champions, Geordie Aitchison and Bill Strelley, both to become legendary names in Scottish boxing circles. Aitchison and Strelley had fallen out and the challenge went out for a bare-knuckler. Venue was to be the Parkhead Club, close to the Cross. Every man in the district and nearby areas of the East End heard about it and so many of them turned up they crowded the street after packing the hall. So they changed the venue to bigger premises a mile and a half away at the Rottenrow. Alex walked along with the huge crowd from Parkhead Cross to the Rottenrow but was stopped at the door by a burly steward. "Away hame boy . . . you're too wee to see a fight like this."

What went on in the ring that day at the Rottenrow Amateur Athletic Club's venue wasn't for little boys' eyes. For this was street fighting . . . in the ring. And it was between two men who had once been friends and were still fellow brothers of the 103 Union and

Crown (Bridgeton) Masonic Lodge. Their trouble had started over their rivalry as fight promoters. Strelley promoted the fights at the Scottish National Club at Bridgeton Cross and his friend Aitchison assisted in the training and matchmaking of the young boxers. Then Aitchison started promoting on his own in a variety of premises, at Clydebank, the Rottenrow and other places. He then organised boxing shows at the Parkhead School of Physical Culture in Dechmont Street. Parkhead Cross and Bridgeton Cross are within a mile of each other and while there were healthy boxing audiences in both districts, there were only sufficient to fill one hall and make money for the promoter. And when Geordie Aitchison started his promotions at Parkhead, his dates often clashed with Strelley's at the National, causing him to lose money at a succession of promotions. The bad blood followed. It started one night at the National Club when Aitchison was acting as second to a boxer. Strelley's brother-in-law needled him about his rival promotions and a fight developed, stopped by Strelley himself. "If there's going to be any fights," he said, "then it's between him and me." Game as they come, Aitchison retorted . . . "Right then, into the dressing room, lock the door and the man that comes out walking is the winner." Strelley refused. "We'll do it in the ring," he replied, "bare knuckle."

"You're on," said Aitchison, "bare knuckle . . . and no holds barred."

Well, it would be a truthful fight at least and Strelley would have appreciated that. When he refereed fights at his promotions he would lambast men on the floor as he gave them the count if he thought they were malingering. It would go . . . "One . . . you better get up quick . . . Two . . . you're just swanking lying there . . . Three . . . you're just lying there to get the easy road and get your money . . . Four . . . right I'll gie you one last chance . . . Five . . .

There was no swanking when he went into the ring with Geordie Aitchison that day. As they agreed, it was no holds barred. Heads, knuckles, elbows . . . they gave it everything and the packed hall cheered them like it was a world title fight. There were no rounds or rules. They just fought. And it was Strelley who had to admit defeat.

Alex was thirteen when he left school in Parkhead. At that time he had been boxing for a year, travelling right across the city by tramcar to Jim Morton's Club in Paisley Road West for training nights. His Dad had insisted he take up the sport for what seemed to him the logical reason that "it might stop the Parkhead boys knocking the hell out of you". Jim Morton was one of the pioneers of Scottish boxing before the turn of the century and had introduced midget boxing to the crowds. Little Alex Farries was to become one of his star turns.

When he left school he went straight on the road with Guest's Travelling Booth, punching his way at thirteen to the cheers of the crowds round all the Ayrshire Fair towns, Kilmarnock and Irvine, Kilbirnie and Kilwinning, Mauchline and Maybole . . . anywhere where they knew they could attract the crowds with their barker's "Hurrah, hurrah, hurrah . . . who's going to challenge the great men of Guest's?" And on a platform in their colourful dressing gowns, the pugs lined up, crooked noses, worn and mis-shapen ears daring anyone to be good enough to challenge them. And at either side of the line-up were the travelling midgets, Alex Farries and little Charlie McMillan. The crowds would gasp then cheer when the stewards helped them on to stools to give punch ball demonstrations, their stick skinny arms beating the ball into a rhythmic blur. Then the barker would announce that the boys would have a "real fight". And the boys would square up in the ring, setting their imp faces as man tough as they could, before the first bell of their two-rounder. If Alex won at Kilmarnock, it was Charlie's turn to win at Kilwinning, Alex at Kilbirnie, and Charlie again at Irvine. But such was their skill, the crowds never knew, never even suspected and they would hail them with coppers for their courage.

The men in the troupe were a mixture of young boxers hoping one day to be a champion and older ones who knew they never would be champ but were still good enough for the booths. And the wages were good . . . up to £7 on a good week. But they had to save off that for it was a short season, and would be even shorter if it was a wet summer. That seemed to be often enough.

Unless they made the big-time, and few of them ever did, none of the professionals made a fortune from the fight game; they called their prizemoney their wages, and that was the measure of their earnings. They were clever with their fists, but few were astute enough to out-deal the promoters; not for them the luxury of agents and managers to wheel and deal and protect their interests. The attitude of the promoter usually was . . . take it or leave it; if they left it, there were plenty of others who would take it, and, besides, there was the wife and weans to think about.

Alex Farries had his fill of them. A lot of his fights were arranged by Jim McOnie, the booth promoter in the Gallowgate. When Alex arranged one of his own fights at the rival arena, Premierland, McOnie fumed at him. "You . . . fighting at Premierland for £5. Well for a start they'll no' let you win there. And you could have got more money had I fixed it for you." The last point might have been debateable. The first wasn't. Alex fought Mouse Higgins in the contest. It was one of his best fights and they nearly had to stop it

several times, such was the punishment he was doling out to the
Mouse. He had him down in the seventh and it looked like he was
going to be counted out. However, he got up, took buckets of more
punishment and staggered on to the final bell. McOnie was right . . .
Alex would never win at Premierland. The referee lifted both boxers
hands and announced . . . a draw.

Alex arranged another fight of his own, this time at the Glen
Waverley soccer ground in Barrowfield, also in the East End of
Glasgow. Jim Gilmour, the Premierland man and Sammy Wilson's
old mate was the promoter and agreed on a purse of £5. When Alex
discussed the money with some old friends they told him he was
being robbed. It was the main fight and he should have been on a
percentage of the gate, they said. Alex went back to Gilmour in view
of this and said he was demanding a percentage. Gilmour smiled at
him and said . . . "Percentage then, Alex! Fine. How about ten per
cent?" Alex was delighted at the offer, even more so on the night of
the fight when he saw the crowd that turned up. After the fight he
went to the promoter's room where he was told, "Great fight, Alex.
The crowd loved you. There's your £5 purse money . . . and your £5
for your share of the gate."

"Five pounds," stormed Alex.

"Aye, five pounds," said Gilmour.

"But there were thousands there," said Alex, "and you said ten per
cent."

"Aye . . . but did you have anybody at the gate actually counting
them so you could work out your ten per cent? Of course you didn't
so you've got to rely on me to tell you. So I'm telling you . . . five
pounds."

They got Alex Farries to fight Scottish champion Jim Maharg in a
non-title fight, fifteen rounds of two minutes each, for £10. But it
sounded much more than that when he read it in the *Evening Times*.
£100 In Stakes, said the heading in the story. It announced the
forthcoming fight making no mention of the prizemoney but related
that Alex Farries was backing himself for £100 in the contest. He
went straight to McOnie who was promoting after reading the story:
"What's this about me backing masel' for £100?" McOnie smiled.
"Surely you've got enough friends to back you for that," he was told.
Alex was a battler; he had lost as many fights as he had won. "If I had
to ask my friends to back me every time I fought," he told McOnie,
"I'd have no friends left by now."

Other promoters were tougher. They wanted Alex to meet Freddie
Tennant at the Caird Hall in Dundee. Tennant had a reputation as an
uncompromising fighter and they were tipping him as a future

Scottish champion. McOnie had made all the arrangements for the
fight. The purse was to be £4. "But I've agreed they'll pay your
trainfare, Alex. No' bad, eh!"

"What'll happen if I go on my motorbike?"

"That's a great idea, Alex," replied McOnie. "It's twenty one bob
return on the train. Your bike will only take a few gallons so you'll be
shillings in. And anyway, Alex, going on your bike will be good
training for you . . . bit of the old toughness, you know."

Alex couldn't quite figure that; a motorbike helping his training?
Nevertheless, despite the fact it was March and the snow was lying
deep on the wide gullies of the Ochils, Alex got set for the trip.

His mate Fred Hardy had said he would ride pillion to be his
second in the fight, but changed his mind at the last minute. Little
wonder. It was a bitterly cold day and threatening a gale. Besides,
Fred had other problems. He had been fighting under the name of
Alex Jamieson so that he could still collect his eighteen shillings
unemployment money. Lots of them did it and mostly got off with it.
But somebody told on Fred and they had stopped his money.

A blustery north-easterly was blowing direct into his face as Alex
headed up the long slopes of the road to Stirling on his new, saddle-
tank A.J.S. He had bought it from Bell Brothers for £51 . . . the price
of five thousand punches on his spreading nose. The rain turned to
sleet and finally snow on the long climb up Cherrybank Hill into
Perth where he had to stop in order to muster some circulation back
into his frozen body, before completing the last of the miles to
Dundee.

Scots are proud of their hospitality. At its best it has few equals. It
also has few rivals when it's at its worst. They don't have the
calculated indifference of the metropolitan south. The Scot doesn't
calculate like that when they are offhand to the stranger or newcomer
in their midst. But some ancient suspicion or hostility towards the
outsider, distilled in past centuries in the Glens and by the Clans, still
runs though the blood of some. And to them the stranger or
wayfarer, tourist or traveller, is an encumbrance; someone to be
suffered. Like Alex was to be in Dundee.

McOnie had given him a slip of paper with the name and address of
a man in Dundee passed to him by the promoter there. "He'll look
after you till the fight," was the message. Alex went straight to the
address when he arrived in Dundee that afternoon, cold and weary
after the slow ride up against the headwinds. A woman came to the
door. "My man's away," she said. "He's at the demolitions . . .
working there for the day. You'll need to come back at tea-time."

It was just two o'clock and he was starving . . . and that night he was on the bill of the biggest hall between Glasgow and Aberdeen. He parked the A.J.S. and went for a wander round the busy town, buying a pie from a baker's and ending up in the Brit Cinema to pass the time and get some rest.

The man was shaking him roughly by the shoulders. "Hey . . . you. Waken up, Mac. We don't let modellers in here. Out ye go." Alex had fallen sound asleep in the picture house and the usher had assumed he was a tramp. "Bloody modeller," said Alex . . . "I'm one of the stars on the big fight show tonight."

It was five o'clock, the traditional tea-time, when Alex returned to the address he had been given. The woman too had just returned and the house was cold. "Ye'll get a hatchet in the shed," she said. "We need firewood to light the fire. The wood's beside the hatchet." With that she left again to fetch the evening meal . . . fish and chip suppers.

The doctor gave Alex the usual prescribed test which was now compulsory prior to all big public fights. He couldn't remember the number of times he had taken the same test . . . two taps at the base of the shouder blades, two on the chest, pulse rate and a stethoscope sounding.

The doctor looked at him, a serious frown on his face. "You shouldn't be fighting," he said. "You've got a bad heart."

Alex sat up with a startle. "What . . . me wi' a bad heart! Tell you what. You shouldn't be doing your doctor bit. I've been fighting fit all my life and I'm still fighting fit and I'm fighting the night no matter what you say." And he did.

After the doctor left the room, Alex asked one of the seconds about him. The reply was, "He's one of the best in the whole of Dundee." Alex was still convinced he had been wrong.

Freddie Tennant was the local boy and they cheered him wildly when the boxers took to the ring. And they cheered wildly throughout the fight for the two men provided a rough, tough contest. At the end of the tenth and last round Alex was pleased with himself. He was sure he had done well, knew he had logged lots of good points with determined, accurate punching, and at the same time had caused Tennant to miss a lot. But the crowd cheered even louder when the referee raised the hand of the winner . . . Freddie Tennant.

Wearied and aching after his long and punishing day, Alex returned to the cold comfort of his night's digs and slept a full round of the clock, wakening the following day just before lunchtime. . . and in an empty house. He had been told to report to Miller the Promoter at his caravan, which was the headquarters for his travelling booth of boxers. He knocked on the door of the van. "I'm here for my £4 Mr Miller." The promoter looked at him. "Oh aye . . . you're Farries." Alex thought the next comment might be something about the fight the night before. Might even say he put up a good battle. But the man had other things on his mind. "What do you mean £4? It's £3.10 shillings . . . ten bob off for your digs. And your trainfare has to come off as well."

When they heard the heated exchange that followed, a group of Miller's booth men came over and stood, arms folded, making it clear whose side they were on. "Come up here on your auld motorbike and think you can claim trainfare. Who are you kidding? There's £2 and ten bob . . . that's your lot."

The money was to last Alex for a long time. When he returned to Glasgow he was so fevered he had to be lifted from his motorbike and put straight to bed where he lay for a fortnight. He had contracted erysipelas. And it was to be many more weeks before he was fit enough to return to the ring.

*   *   *

It was in 1932 and Sammy Wilson was stepping up the opposition for Benny. As part of that campaign he wanted to try him with a new grade of opponent. He had a fair number of fights under his belt now. That year he had been matched with Charlie Deacon, Young Hardie, Jack Riley, Kid Murray, Jim Boal, Scotty Deans, Young McManus, Jim Driscoll, Young Griffo, Tiger Naughton, Young Griffo again, Scotty Deans again, Joe Aitken, Freddie Tennant, Tommy Higgins, Jim Jeffries, Tony Fleming, Paddy Docherty, Joe Aitken again, Freddie Tennant again and Young Beattie. Only one of the fights, against Young Griffo, had been an unavenged defeat. Five were drawn verdicts, the rest convincing wins. "Got a good opponent for your next one wee man," said Sammy. "Alex Farries. He's the kind of man you need next. He's met them all. Knows all the tricks. Can show you a few things and will give you a right good scrap."

Alex was twenty-seven years of age at the time. Benny was nineteen. The fight was fixed by Tommy Kane, the matchmaker, and the venue was the Eldorado Stadium in Leith. The men in the fight trade were, in the main, friendly gladiators; Alex, Benny, and their matchmaker Tommy Kane, met at the Queen Street Station and travelled to and from Edinburgh together for their bout. The fight went the full ten rounds. Alex wasn't over impressed by his youthful challenger and was able to score sufficient points over him that he was surprised when the referee raised Lynch's hand as winner. But he was used to decisions with which he didn't always agree.

Travelling back to Glasgow, Tommy Kane brought out the £5

prizemoney to be divided between them. He handed Alex twenty half crown pieces and was met with . . . "Not on your Nelly. Think I want to walk around with half a ton of silver on me?" Benny laughed. "Give them to me, Tommy. I love to hear the jingle of money in my pockets."

They laughed and joked together about their experiences in their tough and hard trade, Benny telling Alex about the great characters they had in the South Side and some of the capers they would get up to. Alex told him about some of the men he had boxed and about boxing characters with whom he had travelled in his long years at the craft.

"Danny Wiper was a great fellah. We used to go thegether to Jim Paterson's booth at Falkirk. They had shows there every Friday and Saturday. You got thirty bob for a ten rounder . . . and they gave you an old bucket in a caravan to wash yourself afterwards. The punters used to come into the van before the fight and ask us who was gonnie win so they could back us. They thought a' the fights were fixed . . . and they weren't. Danny used to give them a tune wi' a melodion after his fights. They loved it. Mind o' one time we were coming back and there were some men busking at the station in Falkirk. What do you think Danny does? Gets oot the melodion and joins in wi' them . . . and then goes round with his hat!"

"Then there was Bushman Dempster, the welterweight. He used to gie them a speech after his fights. Aye, fight ten rounds and if he lost he would address the crowd from the centre of the ring. Used to tell them he had been sent by the Buroo to a workscheme felling trees up at the Palace Riggs in Cumbernauld."

"Ever fight at Morecambe, Benny? Gees, got some characters down there. I went there with Jim Naughton once and he's looking for his name on the bill and it's no' there so he asks the promoter what happened. 'That's you there' says the promoter pointing to a name on the poster . . . Jim O'Naughton, fly weight champion of Dublin. Christ Jim had never seen Ireland, never mind yer champion o' Dublin bit. And after his name it said . . . 'This is the man who has chased his rival Campbell all over the world and now they meet right here in Morecambe'. All over the world, Christ! Morecambe was the furthest Naughton had ever been in his life."

"Another time we're down there and the promoter had him wi' another name . . . 'Tiger' Naughton. Then he says to him . . . 'Right, Tiger, I want you to take a dive in the fourth.' Jim told him he wasn't on: Maybe he should have done as he was told . . . he ended up getting a tanking and they had to stop the fight in the sixth."

Alex's fund of stories about boxers and the game was limitless and

Benny listened intently to them, throwing his head back in raucous laughter as the tales varied from character to character; hard men to happy men; men with hearts of stone; men with hearts of gold. The Fancy had them all.

"Tell you another story about Tiger Naughton. He was fighting this fellah Bobby Shields . . . you know him probably; he's from the family that owns the cooperage at Celtic Park. Well, Bobby had given a transfusion of blood that day to an uncle and Tiger beat him in the fight. They were talking about it afterwards and auld McOnie was there and when he hears the word transfusion he turns to Tiger and asks him what it means. Tiger said that it meant one person giving something to another person. 'You mean,' says McOnie, 'that if I gave you two and sixpence that would be a transfusion?' 'Naw,' says Tiger, . . . 'that would be a fuckin miracle!' "

About a month after their first fight, Benny and Alex were matched again, the fight taking exactly the same pattern and with the same result. By the time they got to their third fight, their wages had improved considerably. It was at Gourock and the money was £7 a man, win, lose or draw. Again Alex was sure the verdict was his, positively so this time, but once more the referee took Lynch by the wrist.

The more he fought, the more he was winning, and winning them convincingly; the referee stopping the fights of some, the seconds throwing in the towel of rivals in others, some by knock-outs. Tommy Higgins went the distance, but it was a clear verdict in the tenth, Billy Kid Hughes retired against him in the ninth, the referee stopped the fight against Joe Cowley and Willie Vogan was knocked out.

There was an appeal to the matchmakers for one more Farries versus Lynch fight. And, unlike their first meeting which had passed almost unnoticed, there was considerable talk about a projected fourth meeting. Could Benny k.o. Alex like he had been doing some of the other veterans he had been fighting? Definitely not, said Alex's men. He had never been stopped in his life, and that was quite a record for someone who had been fighting as long as him. And there was his great victory over Scottie Adair from Canada, a Golden Gloves Champion. Alex would surely have the measure of the new man by now; and, anyway, wasn't there some doubt about Lynch's previous wins; there certainly was in Alex's mind. A fourth should surely settle matters.

August, 1933, and they met in one of the bars in Dundas Street, which flanks Queen Street railway station and, like the other streets on a hill, had parallel slab tracks set in the cobbles to ease the burden of the horses with heavy carts.

There was Euan Wellwood, bejowled and bespectacled, the boxing writer for the *Evening Times*, who often arranged sparring partners and other matters for managers and promoters, Sammy Wilson and Alex Farries. Benny would be due any minute and as they waited Euan ordered some drinks, a lemonade for Sammy, knowing him a strict teetotaller. "Want to know something about drink?" he told them. "You can have whisky or wine or as much beer as you like if you come up to my place in Florence Street. And you'll no' get those footery wee measures I see them getting in this pub. Aye, I always keep a drink in the house and they tell me I pour a great whisky. Wouldnae touch the stuff masel' though."

They had just started to make arrangements about the deal for the fight when Benny walked in. Farries looked him up and down. It had been several months since they last met and over a year since their first fight. He had matured considerably in that year. Gone was the crumpled suit and in its place a well-cut fifty bob model, trousers neatly pressed, shoes highly polished, his hair slicked back not a strand out of place, his handsome boyish face marked only by the Surrey Lane scar. Standing beside the bulky Wellwood made him look even smaller and as he stared at him Alex thought . . . "Christ, he's just a boy; how the hell have I no' been able to beat him?"

"A beer, Benny?" asked the sports writer. "No thanks, Mr Wellwood." "Lemonade then?" "No thanks . . . I'm fine."

So they set about finalising the details of the fight. The date was set and it was agreed that it was to be outside the flyweight, but only just.

"We'll settle for eight stone one pound," said Sammy Wilson.

"Make it eight two," said Alex.

"No," said Sammy. "Eight stone and one pound is our weight . . . and not an ounce over."

"I don't mind eight two," said Benny.

"Aye you would if you got hit by a man that's a pound heavier than you," said his manager.

Benny was a natural flyweight at the time and had they fought at eight stone two, he would still have been at his natural eight stone, or under. Alex Farries, on the other hand was eight stone ten pounds and going through the agonies of most flyweights as the years advanced and their bodies got naturally heavier.

The other details were settled. They confirmed the earlier suggestion that the purse was to be £10, each man paying £5, winner taking all. Weigh-in was to be on the morning of the fight at the offices of the promoter Neillie McGhie, just up the hill and in the same street as the bar in which they were meeting. Venue, the Parkhead Arena.

Sammy unrolled a big white five pound note from the wad he always carried, Alex counted out five singles. They shook hands. The fourth fight was set.

Alex Farries started serious training the next day. Another old rival, Jim Maharg, came to his aid. Maharg was a contemporary of Alex's, but had more success in title fights. Few men had fought more big-time fights than Jim. Once he had fought three in the space of ten days. Like Alex, Jim was also an East Ender and opened up his club there, in Old Dalmarnock Road calling it the Bridgeton Amateur Athletic Club.

It was still mild weather and the sweat came easy for Alex during his long training sessions. He hadn't trained so hard for a single fight for a long time. But he was determined to win this fight. He needed it badly. He knew the ups and downs of the boxing trade. The ups included being able to get a house in one of the better tenements in the East End, a room-and-kitchen in Palace Street, just behind Celtic Park's football ground, where they used to crowd into the top floor of the houses at the head of the street on a Saturday to see right into the Celtic's ground. The rents in Palace Street—nicknamed locally as Honeymoon Row—were ten shillings a week, twice the average of the houses in Bridgeton and the Gorbals even though, like them, there was no bathroom and the toilet was communal on the stairhead landing. He knew the downs of the game too. Like the incident at Dundee and the weeks after it without a fight when his only income was the eighteen shillings from the Buroo. He knew the mornings after the defeat of a night before when his face burned and his body ached but he still had to force himself out of bed and on the road for some more training. The finances were getting low once more, and with £5 of his own money staked on the fight, he really had to make a go of it.

As well as giving him long sparring sessions himself, Jim Maharg arranged a supply of other lads to help Alex train. They were young lads mainly, hopeful of getting into the one industry available to them where, if they had the right amount of brain and brawn, they could lift themselves out of the set course which seemed to be their destiny . . . £3 a week and a room-and-kitchen if they were tradesmen, a lot less if they weren't. At the end of every punch, hook, feint, weave and tap there could be freedom for them. They thought of that while they completed the weary miles of running and as they skipped and rattled punch balls; as they suffered heavy medicine balls dropping on their stomachs and as they fought countless shadow battles against themselves. And it was on their minds too when they sparred with partners . . . must sharpen that defence block; should exploit his vulnerabilities; shouldn't let him catch me with that left jab; watch his straight rights; keep the mind moving, thinking, always on the alert; the more you do it the better you get. Well, so they say.

Alex was moving well with his sparring partners and he and his aide Jim were pleased with his progress. His weight was coming off precisely as they had planned . . . a pound per day. Can't let it come off too fast or else you get too weak to train and if the weightloss-training balance isn't right, you could become susceptible to weakness and bad form and a target for infections like the cold or a fever. On the eve of the fight Alex was more than confident about his chances. He was tipping the scales at just a few ounces over the eight stone one pound mark and he could surely get that off overnight. He was feeling as fit as he could remember.

The following morning, he walked from his house in Palace Street to Gilmour's club in Barrack Street, less than a mile away, where they had scales which they used at weigh-ins.

Alex stepped on them, apprehensively. His face fell when the figures were read out . . . eight stone one pound and two ounces. "Have ye been to the lavvy, Alex?" asked one of the helpers. He had. The official weigh-in was just an hour away and he pondered as he listened to the suggestions they were putting to him. The most logical, it appeared, was to do what some of them were saying . . . run from the club to McGhie's office up town for the official cere-mony.

In order to get a good sweat up, Alex ran faster than he normally would have in road training and was still breathing deeply when he got to the offices in Dundas Street. Benny and Sammy Wilson were already there and Benny was the first to step on the scales. "Seven stones thirteen pounds exactly," said the official from the British Boxing Board of Control. Alex mopped some more sweat from his forehead and stepped nervously on to the scales, stripped naked and looking straight ahead.

"Eight stone, one pound and two ounces," said the official. Alex was crestfallen. How could he be that heavy? He had been that weight the night before. And that was what they said he was an hour ago before losing all that sweat and energy on the morning of his big fight.

"Right . . . get it off," said Sammy Wilson. "The fight's at eight one."

Benny interjected. "C'mon, Sammy. It's all right by me . . . what's two ounces?"

"It's a punch heavier than yours . . . that's what it is," he came back.

But Benny was insistent. "The weight's fine, Sammy. I'm accept-ing." He held his hand out to Alex and there was a firm shake.

Alex appreciated Benny's gesture but the relief on his face didn't hide his apparent exhaustion. Connie Thomson, the trainer at Premierland, couldn't help but notice his drawn features. He drew him aside. "Alex, get yourself home as quick as you can and only stop at one place on the way—the butcher's. Get yourself a big steak and an oxo cube. Get stuck into them when you get to the house then straight to bed for a sleep and you'll be right as rain for tonight." Alex thanked Connie for his advice, not revealing he didn't have the price of a steak on him. When he counted out his money in the butcher's, however, he had enough for some stewing steak . . . and the oxo cube.

Being the local boy as well as the veteran who had entertained them so many times in the past, Alex got the biggest roar from the crowd, one of the biggest the Parkhead Arena had ever seen. He looked over at Benny loosening up in the opposite corner and the same thought crossed his mind as it had the day they had fixed the fight . . . "Christ, he's just a boy." They touched gloves at the start of the fight and the faint grin on Lynch's face seemed to be saying, "Right, c'mon auld yin." The first round was fast and furious, Lynch penetrating Alex's defence with some hard blows to his rib cage. "Christ this yin's hurting. Really hurting," thought Alex.

The crowd loved the battle, as they always do when two men go for each other hard. By the end of the third round Sammy Wilson knew it was going to be a fourth for his protégé. "You've got him wee man. He had a hard time that last round so don't let up in this one. Give him a couple of hooks . . . and keep him busy."

Benny just nodded in reply. He could read the fight as well as Sammy and he knew he had the better of the man. Might even be able to get a knock-out over him, he thought.

Alex was thinking other things. "Is this Lynch I'm really fighting? Gees, I should know him better than any fighter but this is a different man from the last fights. God he's hurting me."

The fourth round was torture for Alex as burst after burst from the flailing, hooking Lynch hit target. A wicked left hook semi-circled on to his stout, square jaw and Alex crashed on to the cape, winded and hurt. That was it. The referee reckoned he had enough and stood in front of him when he rose, inside the count, and ready to come at Lynch again. The arena erupted in a wild yell when the referee turned from Alex to do the formal raising of the winner's arm. Their local boy had been beaten but they were seeing a man that looked like going places and he got their vocal support.

Alex was bewildered. This was a new experience for him. Fifteen years a fighter he had taken on all-comers and never once had he been stopped like this.

Promoter McGhie came into Lynch's dressing room after the fight and shook his hand before counting out the winner-takes-all £10 prizemoney to hand to Sammy Wilson. "That was quite a tanking you gave Alex . . . great fight Benny." When he left the room, Benny turned to Wilson. "Sammy, give me £4 for Alex . . . he's due it." Wilson handed him the money and he went across the corridor to the other room where the fighters stripped. "You've missed him, Benny," said one of the men in the room. "He left as soon as he dressed."

*   *   *

The mild autumn weather had broken that evening and the first chill winds of early winter were scouring the back streets. The little man walked with a slight limp for each step jarred the bruises and pains around his chest. Alex's father and his brothers Tommy and Willie walked with him down the Springfield Road towards his house in the small, four-street scheme of red sandstone tenements bounded on the one side by the Eastern Necropolis which, in turn, overlooked Celtic Football Park. They said if you managed to get out of the first and into the second then you really were in Paradise. Little was said among the men as they walked son and brother home. For Alex it was a night of reflection as well as crushing defeat. He looked around the kitchen room of his flat. On the wall there was a picture of him in the classical boxing pose. That had cost him a few punches. Got it for topping the bill against Jim Maharg in a benefit fight for a man who had lost his life saving a boy from the canal at Port Dundas. So instead of prizemoney they had given him the offer of either a photo of himself or one of Tommy Milligan, one of Scotland's greatest-ever boxers. Milligan had been surprised when Alex's choice had been for a photo of himself. "Are you the man who refused my photograph," he said to him. "Whatever for?" "Whatever for?" said Alex. "Who would know you in my house in a few years time? But I'll tell you what . . . they'll know me all right." The memory of it all flooded back to him as he stared at the handsome framed photo. "What a game," he thought. "A picture on the wall, and that's about all there is to show for it." No, there was something else. There was a tea service the wife kept in the wee display cabinet.

Aye, they had presented him with that after the dazzling performance he had put up the night he had beaten Danny Conlan of Anderston. Said it was silver, so they did. Then when they polished it the silver came off and now it was black, but they kept it just the same in the display cabinet. It was a reminder, wasn't it . . . and there were precious few of these for the journeymen boxers. Tonight, though, there were the other reminders; a body that was nearly a stone lighter than its natural weight and wracked with Lynch's jabs which pained with every breath.

"You could get yourself into bad health, Alex," said Dr Beveridge from Westmuir Street, called by his wife Peggy the next morning because of his condition. "How much did you earn to get yourself in a state like this?" Almost sheepishly, Alex told him. "You see it was winner take all, doctor. It's like that in the fight game."

"For God sake, Alex, You look like you had been run down by my car. Do you know how much you get if you get knocked down by a car and get in a state like this? A small fortune. Makes you think . . . doesn't it?"

That same day promoter Neillie McGhie called and was told by Peggy that the doctor said he should stay in bed for a while. "Benny was looking for you last night after you left," he said. "Here . . . he wanted you to have something; there's four from him and six from me. We both think you deserve it for the fight you put up."

Alex was confined to his bed for a fortnight. He never fought again. At twenty-seven he was back to being an ordinary working man again. Ordinary meant he could no longer afford the ten shillings rent for the house in Palace Street. They would get a place for five shillings a week down in Fielden Street, Bridgeton, and sink into the anonymity of the ordinary working people. Well, thought Alex, at least there were the memories of the good times; a lot of people didn't even have that.

And there was the tea service and the big photograph on the wall.

9

Comedians and Confidence Men

Percy Joseph Sillitoe, Chief Constable of Sheffield, was one of the many senior police officers from all over the world who applied for the vacant job as Glasgow's Number One policeman. He told the interviewing committee that he would stop the graft in the force as well as completely reorganise it. He got the vote and the £1500—rising to £2000—a year job.

His drastic reorganisation programme caused great consternation in the Force, as well among the men in the street. He had hundreds of police boxes—323 of them—built throughout the streets of the city and suburbs. The purpose was communication. Each was its own miniature police station, available for holding suspects until a Black Maria was called. From these boxes the beat policemen could keep in touch by 'phone with their main police station. The boys at the corner laughed at them and said they were only there so that the Busies could eat their pieces and get a doss after drinking the booze the publicans gave them. Sometimes that was true as well.

Long, sleek Alvis patrol cars began prowling the streets and the loiterers were watched like they had never been watched before. The crews of the cars wore the new hats Sillitoe had introduced . . . flat caps with black and white check like Army Guardsmen. Sillitoe's theory was they were now in the motor age and the caps would help his men to be observed more easily at night.

It was Tash Conlin who had told them. He had made a study of the new man Sillitoe by reading all the reports about him in *The Glasgow Herald* at the library. "The new caps and the police boxes are just the start," he told them. "He's gonnie introduce all kinds of science into the force. They've got this thing called forensic science and they say they can actually prove with it that you were at the scene of a crime. And he's been warning a' the Teuchters that they're no' getting promoted in future just because faither is Big Donald frae Skye. In future, so it says in the *Herald*, they've only to be promoted on merit."

"What's merit, Tash?" one of the group asked.

"Ah know," said another. "You know when they broke into Cameron's Bar the other night there. Well, the Busies caught two of them red-handed. They were just going off shift at the time so they says to the robbers 'leave two bottles of whisky in the back close . . . then fuck off.' That's merit."

They laughed and laughed louder when another added his bit: "Ah thought merit was whit ye did after you left your lumber wi' a bun in the oven."

Someone then said that one of the Sergeants at the Lawmoor Street Police Station had told them that Sillitoe's men were going to crack down on the Billy Boys, the Protestant gang in the East End under Billy Fullerton which continually harassed and taunted Catholic gangs and groups. "Sillitoe must be a Catholic then," was the conclusion; a perfectly logical one at that as the Force was Protestant -dominated and the Billy Boys had been the least of their problems.

The conversation switched, suddenly, when one of them turned to Benny Lynch. Benny Lynch loved company. He loved the company of the boys and men with whom he had grown up. He loved the chat and the patter of the corner boys and especially the group who would hang about at Sammy's bookmaking pitch in Florence Street. "Hey Benny, did you tell the boys how your boxing career nearly came to an abrupt end yesterday."

'Aye, did you hear about it?" he replied, adding . . . "the bastard." "I was fooling about in the back close wi' Arthur Holding. Kidding him on, like, doing the old one, two, on him . . . no' hitting him like. Just taking the mickey. Then he loses the rag. And when I put my hand on the ledge at the window he had this big brick and brings it right down on my hand . . . and I just managed to get it away in the nick of time. Just as well or I would have ended up wi' a hand worse than Sammy's knuckle-rattler."

"Did ye sort him out after?"

"Naw. Nothing like that. Sammy saw to him."

"Hey, Benny," said another of the chinas. "Did ye hear about what they did to Jimmy the Bam last week?" Jimmy the Bam was one of the local beat constables, a big rough Highlander. He once brought his wife to meet the corner boys and told them to tell her the nickname they called him and they had all shaken their hads saying . . . . "What Nickname Constable?"

"Well, your man Sammy was standing with some of the boys . . . Neillie, Alex, the Gunner, Josie and Eddie, when they see the pony and cart of the ragman, you know the one that plays the bugle, it was tied to the lamp post outside Knotts's Restaurant and he was inside at his scoff. They knew Jimmy the Bam was due on his beat so they get the ragman's horse and unhitched it, upended the cart on its side and took it through Knotts's close, you know that narrow one. It's that thin Fat Sarah cannae walk up it straight wi' her message bags. Then they took the horse through, tipped the cart back on its wheels again, hitched up the horse and left it standing in the back. The back's that wee there a' the horse could do was stand wi' its nose up against one wall with the back of the cart touching the other wall. And all the time they're doing this, the customers from Mitchell the Pawnshop are coming through the close to go up the back way to the pawn so's their pals will no' see them in the street and they're a' gaping at the horse and cart but feart to stop in case they're seen going to the pawn. Then the Bam turns up and the ragman is doing his nut in the street an' shouting . . . 'Haw polis, look what's happened to ma horse an' cart.' Christ big Jimmy nearly had a wean when he saw it. He stood for about ten minutes just staring at the wee pony wondering how the fuck a cart six feet wide gets up a three foot close. then do you know what he did . . . starts looking up at the sky. The Big Bam is such an eejit he thought it had somehow dropped down from the top of the building. And he wonders how they call him Jimmy the Bam. Mind you, he hasn't been the same since he rattled the lock of Cameron's Bar one night on his rounds . . . and we had it covered in shite!"

Benny loved the stories that happened in the street, particularly the escapades surrounding his manager Sammy Wilson. He would tell many himself, one of his favourites being the one about Sammy and his skeleton suit. It was a joke suit somebody had given him, a black damask overall with a hood and, on the front, the neatly stitched white outline of a skeleton. "He had been dying to wear it for ages then one night at Hallowe'en he gets it out. He says to us . . . 'I'll show them what a real fright is.' So where does he go . . . the cemetery. You know the old graveyard in Ru'glen Road? Well he creeps in and climbs up on the wide sill of the big window at the back of the Camden Street billiard hall. It was packed as usual and he starts knocking on the window and dancing on the sill making a' kind of weird noises. Christ, they shit themselves . . . and scattered in all directions. They thought somebody had jumped out of one of the graves. Sammy spots auld Mick McCafferty, the Irishman, among them, running for his life. So he jumps down from the window and sprints round to Camden Street and gets to Mick's close just as the auld yin is running up the street. 'Bejassus' he screams and scrambles back out of the close again wi' Sammy on his tail shouting . . . 'wheeee'.. Know what happened? He ran straight to the Lawmoor Street polis and made them keep him in the nick all night."

The story convulsed them and they rated it so highly one of them compared it with the laugh they had got the time they had put the horse-jalop in Snack Kelly's dinner. He had been having his dinner in Knotts when, unknown to him, they had poured it into his mince and potatoes. Snack, the trencherman, never knew . . . till it took effect. The nearest toilet to Knotts was in the narrow close . . . and knowing he would head straight there they had it nailed up. "Christ, have you ever in all your life seen a mess like that? And the stink? But it made him think twice about stuffing his face that much."

They liked to laugh and joke and when they did their loud guffaws could be heard a half a street away.

They would cup their hands and give a loud single clap, rub them together and shuffle their feet, their symbol that the patter was good and they were enjoying themselves. The subjects they covered in the course of a day were wide-ranging; tales of old practical jokes and comical situations involving the Busies were a favourite; they would scheme new dares and manoeuvres; create pastimes and diversions which were like adult versions of the street games they once played . . . "Bet you can't get from one side of Ru'glen Road to the other without going over a tramline. How much? A tanner." And somebody would accept and spend half a day or more trying to prove it could be done. (It could. You had to walk more than a mile towards Rutherglen then crawl under the road with the Polmadie Burn, going under instead of over the tramlines!) There would be long discussions on the two sports which mattered most to them, football, especially Celtic and Rangers, and boxing. They treated both subjects with the reverence of an art form, every subtlety, nuance, detail and minutiae discussed, dissected, debated. If it was boxing, Benny would be appointed arbiter if there was a dispute in the debate and if he said someone was or wasn't the best, then that was a fact. For nobody knew better than Benny, they reckoned. Sometimes John Neagle would join them. John had a special rating among them, just as Tash Conlin had, for his knowledge about matters. John loved boxing talk too and could hold them enraptured with his blow-by-blow account of some of the classic fights. "Best ever," he would say, "was Tommy Milligan and Mickey Walker. What a night that was."

He would begin the same way every time . . . "June 30, nineteen hundred and twenty seven, and Scotland's Tommy Milligan faces up to Mickey Walker at Olympia for the Middleweight Championship of the World. You should have seen the job they had trying to get the Yank to come over. He was the biggest name in boxing and could name any price he wanted for a fight. And he did. Said he wanted £20,000 to fight Milligan. Aye, right, £20,000 for one night's work.

Christ, and here's us wi' boys doing it for £1. But no' content wi' that, he wants to nominate the referee. So they start putting names up to him and he and his manager keep turning them down. Then they made a suggestion . . . the Prince of Wales. Right. They were serious an' a'. Wanted the fuckin' Prince to jump about the ring with them. Eventually they gets Eugene Corri and the promoters sent him to the boxers' two camps to spell it out to them just what he wanted of them in the fight. He came up here to Craigneuk where Tommy was training. That's big-time that, so it is . . . sending the referee to your camp to tell you the rules."

"The fight was a cracker right from the bell. Walker comes out and straightaway it's the real bulldog stuff, two hands flying like a windmill at our Tommy. But Tommy gave the Yank a fright and gets stuck right in as well and there they are, toe tae toe in round one and there's another nineteen rounds in front of them. What a start! They called Walker the miniature Jack Dempsey . . . no' much of a miniature when you're a middleweight. But he fought like Jack and didn't let up when they came out for the second. He got his first good punch at Tommy in the second, then followed it with a wallop right in the guts. But Tommy didn't flinch and came right back at Walker. In rounds three, four and five he's punching more than Tommy, getting three hard punches in at our man for every one he's collecting. But the odd ones Tommy does get through let the Yank know that our champ is no mug. In the sixth Tommy goes on the attack but Walker stands his ground and gets in some heavy bombardment at the body. Tommy side-steps one of these big ones and stumbles as he does so and nearly goes over. Walker, quick as a flash, catches him off balance and in he goes with a one, two right to his solar plexus."

"In the seventh the Yank is gaun hell for leather, hooking and swinging at his face and body and Tommy starts to get a bit tottery and you could see it when he went to his corner at the bell. But he comes out for the eighth, game as they come, and Walker goes straight for him, gets a couple of stotirs to the face and Tommy hits the deck for a count of eight. As soon as he gets up Walker leaps on him and down he goes for another count of eight. Up again and Walker's at him like a tiger and do you know what . . . he couldnae get him down again. What a fight! Nane o' us had any voice left by this time. Out he comes for the ninth and it's the same again, one to the face then an uppercut and you'll no' believe it, but it lifted him right off the ground. Christ, what a man! He gets up again after a count of six but he doesnae know what time of day it is and he's wandering about looking for the Yank and the ref has to grab him

and point him in the right direction. I'm telling you, we were amazed
when he comes out for the tenth . . . and he actually has a go at Walker.
What recovery! But Walker knows he's on top and gives him a left
and right to the stomach, then a left and right to the jaw and
Tommy's flat on his face again. And Christ, does he no' get up again
wi' Walker thinking he's gonnie have to shoot him to get rid of him.
But he's staggering all over the place now and Walker gives him two
more to the jaw and he's down again. The ref was getting to ten when
the towel comes flying in. That was it. I'm telling ye . . . that was some
fight."

They had listened, hushed, as Neagle shadow-punched and hooked
at appropriate points to emphasise the vital moments during his long
commentary.

"Aye, never been a fight like it, or ever will be," he would
conclude. And somebody would invariably add . . . "Aye, an' it killed
Tommy as a boxer. He fought a couple of third raters after it and got
clobbered and had to chuck it at twenty-four years of age."

"Och well," Neagle would say. "He came to the Gorbals after that
and has a good pub now. But he hates it when I go in and say . . .
'Gies a Johnny Walker, Tommy. I said Johnny Walker, Tommy . . . no
a Mickey Walker.' And they would fall about laughing."

Ploys and schemes to make money, legitimately or otherwise, were
always a great talking point among them. They would speak about
the police who were always on the lookout for a 'take'. Despite the
presence of Sillitoe, Sammy was still paying the regular constables
and sergeant their weekly money to prevent harassment. But one of
them had tried to be greedy with him and the tale which ensued took
the legend of Sammy Wilson of Florence Street to new heights.

The constable was a new man to the Gorbals and its characters and
had been told by his beat mate that Wilson was all right for £1, but
no more. The new man smiled to himself when he saw the slim and
slender Sammy and, without saying to his mate, decided to lean on
him for more. "Hello boys . . . oh a new fellah," said Sammy when
the two policemen stopped by his pitch close. He had anticipated
them and had two single £1 notes neatly folded in his pocket and he
slipped them, without comment and without interrupting his
observations on the weather, to each of the constables. The new man
shook his head. "Just the one, eh! I've been used to getting two from
my last beat so from now on it's double . . . all right Mr Wilson?"
Sammy flushed with rage and grabbed back the pound note he had
just given the man. "See you," he said looking violently up at the tall
policeman, nearly a foot taller than he was. "See you . . . you'll be
dead pal before you get another fuckin' chance to tap me." The

policeman didn't argue back and was visibly shocked at the rough verbal handling he got from Wilson.

It was some weeks later when the regular beat man came to see Sammy. He was in plain clothes and obviously anxious to tell the bookie something and the pair of them moved away from the crowd standing at the pitch. "Sammy," he said. "I hope you never ever say to me what you said to that new man that came round with me. You know what happened . . . he died. Aye, snuffed it digging his garden. Sammy you know me . . . £1 does me fine." Sammy looked into the man's eyes· and didn't say anything for a few moments, then gave a slight, wry smile . . . "Aye. Aye . . . fine."

Dan Cronin was a well known hardman in the South Side. You didn't tell Cronin to fuck off . . . unless you had a smile on your face. But Sammy did. And he wasn't smiling.

It had been a "try on" for Cronin. He was figuring on the basis that if he could hit Wilson once for some money, he could be a regular "tap". He came in a taxi with another man. Sammy was standing with a group of the men when the car pulled up and a window lowered. "Sammy," called a voice. It was Cronin. "Sammy, can I see you for a minute."

He went over to the car and recognised him, but didn't know the other man. "Hello there Sammy," said Cronin, with a smile which vanished the moment he gave the greeting. "Right, Sammy . . . £1 for each of us."

"Oh . . . a pound is it," Wilson replied. "Tell ye what, then. I'll make it £2 for a go wi' each of you, one at a time, up that back close there."

The window slammed and the taxi drove off. Cronin never returned.

Communications were poor and the bookmakers were always liable to someone devising some kind of method of getting an illegitimate bet. The bookmaker's own pocket watch decided when bets would close for a particular race and when they did they would gather all the lines and put them in an envelope and seal it. They knew that as the "packet". Many of them, like Sammy, would take a late bet, but only if the punter had been standing with them before the "off". Other bookies were more loose on their arrangements for taking late bets, like Patsy Lannigan, who ran a pitch in Camden Street. The fact that he took such late bets was a challenge to the imaginative to make some quick money . . . but how? One group perfected what they thought was a foolproof method of cheating Patsy.

Tradesmen going about their various callings were a common sight on the streets; plumbers with their long water-main keys slung under their arm, the gasmen with their heavy bags on a shoulder, joiners

with their big canvas holdalls, and glaziers shouldering whole panes.
So no one thought it out of the ordinary that a glazier with a large
pane of glass regularly walked past Lannigan's pitch during racing
time. The glaziers always chalked their glass, either with sizes or with
a detection line. But the glazier that walked past Patsy's had marks on
his glass which had another meaning. A team of them had got access
to instant results by phoning the Exchange Telegraph, the news and
sports agency which served the bookmakers with results from all the
courses. One of their contacts worked there and gave them the same
instant service. They then marked the horse's number on the pane of
glass . . . and the glazier went for a stroll past Lannigan's pitch where
the last in line of the team put on the late bet. He had to be changed
regularly, of course, in order to avoid suspicion. Patsy eventually
smelled the bad egg, but couldn't identify it. All he knew was that
when he stopped taking late bets his losses were instantly adjusted.

After a round of laughs about the comical situations in which they
were regularly involved, the conversation often drastically changed
course to the serious issues of the day, particularly if John Neagle or
Tash Conlin, their intellectuals were there. "Don't say politics has
nothing to do with it," Tash would say in answer to any of them if
they argued otherwise. "Politics," he would say, "has to do with
everything . . . everything whether it's the price of a plain loaf or how
much you pay the factor." They believed Tash when he theorised, for
unlike them he had read books. Tash knew his Marx, Engels and
Trotsky, his Connolly, Collins and Griffith, and his McLean, McShane,
and Maxton. "Your whole lives are ruled by politics, whether you like
it or no'. And the politics in this country stink. Do you know what
they're about . . . property. Those who have got it have got a' the laws
on their side to help them keep it and nae Government is interested
in changing them. I've lived under a Tory Government, a Labour
Government, a Coalition Government and now it's what they call a
National Government, same thing as the one before it wi' a different
name just. And they were a' the same. Not one of them did anything
for us. They were quite happy for them wi' the money to make more
money out of them that has nae money. You take these houses we
live in. Bet not one of you knows who owns them. You a' think it's
the factor. Oh, aye, we know they're bastards, but they don't own the
houses. But I know who owns them."

He would rumble in the inside pocket of his old blue, pin-striped
suit, the stripes now completely worn from the front of the legs and
the jacket glazed, and from it would pull a pile of letters, a wallet
struggling to stay in one piece, stuffed with more letters and
envelopes, an E.P.N.S. cigarette case on which he had his initials

engraved in copperplate, his old Army paybook, and a thin school
jotter, neatly folded in two. He would separate it from the rest of his
pocket contents, which he carefully returned again. He would hold
the jotter up, like the evangelists did with their bibles on a Sunday in
the Candleriggs and other streets off the Trongate, and say, "This is
the evidence. Inside this book are all the facts about who owns your
houses . . . all supplied to me by my wee china Davie who works for
Macfie the factor and who knows through his work there how to find
out anything and everything about houses in the Gorbals. I once
asked Davie to find out for me who owned all these bloody houses
right here in our street, as well as some of the others roundabout.
And it's amazing the names of some of them. Wait till you hear this,
starting with our ain street. These are our owners, the ones that get
our rents . . . number 65, the Trustees of Mrs Rose Hyland, Kingsway,
London; number 73, J.Y. Gornall, Woodland Park, Prestatyn,
Flintshire; number 99, Mrs Norah Thomson, West Byfleet, Surrey,
executrix; numbers 121 and 125, James Marquis, Rouen, France, and
others; numbers 178 to 190, Ann Hendry and Frederick Hendry,
clergyman, Craigellachie; number 150, Mrs Isabella Schweder,
Worthing, Sussex; numbers 118 and 120, Mrs Georgina Dow,
Dundonald Street, Edinburgh; numbers 80 and 82 Mrs Jane Craig,
Knaresbrough, Yorkshire. There's three closes in Cumberland Street
owned by Mrs Esther Massiak of Stockholm, that's in Sweden, and
others. Four closes and shops in Crown Street owned by Clive
Cuthbertson care of the East India United Services Club, London.
And another two closes and shops owned by Mrs Annie C. Miller, St
Brededes, Jersey. I've got three more pages like that and Davie is
getting me more."

They were always impressed when Tash reeled off facts and figures
about anything, but particularly the housing speculators and would
whistle in astonishment as he related them, muttering disapproval
and chorussing "Fuckin' terrible so it is."

"Now tell me, for I don't know," Tash would go on. "What's a
minister up in bloody Craigie-lachy, or whatever they cry it, doing
owning closes in Florence Street? And a wife in Sweden wi' closes in
Cumberland Street? And some auld geyser sitting back in his big
chair in the India Club surrounded wi' flunkies feart tae talk to him in
case they waken him up and getting his cheque brought to him in a
silver tray. What's he doing owning a chunk of Crown Street? And a'
they others that live in the South of England. How should they a' be
sitting back in their big fancy villas and you and me having to scrape,
and that's what it is and you a' know it, scrape, scrape, scrape, to put
money in their pockets."

The thought of his words, no matter how many times he said them, always roused him and though he was the most placid and gentle of the men in the street, his pale, thin face would flush with anger. "You see the trouble wi' youse is that you don't think about these things. You just pay your money to auld Macfie and think he's the bastard. He's only the factor, the collector, the conductor taking the fares. I'm telling you, it's them in the big houses and the politicians that let them rake in the money that's to blame. The only time the politicians take action is when they think we might get out of hand. Land of hope and glory mother of the free they tell us and they bring in ten thousand troops and tanks ready to use against us right here in Glasgow the first year I was back from the war . . . for what? Because they were striking to get the forty-hour week. That was your Lloyd George and his Coalition Government for you. And I was there in George Square the day they read the Riot Act and the polis charged everybody wi' their batons drawn. That was the day they showed us whose side they were on. Nae wonder the men broke into the pubs in North Frederick Street and let them have it wi' beer bottles. Christ, one year they're in the trenches fighting the Huns that Haig and a' them said were the enemy, the next year they're back here and fighting wi' another enemy . . . the real enemy, the ones that are trying to keep us down. Dae ye no' wonder how a lot of the boys are wondering who really was the enemy in fourteen tae eighteen? Well, I've got nae doubts. And neither did John McLean . . . and they got rid of him because he tried to do something about it. See if any o' us is too clever and start getting things organised to change the system they're right on to you. Land of hope and glory . . . mother of the free . . . that'll be right."

Some of them hadn't heard about McLean and asked about him. Tash's tone of voice would change when he spoke about McLean. "Great man. A truly great man," he would say, and would turn to Benny . . . "He stayed out in Pollokshaws near your Aunty Beck. Aye, was born just near the wee round Toll house at the far end of the Shaws. Frightened of no man was John McLean. Told the Labour Party an' a' what he thought of them for stopping the workers' direct action campaign. Told the Communist Party as well for they were selling out to Moscow. I can see him now, standing there at the corner wi' Cumberland Street when he stood for election here in the Gorbals. It was the week I came back from the Army and I'm telling you I was thinking a few things masel'. But John McLean put them into order for me. I followed him round a' the streets just to listen to him. I had never heard of the propertied class till John spelt it out for me. I heard him that often on the subject, his very words are imprinted in my mind. The root of all the trouble in society, he would say, is the inevitable robbery of the workers by the propertied class . . . simply because it is the propertied class. To end that robbery would be to end the social troubles in modern society. And if Scotland had to elect its own Parliament it should sit right here in Glasgow . . . the workshop of Scotland. And it would be a working class parliament."

"Aye, he was great. Well, they got him in the end. Charged him wi' sedition and he was in an out of jail . . . for speaking his mind. They drugged his food when he was in Peterhead and when he went on hunger strike the warders held him down and rammed the food right into him. When he came out the jail he was like an auld auld man. Died at forty-four. I was at the funeral out at Eastwood Cemetery. He got some send-off, I'm telling ye."

Another voice would dramatically change the sombre mood of the gathering.

"Anybody got a *Noon Record?* I want to see who they're tipping for the three o'clock at Ayr."

10

Dancing at the Tripe

The Gorbals slept but never died. Compressed within its near-mile triangular boundaries lived 45,000 people. The black canyons of tenements were interspersed with buildings which had been there before the houses, a range of industrial factories and premises. By day the suburb throbbed with their activity, their tall chimneys belching black nimbus clouds, some so heavy they became instant fog, and the aromas of the products gasped to the sky in big puffs of steam and gases. There was a biscuit factory, a confectionary works, bakeries, a jam factory, a sauce factory and a wine and cordial factory, which gave a variety of homely smells. They gave the Gorbals its blossom fragrance to relieve the senses from the harsher fumes of the skin warehouse, heavy and fetid, the dye and chemical works, strange and choking, and the twenty-four hour inferno of Dixon's Blazes iron works. The Gorbals also had a cotton mill, a smithy, two cemeteries, a tube works, an industrial school, and the famous Hutchesons' Grammar School, an academic factory for the offspring of parents who lived in the grander tenements of Crosshill and Shawlands and the pomp stone villas of Newlands and Pollokshields, and who could afford to pay up to twenty one guineas a year for their education, that being about as much as would keep a working man for nearly three months.

The street never stilled. Even when the Catholic and Protestant children went to their separate schools, the Gorbals children being the same victims of the 1918 Act and its religious apartheid as other Scots pupils, there was always activity and noise of some kind in the streets. The ragman fluttered a bounce of balloons from tall canes at the rear of his little pony and cart and blew as good a reveille or cookhouse-door as they did at Maryhill Barracks.

The man who came with the sheeps' bags and reeds had a loud deep voice, baritone going on bass, and you could hear his call thirty closes away . . . "Trrrrrr . . . iiiiii . . . yepppppp". The fish hawkers would summon wives with their "Loch Fie . . . yennnnnnnnnnn herrrr

. . ennnnnn" whether or not their herring came from Loch Fyne,
tender and pink and, they said, tasting like no other herring on earth.
There were the sticks and briquette men, like Darkie Marshall. Darkie
was a West Indian and he had a little brick shed in Surrey Lane
where he and his boys chopped old boxes and wood into firewood
kindlers which they tied in six inch fasces, bagging the sawdust to sell
as floor covering for the butchers' shops and public houses. Darkie's
boys would also carry hot briquettes, fresh from the Gushet coalrea,
and trade them in the streets, a dozen to an old Lanark tomato box,
with their cries of "Breeeeee . . . kettts; breeeee . . . ketts." The fruit
barrows would be stacked high with Granny Smiths and Macintosh
Reds, Victoria plums and pomegranates, but the call was invariably for
their pears, for they made a good call did their pears, their
"hunnnnneeeee . . . pey . . .yerrrrs."

And various evangelists, sandwich-board men, and other itinerants
wandered the streets with their own particular message . . . men like
Bum Brady who had his own one-man campaign against nicotine. He
would proclaim his message to all who listened as well as distribute
cards which recorded his words . . . "Did Jesus Smoke? Never! He
never used tobacco."

But it was the shouts of the coalmen which dominated. Next to the
midgie men, the refuse collectors, the coalmen had the next dirtiest
and most arduous job in the street. They would be up before dawn to
feed and water their horses, many spavine hocked old nags, in the
railway arch stables in Cumberland Street before going to the
coalreas to load their carts, double and sometimes triple stacked with
hundredweight hessian bags of what they called "best house coal".
Each of the coalmen had their own distinctive shout. They toured the
streets every day and even though there may have been six, or more,
of them in one street at the one time, they always knew that their
coalman was among them.

Most of them would deliver on tick and collect on Friday, pay day.
Orders for regulars would be delivered whether they were at home
or not, for you could leave the key in your door and only the
coalman would dare enter your house. And the regular coalmen were
the good coalmen, laying their big bags gently to rest in the kitchen
or lobby bunker so that the dust didn't pollute the house so much
that it settled in a fine film on the bread and butter slices laid out for
Da's tea an hour after they had left.

At night in the Gorbals most forms of social communications could
be found. The Gorbals had more pubs per head of population than
any other district in Glasgow . . . 118 of them; one for every 383 of
the 45,146 population. Some streets had more than others. Florence

Street only had them at the corners with other streets, like the Moy at the corner of Cumberland Street, Cameron's at the corner with Old Rutherglen Road, and Elder's and Eadie's at the corner of Caledonia Road. But in many streets a man could get more than his fill if he walked, and drank, from one end to the other. Only the hardiest could stand a pub crawl of Crown Street. It had 14 pubs. Eglinton Street had 11, Gorbals Street 10, Cumberland and Ballater Streets each had seven, Adelphi had six, and the rest of the streets averaged three to four apiece.

The pubs, in the main, were named after their proprietors. There was Morrison's, Elder's, Moir's, Winton's, Lorimer's, Flanagan's, McKillop's, McNee's, Marr's, Robb's, Munro's, Hanlon's, McNab's, Sharp's, Beacom's, Brechin's, Holmes, Brown's, Stephenson Taylor's, McLaren's, Hurrel's, Kennedy's, Archibald's, Souter's, Teacher's, Meiklejohn's, Cairns, McCann's, Goldie's, Sproule's, Keith's, Doyle's, Cleland's Finnegan's, Leonard's, Roper's, Sweeney's, Vogt's, Webster's, Quinn's, Molloy's, McNulty's, Watt's, McKenna's, McCondach's, Watt's and Cook's.

A lot more imagination, and promise, was used when they chose other names for their bars. There was St Mungo's, The Glue Pot, Rosie's, Waverley, White Horse, Old Judge, The Clachan, The Pig 'n Whistle, The Orchard, The Splash, The Cecil, The Struan, The Ivy, The Moffat Arms, The Oval, The Challenge, The Railway Tavern, The Ferry, The Birch, The Coronation, The Braehead, The Logan, The Wee Mill, The Stag, The Hole in the Wall, The Four Ways, The Why Not, The Moulin Rouge, The Boat House, The Hampden, The Thistle, The Emerald Isle, Doake's, The Wellington, The Bhoreen, The Cloch, The Bellwood, The Holly Tree, The Camden Vaults, The Bible Class, The Carlton, The Granite City, The Cavendish, The Locheil, The Grapes, The Lion, Jackson's, The Wheatsheaf, The Wee Man's, The Tap, The Apsley, The Havanna, The Windsor, The Subway, The Lorimer, The Kildonan, The Erigoil View, The Devon, The Gordon, The Star, The Errol, The Moy, The Loudon, The Globe, The New Era, The Princess, The Seaforth, The St John, The Glenbervie, The Turf, The Tyre, The Central, The Haven, The Oxford, The Mill Inn, The Glen, The Cockatoo, The King's Arms, The Surrey, The Balmoral, and The Mally Arms, special to Benny for he had sold newspapers outside it as a boy.

The pubs were men's places. They would stand at the bars, one foot resting on a brass rail, the other in the scattering of sawdust to soak up spills and bronchial spits. There was no place for women in their kind of drinking world, and many pubs would boldly point out that fact with a "No women permitted" sign painted in neat white lettering above the licensee's name on the entrance door. Some women, usually the older ones, would accompany their menfolk to the bars which did allow females, but they had to be kept out of sight behind divisions of opaque glass called the "sitting room", which often had its own entrance from the street so that the men at the bar, getting on with the serious business of drinking, would not be disturbed by the sight of them.

Women too could use the Family Department, a small compartment set aside from the bar with its own entrance from the street, and which only sold liquor for carrying away. The favourites were screwtops, large dark bottles of beer which most shops stamped with their own mark and only that shop would accept them back for the penny refund, and a flat muskin bottle of whisky the contents of which were only sufficient for one small glass, or, if the horses and dogs had been good to them, a half-giller in a stone bottle.

When the pubs closed there were shebeens like Oily Gregg's or Red Nose Andrews and many others. There were theatres, cinemas, dance halls and if you couldn't afford the price of them, there were entertainers who came to the streets and back-courts, the last remnants of the wandering troubadours and minstrels of the Middle Ages. They would sing, play fiddles and saxophones, and bring their own dance boards, their very own miniature stage, on which they would rattle out tap-dance routines fit for a Command performance. The house windows would fill with "hings" if O'Leary, Tracy and O'Leary came to the street. They were a great trio. The O'Leary brothers wore kilts cut ridiculously short with old military tunics to perform a rookie soldier act, rifle drill and all, which brought roars and howls from the stalls, balcony and gods of the tenement audiences. When the brothers finished their act, Tracey blacked-up and gave them the best Jolson act they had seen since they waited four hours themselves in the Coliseum queue to watch *The Singing Fool.*

One group came from as far away as Coatbridge and the children would shout "Here's Mr Watson the Charlie Chaplin man." There was Tommy Hughes, songs with banjo, Teddy Downie, songs with accordion, the Shearer brothers, dancing a speciality, Larry McGriskin, on clarinet accompanying his partner Eddie Gauchan who danced, and Davie Able, better than any of the banjo players who played to the theatre queues up town.

Many came unaccompanied . . . Poncinello with a shiny black piano accordion he could make sound like a small orchestra; Tommy Lennie, just one leg, a crutch and a clarinet with a repertoire that included all the latest American jazz; club-footed Limpy Dan, whose only showbusiness offering was *By Cool Siloam's Shady Rill* and when he got to the line "Whose years with changeless virtue crowned" would deftly start at the beginning again because he didn't know any more; and Old Granny with a pram and a gramophone with only one record, *The Old Rugged Cross*, and if the pennies came down by the time it got to "The emblem of suffering and shame" she would take it off and move up three closes.

But all of them were better than old Tommy McLean, a modeller. For Tommy only knew one tune, but he sung it very badly, to say the least, despite the fact it was his own composition. It went:

When it's Springtime in the model
The model in Carrick Street
The bugs begin to yodel and
Ye cannae get to sleep
You get up to read the paper or
Wash your dirty feet
When it's Springtime in the model
The model in Carrick Street.

Tommy had to work hard to get his pennies.

Maybe they didn't have a banjo player as talented as Davie Able, but the real theatres had their own magic. There were ones a short walk away from the Gorbals, like the Metropole, just down Gorbals Street and over the Victoria Bridge to the Stockwell, where Charlie Chaplin himself had played and where Stan Laurel's dad was the manager, or the Queen's behind Glasgow Cross, a few hundred yards further on. But there were stars as good as any in their own theatre, the Princess's. It had been going since before the turn of the century and had entertained generations of folks from the Gorbals. The favourite stars were Tommy Morgan and his old pal Tom Yorke who could fill every one of the 1439 seats, as well as stack in the 162 the Firemaster allowed in the standing area at the rear of the stalls.

If Morgan and Yorke were the stars at the Princess's the highlight shows were the pantomimes . . . Handy Andy, Goody Two Shoes, Hanky Panky, Jack O'Hearts, and Prince Charming. Heaven on earth was a bar of Fry's Sandwich, a seat in the circle, "Big Beanie" Tommy Morgan himself on stage, skinny pal Tom Yorke feeding, and a programme which told you about all the fun that was to come, and packed with advertisements offering the best things in life, few of which you could afford. "Thomson's Piano of Govan Road are stocking Collard and Collard, Eungblut, Windover, Brindsmead and Burling and Mansfield pianos. Reconditioned from £16. New uprights £30"; "Morris Minor car . . . £130; Oxford £275; . . . from A. & O. Fraser. Official distributor". But being a theatre in the Gorbals, the liquor advertisments predominated. "Where Men Meet In Town .

. . His Lordship's Larder." "Have some beer . . . it's great stuff . . . at McKenzie's Seaforth Bar, 109 Gorbals Street." "What about a 'Happy Day' to guarantee a perfect night!" "Happy Days" came from the little bottles of strong ale they called Wee Heavies, Wee Fowlers or Wee Dumpies and which they poured into a pint glass filling the remainder with heavy ale, the dark oak of one mixing with the red walnut of the other creating a nuggety brown blend, a pint of which, if preceded by a quarter gill of whisky the last drops of which were kaleidoscoped into the beer froth, was a true working man's relish. Two of them and your happy day well and truly started.

Tommy Morgan and Tom Yorke were, like so many comedians, laughed at and loved not so much for what they said, which at times wasn't really all that funny. They were laughed at because it was "them". It was seeing them, watching their antics, listening to that gutsy voice of Morgan and his catchphrase Clairty, Clairty which meant "I declare to goodness". It never mattered whether they knew or not, he made it sound funny.

Tommy was from Bridgeton, although he never said it that way. It was Brigton. The East End, and predominantly Protestant. Tommy's humour was raw and rough, a corner boy's corner boy. They would have loved him in Florence Street as they passed the time of day, for he was as much of them as they were of him. One of his popular routines in the Princess's pantos was playing the part of Andy Andrews, described in the programme as "a poor Scot". Tom Yorke played Lochinvar, "a wealthy Scot". A typical sketch would go:

Lochinvar . . . "Ah weel . . . my steamer wrecked upon the shore. Who cares? I've cash to buy a dozen mair. Now 'spose I was to be generous and gi'e you £1,000. Whit wa'd ye dae?"

Andrews . . . "Count it!"

And the audience would be convulsed. For that was their humour, street humour. If someone were to give them £1000, a first instinct would have been the same as Tommy's poor man Andy. Count it.

Lochinvar . . . "Spose I gi'ed it to you all in gold?"

Andrews . . . "I'd bite it."

Lochinvar . . . "Well, if I gi'ed you Treasury notes, what would you do?"

Andrews . . . "Sterilise 'em."

With no reason, their subject matter would suddenly change.

Lochinvar . . . "We'll climb Ben Nevis, if ye dinna mind."

Andrews . . . "Ye push me up, I'll push masel' behind".

Even without the benefit of a Happy Day, lines like that could rock the theatre. They had no mountains to climb with their audiences.

The other great Tommy who was a regular at the Princess's pantos was Tommy Lorne, who many swore was the funniest-ever man on a Scottish stage. He too could miraculously transform similar infantile scripts, with his gangling innocuousness, into almost realistic domestic, and very funny situations. He would be Tam the Postman and some of the other characters in the production would be Sir Anderston Cross, Fairy Harmony, Fairy Spice, Simon Slyfox, Captain Put and Bosun Take.

Mistress McIntyre . . . "Tam what's the latest at Kildaldcumkirknocton?"

Tam .... "Dinna swear at me missus."

Mistress McIntyre . . . "We'll cook a haddy first . . . what shall we stuff it with?"

Tam . . . "Sassages!" He would then pick some up from the stove, sniff them and exclaim . . . "They've got sunstroke!"

Mistress McIntyre . . . "Despatch them with a humane killer."

Tam . . . (raising a mallet to the sausages) . . . "They'll never smile again."

Benny Lynch loved the theatre, especially the pantos. But he liked the dancing even better. A man could dance once a week at a different dance hall for a year and a half in Glasgow without going to the one place twice. Many of them were in halls owned by the local burgh, their names being from the locality of that particular burgh; but that didn't worry them or in any way detract from the glamour and excitement that a "night at the jigging" provided. With a lively band and a good partner, the functional local community hall could be paradise itself.

There was the Govan Town Hall, St Mungo Hall, City Hall, Trades Hall, Parnie Street Halls, North Woodside Halls, The Pollokshaws Burgh, Partick Burgh, Springburn Burgh, Shettleston Public, Bridgeton Public, Elmbank Street Halls, and the Ancient Order of Hibernian Halls. The Tollcross Co-operative and the Shettleston Co-operative had halls, so did the Riddrie, West Regent, and Quarryknowe Masonic. There was the Couper Institute and the Pearce Institute. The Ballieston Welfare and the Shettleston Welfare. There were the Wilton Street Halls and the Whitehill Street Hall. Then there were the private enterprise halls, mainly custombuilt for the dance craze, riding on the wave of the foot-tapping beat they called jazz, but which still incorporated more traditional melodies to let them foxtrot and waltz, one-step or tango like Valentino had done. Uptown had its Berkeley, Playhouse, Albert, Locarno and the West End Ballrooms; the suburbs had their Dennistoun Palais, the Plaza, F & F, Tower, the Garage, the Top Hat, the Marlborough, Lido, Mascot, Ruskin, Pirolis and the Coffin.

But for those of the South Side, one place was incomparable. Its official name was The Kingston Palais and it was in Gloucester Street, which they pronounced the Irish way, Glow-cester, in the district of Tradeston, the cheek-by-jowl suburb of the Gorbals. The Kingston Palais was a small restaurant by day, a few trestle tables, serving the basic staples of life—all that was required of a restaurant in a suburb like Tradeston, or the Gorbals. And when lunchtime was over, they would clear the tables and stack them, the band would arrive, a humble group of three or four, and the Kingston was instantly transformed to a place of magic.

They called it . . . The Tripe.

The Tripe was run by James Sweeney, a former policeman, a tall, well-made man who made sure his daily dancing, matinees, evening, and sometimes late night, was run with order and decorum. The Tripe was for good dancers. That's why Benny Lynch and his mates went. A man's ability, or lack of it, as a dancer was spoken about. Being a good fighter was a character reference to the men at the corner; so was being a good dancer. And when the women spoke of a man, his dancing prowess was of prime importance.

Dancers who went to the Tripe were heading places , just like the boxers were. Dancing, like boxing, was for real. You could go places if you were good at either. The Tripe to the dancers was like the LMS Rovers to the boxers. Survive it and you would survive anywhere. The legendary Wyoming Dance Formation team, one from Florence Street, one from Oxford Street and one from the Gallowgate with their partners perfected some of their initial skills at the Tripe. So did Johnny Bryden, Willie Lewis and Jimmy Forbes, great men to get a classy foxtrot with for they had the real ballroom style, poise and an aloof indifference to those who watched them, envious of the way they could weave and glide through the throng.

"Gonnie gees a dance?" Feet Milvanney would ask Benny. "You're rerr on the flerr," she would say. Feet had feet, large and splayed, and because she wore half-inch heel flatties, they looked even more splayed than the ones who could afford the new fashionable short high-heels. Paddy, Benny's pal, and others would laugh at him when he got up to dance with Feet. "Gimme a birl, Benny," she would say. "You're really good when you birl." And he would birl her. And in the middle of a birl . . . drop her. They would laugh when Feet landed on her knickers and Benny would walk away to look for another partner.

Like the boxing, the dancing could be a hard and competitive game. If you fluffed it at the Tripe, bumped and trod on dainty toes, they would talk about you; you would never be refused a dance, but they would prefer to dance with others.

Above the Tripe was a golf ball factory and, at times, their machines would be clacking at such a pitch you could feel their vibrations shaking the building so much it seemed to come right up through the floor.

The Salvation Army (Kingston Corps) also had a practice room and you could hear them too. They would blast it out with all their Christian fervour:

> What a Friend we have in Jesus,
> All our sins and griefs to bear!
> What a privilege to carry
> Everything to God in prayer!
> O what peace we often forfeit,
> O what needless pain we bear,
> All because we do not carry,
> Everything to God in prayer!

This made the little band of the Connelly Brothers and Paddy Cassidy pitch up with their latest hit.

> Give my regards to Broadway
> Remember me to Herald Square
> Tell all the gang at 42nd Street
> That I'll soon be there
> Whisper them I am yearning to mingle
> With the old time throng
> Give my regards to old Broadway
> And say that I'll be there ere long.

An enthusiastic tenor sax, piano and drums could work wonders against a *Friend of Jesus* and the machine that made the golf balls.

Heaven, hell and paradise . . . all in the one building.

Sometimes the tension of the dance rivalry would boil over, more likely on a holiday when it would be very crowded. But James Sweeney and his two sons Ownie and James Junior could always provide a solution, the ultimate sanction being a rapid propulsion into Gloucester Street for which they got one reprieve. "You can get back in but only if you pay again." If there was more trouble, they didn't get that second chance.

Being the kind of meeting places they were, with street rivals meeting street rivals and that rivalry being forefronted with the competition of the dance and for the women, trouble could often flare. And sometimes with tribal ferocity. That was the way it was one night at the nearby Bedford Parlour and they spoke about it in hushed tones at the Tripe and other gathering points for years afterwards.

James Dalziel was the chief runner and collector for Pat Donnachy, the Herbertson Street bookie, and was one of the best dancers at the Parlour. Because of that, and the way he dressed and his name, they knew him as Razzle Dazzle. He was so well known as that there were many who didn't know him as anything else. Razzle Dazzle's enthusiasm for the dance was such that he used to organise clabber dances . . . alfresco dances in the open coupled with a Sunday outing—similar to the ones they had over in Donegal and called Crossroad dances. Two shillings and you got a return trip to Lunderston Bay, a cup of tea, two cakes, and clabber dancing to an accordion, and if you were lucky a clarinet and a trumpet as well, for the whole day.

It was on the first Saturday in March 1934 and during a violent rainstorm that a group of men entered the Bedford Parlour during a dance session. They were from across the river in the Calton and ignored the normal customs and courtesies of the hall, like drying the soles of their wet shoes on the big coir mat at the door . . . and paying their entrance money. That was two straight fouls and they laughed and joked among themselves at the resentful reaction of the Parlour's regular cutomers. They had all been drinking and showed it and that combined with the fact they were now recognised as members of the San Toy and Calton Entry gangs was bad news.

Mrs Stephenson, the owner of the popular little hall, knew all the signs and was considerably alarmed before the eruption came, just a little over a half an hour after their invasion of the Parlour.

Trouble was signalled by the loud shriek of one of the girl dancers who had seen the first spark as two men made for each other. Almost immediately the knives came out and within seconds the dancehall was the setting of a fullscale gangfight, Calton versus South Side and every punch, boot, strike, butt and blow delivered with but one purpose—to kill. They carried Razzle to the ambulance but he was beyond all help. The deep slash in his throat went most of the way from one ear to the other and when they spoke about it at the street corners and in the dance halls of the South Side they would say "the Calton bastarts nearly cut his heid aff". They closed the Parlour after that and a little light went out of the South Side.

It was a straight walk back from the Tripe to the Gorbals, Gloucester Street becoming Cook Street then Bedford Street narrowing into Bedford Lane, where you could hire a barrow from old Mrs Elliott and go into instant business as fruit or fish hawker, briquette or stick man, or furniture removals man. From Bedford Lane the route led to Cleland Street and then Gorbals Street where someone would invariably say, "Fancy Knotts's?", and if they had the few coppers which was all that was required, Knotts would be the next stop.

They didn't think of Knotts merely as a restaurant at the bottom end of Florence Street near Old Rutherglen Road, on the opposite side from Sammy Wilson's bookie pitch. Knotts was no mere restaurant. Of course, it sold the best-cooked and tastiest food in the whole of the Gorbals except, that is, for the sizzling fish suppers they created in the ocean of boiling lard in the long stainless steel range of the Deep Sea chip shop in Crown Street. They didn't have fish and chips at Knotts, but there was everything else that they wanted, and that consisted of the full range of the average family's weekly diet; although it always seemed that they tasted better in Knotts.

There were platefuls of ham bones, so many they had to fight to stay on the one plate and from beneath the hot steam that rose from them, the juice oozed from the red pig meat which draped the bones and which had its flavour heightened by its proximity to the bone— "the nearer the bone the sweeter the meat" they would say—and by the smoke-curing process undergone at the bacon curers. There were houghs and pigs feet, the top end of which had meat that was tastier than the hen they had at Christmas. A shilling could buy a banquet; Scotch broth in deep bowls, white with a single blue stripe, each the size of a dinner plate; and spoons so big they would joke that the Paddy navvies had used them to dig the Mickey Dam at Milngavie; mince with the best potatoes in season, Kerr's Pinks or floury Golden Wonders cooked with their jackets on, but better still if it was early summer and they were the little Ayrshire epicures, straight from the sandy loam at Girvan, so tender and sweet you could skin them with a good scrub; rice pudding the likes of which only granny made; and a fourth course from the most talked-about single item of food in all the Gorbals . . . the Knotts dumpling. Robert Knotts would prepare the dumplings first thing in the morning for they needed a long boil on the coal-fired galley range, black and furnace hot, in the back kitchen of their little restaurant, a conversion, like most of the shops, of a two room and kitchen house in the tenement row. What the Tripe was to dancing, Knotts was to eating . . . basic. It was unpainted, amply stained, and well worn, but the bare wooden tables were always scrubbed and frontal imperfections were amply compensated by bonhomie, cameraderie and honest home cooking.

Robert did the preparation of the dumplings for, as he said, it was a man's job. He used a two-handled galvanised basin, the kind that some people used as a child's bath, for his mix . . . flour, eggs, suet, currants, raisins, grated breadcrumbs—"great for holding it all to-gether," he would say—milk, some sugar and some treacle and a precise amount, only he knew how much, of the aromatic Allspice which was said to have the flavour of cinnamon, nutmeg and cloves all in the one. When his mix was right he would empty the contents, scraping the last pieces out with his hands, into a muslin cloth that would have covered half a bed, knotting it neatly at the top then lowering it gently into the boiling cauldron of the enormous saucepan, the like of which was used by Desperate Dan in the *Dandy* for his Sunday stew. It took three to four hours of gentle simmering, and the same time again puffing out wisps of steam before it had sighed itself cool and solid enough to be carefully placed on a mammoth willow-pattern serving plate and carried to the marble-topped counter by the entrance door. There it would sit in all its gourmet glory, the king of all dumplings, round and dark, sometimes so dark and rich with dried fruit that they said Annie Knotts had zebo-ed it. Its size and presence challenged everyone who entered the restaurant. Unless they had been to Knotts before, it was the biggest single dumpling they had ever seen. You could always tell a first-timer for they would pause by it and look at it in wonderment. Some would touch it to test if it was real; men would clap it like they would a friendly dog as they left the restaurant. It was so firm and solid they would tell their friends that Minnie Smith, whose father was Gunboat Smith, a fine battler of a man, and Lizzie McKenna, the waitresses, would use it to stand on to wash the top of the front window. Benny Lynch loved Knotts's speciality. If it was whole and uncut when he came in he would square up to it, shadow box with it and give it an imaginary knock-out and tell them, "That's what I do wi' dumplings". And it never failed to bring the house down.

They had their poverty in the Gorbals. They had their insanitary houses. They had their unbearable overcrowding. There were days when the worst prospect was tomorrow for tomorrow would only bring them more misery. But in the midst of it there was life to be relished and enjoyed. And it could seem that after a night at the Princess's or the Parlour or the Tripe or to a pub followed by a visit to the Deep Sea or Knotts or even Bridie Travis's chipshop for a ha'penny of crispy crumbs, in the company of good friends, life could be not so bad after all.

A night like that could make them feel that even their world was a great place. And tomorrow might even be a better day.

11

Was The Horse Painted?

The Dingleys were not like Gorbals people. They were in the money. Big money. And when they said a word like rotter or bottle, it was pronounced rotter . . . and bottle. In the Gorbals it was "raw . . . er" and "boe . . . el". But you didn't speak that way when you lived on a small estate with your own stables and an orchard round you and with servants and staff to look after you. No one in the Gorbals lived like that. But John George Dingley was like Sammy Wilson in many ways. He came from a frugal background. He loved sport. He was a gambler. And because of Benny Lynch, the lives of the two families were to cross.

John George Dingley was known as George Dingley. Like Sammy he was a bookie. But big-time bookie. No standing in the street or mixing with the corner boys and sorting out the pitch-and-toss ruffians for him. George Dingley aimed for the big time even before he left school. And he got there.

The family came to Glasgow from Edinburgh and George was born in 1873. At school he was brilliant at arithmetic and could total lines with uncanny ease, a skill the course clerks appreciated on the many days he truanted to work as a helper at the races in Bothwell, Hamilton and Ayr. He studied the bookies and their clerks as they bagged their stake money at varying odds, mentally tallying their takings for counting practice. This, he decided, was to be the life for him. After leaving school he worked around the courses until he had saved enough money to start his own book as an illegal street bookie, making his pitch in Steel Street, just round the corner from the first close in Greendyke Street, off Saltmarket, where he and his bride Mary had got their first house.

But standing in the street like the other illegal bookies was not his idea of making a living. He could make a lot more if he had the street bookies working for him; that was simple arithmetic. He started with two, then three and soon there was a small team of them working on a commission basis for George, now settled in his own Turf Commission Agent's offices at 47 Waterloo Street . . . with real carpets on the floor and a staff of assistants. One of them was a cockney and his name for the boss was to become the name by which he was to be known throughout the racing world, at York and Newmarket, at Lincoln and Haydock Park, the Scottish courses, and to his friends everywhere . . . even his growing family knew him by the name. It was . . . the Guv'nor.

Before leaving Greendyke Street, the first of the Dingley children had arrived. George Junior was born in 1900. By the time they had settled into their small estate there were six others, Willie and Harry, May, Bunty, Betty and Anne.

Roxburgh Villa, the little estate at Bothwell, where the covenanters suffered their crushing defeat in 1679, was just eight miles away from the Gorbals by road. The variation in their life styles was much greater. The young Dingleys lived an idyllic life at the Villa, the girls riding their ponies—Duchess was their favourite—and the worst trouble that could befall the boys was when Stevie the gardener would chase them when, with other pals from the pleasant houses nearby they would steal fruit from the orchard. Bullies from the village stayed clear of them for the Dingley boys, particularly Harry, had the reputation of being the best fighters in the district. And they made sure no one ever went near brother Willie for he had suffered meningitis as a child and it had left him permanently weak.

The Guv'nor had prospered and had widened his sporting interests. He had a string of successful racehorses, all well-known names to the punters : . . . Bargate, Dreamy Donna, Muted String, Bologna, Amadine, Southern Sea, Inlaid, Royal Pilot, Polydeuces, Peter Pax, Kirk-Alloway, Buttertubs, Silverwells and White Bud. He had started the Victoria Club for professional prizefighting, just by the railway bridge which crossed Dalmarnock Road in Dalmarnock, and he was negotiating to buy an even bigger house, Johnstone Hall at Holytown, a village about four miles east of Bothwell. Johnstone Hall was a house befitting a man of his parts. It was a three-storeyed early Victorian villa of fifteen rooms, stables, kennels, garages, billiard room, its own electricity plant and with even more house-staff then Roxburgh Villa.

John George Dingley, the Guv'nor, tall, distinguished, walrus-moustached, dressy as a Duke, patron of the turf and other sports, had the making of a legend. And his involvement with one particular horse was one of racing's great sensations. The horse was White Bud and as a result of two specific races, one at Haydock Park in Lancashire, the other at Ayr in July and September of 1923 the Guv'nor's racing career was brought to an abrupt end.

White Bud had been his favourite horse. With it he had triumphed in one of the classics of the English turf, the Lincolnshire Handicap. The odds were all in his favour and it brought him one of the biggest single fortunes ever won from one race. But later White Bud was to run in a fashion which, to say the least was "erratic". So erratic, in fact, that some men swore it wasn't White Bud which had won the Lincoln. Others vowed that the White Bud which had won the English classic hadn't been White Bud at all but another horse painted with the long white forehead streak which had been a feature of the horse. That was the God's honest truth, they pledged, and old George had cleaned up a quarter of a million into the bargain. And that was the truth too, they said.

Wherever racing men meet the story of George Dingley and White Bud is remembered. Whatever the truth of the story, the Jockey Club held their own inquiry. Their findings were couched in the fustian fashion of the sport's ruling authority: "The Rules of Racing, Part 24 (Corrupt Practices and Disqualification of Persons), Paragraph 6 read as follows. Every person so offending shall be warned off Newmarket Heath and other places where these rules are in force." In short, it meant he was banned from every racecourse in the country. His jockey had his licence withdrawn and his trainer was severely cautioned.

In almost disbelief, the Guv'nor turned up at Doncaster in Leger week and was shocked when his friends Campbell Russell and the famous trainer John McGuigan told him that he would not be allowed "inside" at the following day's racing. They advised him, however, to confirm their views with Mr Weatherby, the Jockey Club Steward. The official was polite, but firm: "Mr Dingley," he said, "you cannot again enter the Jockey Club enclosure." He left immediately for Glasgow where his first instruction was to sell every one of his big stable of racehorses as quickly as possible. The Guv'nor's world had turned upside down. He was Page One news for his deeds on the racecourse.

He was also Page One news in the domestic front. His estranged wife Mary, living in impoverished circumstances in a rundown tenement in Albion Street, one of the oldest streets in Glasgow, had raised an action in Hamilton Sheriff Court to get a more equitable share of her husband's wealth as aliment money. He had been paying her £1 a week. She was asking the court to raise the weekly payment to £12 a week. As her lawyers put it, Mr Dingley was a man of considerable wealth. "He owned a stud of at least ten horses which were pedigreed and of considerable value. One of these horses was White Bud and as a result of its winning the Lincolnshire Handicap, Mr Dingley was reputed to have won on that race alone the sum of

£50,000. He had paid the jockey, a lad of sixteen named Beasley, £1000 for winning the race. He was now regarded as one of the most successful Turf Commission Agents in Glasgow, employed a large staff and owns a pleasure motor car for which it is believed he paid over £900."

Dingley's own lawyers countered by saying he wasn't nearly as well off as he had once been and, as an illustration, pointed to the fact that he now only owned one car whereas at one time he had eleven. And, anyway, Mrs Dingley had intemperate habits, a low style of living and had no desire to better herself.

Like their father, young George and Harry Dingley both knew what they wanted to be early in life. Their choice was in the same industry . . . boxing. Harry said he was going to be a pro' boxer, but the Guv'nor put his foot down. "Fight as much as you like, but not for money," he ordered. So he did . . . and became one of the best amateurs in the country. He was fly, feather and lightweight champion of Scotland, in the British team at the Paris and Amsterdam Olympics. At the Tailte Games in Dublin, Gene Tunney, conqueror of Dempsey and world heavyweight champion, presented him with the Best Boxer medal.

George Junior had no ambition to participate in the sport at the hard end. There were other ways of being involved and he was astute enough to know there was plenty of money to be made from it . . . without the pain. He was to be a promoter.

He learned the Turf Commission trade in his father's office in Waterloo Street, later opening offices of his own in West Regent Street and in Hope Street, having established himself as a successful boxing promoter, billing all the top British professionals in his shows at the Victoria Club, men like Jimmy Driscoll and Jimmy Wilde, the man they said was the greatest-ever of the little men to enter the ring until, that is, another wee man, one from the Gorbals, was to part the ropes. George also became a licensed fight referee, a manager, a businessman, and a council member of the British Boxing Board of Control. A veritable pillar of society.

George was clever and shrewd. As Sammy Wilson was the son of Jocky, the Florence Street hard man, George was the son of George, the White Bud man, and as the years fostered the legend of the famous racing incident, George Junior's own success in life as a prosperous and thrusting promoter went ahead in the same leaps and bounds as his father's life had done. He had married Rita Smellie, glamorous daughter of a wealthy Ayr tavern owner, and they lived in a spacious villa, first of all in Pollokshields, Glasgow's wealthiest suburb where the smallest house would have been a castle in the

Gorbals and where the biggest ones really were built like castles, squared gunloops, crenellations, angle turrets and all. And from wealthy Pollokshields George and his young family moved on to an even better house, one he had built to his own specifications in the best part of his wife's hometown, across the way from the racecourse. They called it after one of his father's favourite horses. But it wasn't the one that everyone knew, White Bud; instead it was Silverwells, a name that brought pleasant memories to the family. As well as being the name of one of the Guv'nor's best horses, Silverwells was the name of the street in which they had their home, Roxburgh Villa, in Bothwell.

George Dingley moved around the parts of Glasgow which Benny Lynch and Sammy Wilson never knew; Sammy could have afforded them and, later on, so too could Benny. But they were not their kind of places. Accent was the sharpest cutting knife of all in Glasgow. To speak like they did in the Gorbals meant that you could never speak like they did in Pollokshields. The accent graded them; degraded them. It could make you Untouchable or Brahman. It was the passpartout to an acceptance that no amount of money could buy. It was the caste mark which closed doors, or opened them. The right one could inspire servility. The wrong one hostility. The right one could be benign; the wrong one malign. It divided and was devisive. The top bore no relation to the bottom. Pollokshilds was top. So too was West End and Newlands. Gorbals was bottom. So was Bridgeton and Calton and Dalmarnock and Townhead. Mount Florida was in between but more top than bottom. So was Cathcart and Hillhead, Hyndland and Langside. Crosshill was in between too, but more bottom than top. So was Tollcross and parts of Shettleston. In some streets the accent could run the full gamut from one end to another. Cathcart Road started in the Gorbals all glottal stop and as it became Govanhill, Crosshill, Mount Florida and finally Holmlea where the tenements were solid redstones and the closes were ornately tiled and with gates, the t's had returned to their speech and they spoke like they lived in a different world. They did.

George Dingley had the kind of accent which was fitting for the kind of places where the people who thought of themselves as the best people would meet. Dad had wanted him to go to an expensive boarding school, like the one the four sisters had gone to in the Lake District. But the three boys opted instead for Uddingston Grammar, the local state school and with one of the finest academic records in the country.

The lifestyle of those with money was, in many ways, similar to those without it. One lot would wine and dine, the other would drink and eat. One lot went to the ballroom and theatre, the other lot to the jiggin' and music hall. It was horses for courses. The best courses were varied and numerous. There was the Rogano, art deco and fine food, especially the good Scottish seafood; the Marlborough and Plaza Ballrooms, the latter so classy it had real velvet flock wallpaper and a focal point fountain with changing colours; the best seats in the La Scala where you could be served with a High Tea of whiting or haddock and ornately scrolled French cakes from the City Bakeries served in a three-tier chrome cakestand while watching William Powell and Myrna Loy frolic. There were the better theatres, like the Royal for one of the productions from a season of Brandon-Thomas plays, Half Past Eight at the King's, variety without vulgarity, or even Stanley Lupino at the Alhambra.

George Dingley liked going for drives in his car too. Only the best people could have a pastime like that. Driving was fashionable and so few could afford it that whenever a car approached one of the big groups of cycling clubs on week-end runs, the rear man of the two-abreast platoons would shout the warning . . . "Oil".

A favourite run would be to the Campsies, the eight-mile-long escarpment of hills which form the northern rim of the Glasgow saucer and protect the city from the worst of the chill wintry blasts off the Grampian Mountains and the high Cairngorm Plateau. There were lots of welcome inns and tea rooms in the little villages which dotted the slopes in front of the steep rise of the hills, Kirkintilloch and Lennoxtown, Torrance, Milton and Strathblane. There was a particularly nice tea room at the Clachan in Campsie Glen, a romantic little village looking up on the precipitous ravines which slashed deep grooves in the hills. The local guide described it as "very attractive for picnic parties . . . excellent catering . . . hot luncheons, teas and dinners a speciality." And, if the sun shone, you could have tea served in the rose garden. It was called the Red Tub Inn.

In the early Twenties the Donaldson family, local lairds, put Aldessan House to what they considered a better use. They had converted The Red Tub into a non-licensed coaching inn to cater for the six-in-hands which came out from Bishopbriggs and later the red and yellow solid-tyred charabancs run by A. & R. Graham which operated one shilling return trips from Glasgow. As part of the decor for their new business, the Donaldsons had Aldessan House brightly limewashed in country white, offset by black window frames and rones with a scattering of half-barrel flower tubs around the courtyard and painted a challenging red. Their attractive new tourist business got its name from them.

Behind the Inn was and old harness house, set in a large garden backed by a copse of connifers through which you could hear the deep rumbling of the Aldessan Burn, slowing after its headlong tumble down from the shoulder of the Black Hill which towered over the Clachan. It was difficult to conceive that such a beautiful setting was a mere twelve miles away from the grime of Glasgow.

The setting of the Clachan was a stage designer's Scotland . . . steep mountains, crystal burns, pungent, heather-perfumed air, horned blackface sheep, stone houses, rubble-constructed and crisp white, skylarks whistle hovering, peewits panicking and in the high trees flapping crows convening. Heaven on hell's doorstep.

"What a .wonderful, truly wonderful, place for a training camp," said George to a friend one day while strolling in the lane which went to the head of the glen from the Red Tub. "It has everything for them. They could run up the hills, take in all that pure air . . . what air! . . . and there's the Inn to look after them. Nothing could be more perfect."

12

Fighting Times

The boxing lesson that had been given to him by his old school mate and friend Paddy Docherty had, like the other few who beat him in the early days, to be avenged. Paddy had moved from the South Side Gorbals and was now living in the East End which gave their second fight more spectator appeal. The South Side loved to see someone from their district knock hell out of someone from the East End . . . just as much as they delighted to see someone from the South Side on the receiving end. The fight itself had both sections of the crowd cheering wildly for any of the two could have been given the verdict. As it was, Benny got his wish. His loss had been requited.

"You were like a wee boy against him the first time," Sammy told him that night. "Now you've got the edge on him. See what I mean by improvement. That's what you're doing a' the time . . . improving." There was plenty of scope for it in 1932, his busiest year as a fighter. There were twenty-eight recorded fights. And as many, at various booths, not recorded. The opponents came in all forms of experience and skill, ranging from the young thrusters to the pork and beans men; scrappers who would drop everything and anything they were doing if someone said, "Do you want a fight?" Some used other names in order to dodge the Means Test inspectors who would have cut or suspended their meagre dole money payments if they knew they were prize-fighting, even though that prize was a few shillings. Others would end up with bruised faces and a set of aching ribs and then disappear back into the anonymity of the back alley boxing booths. All were a lesson to him in one form or another in his chosen profession of ring craftsman.

There was Charlie Deacon, whom he met at Greenock on the very first day of 1932, Ne'erday itself, and who later in the year was to be the cause of him coming to one of the vital stepping stones in his life. Young Hardie was next; he went on to fight as a featherweight. Then Jack Riley, Kid Murray and Jimmy Barr, the first two sinking without trace, Jimmy going on to fight around the shows. There was Scotty

Deans, one of the scrappers, then Young McManus, Jim O'Driscoll, Young Griffo and Tiger Naughton, who the unkind said was a tame Tiger, but who, nevertheless, could take a punch, and his face showed it. Joe Aitken, the Paisley man who was later billed as a Manchester man because he was domiciled there for a while, had been due to meet Paddy Docherty on June 9 but Paddy had called off. It was to be a ten-round fight. Benny had never won at that distance before but was given the chance and another vital hallmark was knotched up.

In the summer of that year, when the young boxer had more than 30 good professional fights tucked away for experience, Tommy Watson, the Greendyke Street booth promoter, considered Benny Lynch good enough to top one of his evening's bills. He was due to meet Charlie Deacon in a return fight, the referee having stopped their first fight in Benny's favour. Despite that, Tommy had reckoned they would make a good return over ten rounds. Charlie, however, couldn't make it because of a last-minute injury and Watson was faced with the dilemma of finding a boxer good enough to be an attraction, as Lynch's name still meant little. There was always one man who would leap at the chance of a fight and would always make himself ready for one. He was one of the few fighters who didn't need to split the ropes in order to earn himself some shillings, for Andy Smith, of Johnstone, in Renfrewshire, had a good-going fruit business in the town with his own lorry and his own car.

And they would talk about you if you were one of the ones who owned your own car. Despite his relative prosperity, Andy was a Follower of the Fancy. Were he to describe it himself, he would have said a Fanatic of the Fancy. He had lived for the game since getting his first lessons from Mr McNab, the strapping big instructor who taught the Boy Scouts at the Constitutional Hall in Howwood, where the family lived at the time. The Smiths were country people, both his mother and father from farming stock, tall and robust. Andy was the very opposite. "I dinna ken how you turned oot sae wee," his mother would say. "Nane o' us like that . . . must have been from your granny. She was a wee wumman." Despite his size, Andy loved a scrap and after the Scouts became one of the best amateurs in the district. The work in his folk's dairy was tailormade for building up his stamina. Up at five o'clock every morning, down to the stables, dress the horse, harness it to the cart then run alongside it as it galloped the two miles up the steep Uplawmoor Road, past the mill girls' home they called The Women House, to Bowfield Farm, load the heavy, galvanised milk churns, then run back again to the dairy, set the cart for the morning milk run . . . then home to the house for a shower and breakfast. The rest of the morning he delivered the milk, running most of the way, especially up the stairs of tenements. For the trainers told him they were the best work for young boxers.

At the week-ends, young Andy would head for the place the locals called Glesca. He would take the long distance tramcar that came all the way from the city, twelve miles away, to Kilbarchan, where it reversed at the police station to return to Glasgow again.

Local boxers had told him there were great clubs up in the big city where you could get training on all their fancy equipment, heavy punchbags, standing and hanging punchballs and if you were good enough you could even get a massage. The boxers there were always looking for another sparring partner, someone who was another test for them, no matter the weight, and he found himself limitless practice bouts at Morton's Club at Paisley Road Toll and later, as he got to know the city better, over on the East End at Geordie Aitchison's School of Physical Culture at Parkhead and on the South Side at the L.M.S. Rovers.

Andy was eighteen when he turned professional in 1922. Billy and Tommy Watson, old boxers and now scrap merchants, lived nearby at Murphy's Toll on the Howwood Road. They told him he was old enough to pick up some extra earnings by mixing it with the professionals. "Come along to my booth in Greendyke Street, just by the Glasgow Green, sometime," said Tommy Watson. "You can't miss it. It's a big tent between two buildings and you'll see big pictures of us outside it. I'll see what I can do for you."

He was paired with Sandy Brown of the Calton. Sandy had been a sparring partner to Elky Clark who they were saying was going to be Scotland's first world champion. Although he was showing signs of being a bit worn around the edges, Brown was a highly rated fighter and Andy had to work hard and use every trick he knew to get a points decision. It was his first professional victory and he was thrilled to return home that night with his thirty shillings prize money and the prospect of more professional fights to come. "By gees, you've got to put up a fight at the booth," he told his pals back in Johnstone. "The spectators have a good dram in them and see if you let up . . . they're shouting they'll take their jackets off and come in and give you a hiding." Andy wasn't spectacular as a boxer. But there were few as game and none could—or ever were to—get through to him with a knock out.

Benny was nineteen at the time. Andy was twenty-eight. Benny had now been in the ring as a professional for about thirty official fights, and as many unofficial booth fights. Andy had lost count of his. "About a hundred," he would estimate if asked. He hadn't reached the championship heights, but had fought around the booths, the stationary ones, the travelling ones, where they threw the gloves at any man drunk or sober, game enough to get into the ring with them; he had fought Packy Cassidy and Tommy (Mouse) Higgins and his brother Jim who went on to be British and European Bantamweight champion; taken on aspiring champions, former champions. Tommy Watson knew the reply to his telegrammed message before he even sent it. Andy, reliable Andy, was there on time for the fight.

It was the first time the two boxers had met and Sammy had warned Benny not to treat his stand-in lightly for his long experience in the ring more than compensated for whatever lack of skills he might have. And, sure enough, the pair of them turned on a display that more than satisfied the Watson customers. Andy wasn't unhappy when the verdict was announced at the tenth bell. He was the loser, but had been thrilled to fight someone who, he said, "really had it".

The pair of them spoke to each other for the first time after the fight and took to each other like long lost friends. "You from the country," asked Benny. "Green grass and that?"he joked, and they laughed. "Why don't you come and see it for yourself," replied Andy. "I've even got my own club . . . started it in the hayloft of my father's stables. One of the first places with electric light in the district, so it was." "Might take you up on that."

Andy and his wife Mamie took in their new charge and he helped them with their thriving fruit business, learning to drive Andy's slender but reliable Model T Ford lorry as they made all the regular calls in the area . . . to Quarrelton and Millikenpark, over the railway to Kilbarchan and on to Houston, Crosslee and Bridge of Weir, always working late on a Friday; for that was pay night and there was always a good sale then.

"Fancy coming with me to the booths for the holidays," said Andy to Benny one day. He had never thought about the travelling booths before but it sounded like a good idea. Sammy was contacted and he agreed it could help him. Andy laughed when Benny said that he thought he might have been off to the Isle of Man or some of the other English places with the wife and kids instead of the booths. "Not on your Nelly," said Andy. "I love the booths and that's the way I spend the holidays every year. Besides the money is good and I can come back with about £30 in my pocket . . . and so could you."

The travelling boxing booths tailed on behind the amusement shows and circuses which toured the country from Easter till the September holiday. Although they were all scrappers of one sort or another, their booth performances were tinged with Barnum; more show than skill, more pretence than punch, more fairground than fight. Fighting every day, often more than once, none could have survived a season of it had they been fighting for real. Nevertheless, between the show fights, there were the real scraps when they threw down the gloves after the barker gave his hoorahs.

The booth was a large tent with a false front. Inside the tent was the ring around which the audience stood, or sat on tiered planks. Outside, before the false front, was the stage on which the pugs paraded with all the arrogance of itinerant gladiators, satin dressing gowns and bright scarves, hack faces challenge set at the gathered audience. Behind them a wooden backdrop gaily painted with showground scroll and depicting some of the fighting legends every man knew . . . John L. Sullivan, Jack Johnson, Jack Dempsey and maybe even some of the bare-knucklers like Mendoza and Bendigo.

"C'mon, c'mon, c'mon," the barker would bullhorn. "C'mon, c'mon, c'mon. Here we have the finest boxers in all the country. Champions every one of them. Have you ever, ladies and gentlemen, seen such a splendid bunch of men?" And nobody laughed. "Flyweight to heavy weight . . . take your pick of them gentlemen and we'll accept your challenge. Show the ladies and your townsfolk just what a really good fighter you are. Just stay on your feet with any one you care to pick for three rounds and you will earn yourself three pounds . . . all for a few minutes in the ring. C'mon, c'mon, c'mon, who'll take the gloves . . . did I hear you, sir, say that you would?"

The challengers would move about the stage, as if to show they were for real. They would shadow box and grunt, rattle a punch ball like it was a toy balloon and make fearsome snorts. They were a mixed bunch the booth men. Some had been to the heights. Some were heading for them. Some had tried for them but had never made it. Some didn't care. They were drifters and this was a job they could do. Others had no home; the booth was their home, their life.

"You'll need to learn the booth language," Andy told Benny before they left for Sunderland fairground to join the booth run by Len Johnson, the famous Manchester middleweight of the Twenties and a man who had been to the heights. He had been the Empire Middleweight champion and was highly respected not only as a man but as one of the great boxing masters. "First, you don't call them fairgrounds or showgrounds. They're gaffs. So you see we're going round the gaffs. And you don't say audience, spectators or members of the public. The word is flatties. If you fake a fight it's called a gee fight. And the guys we plant among the flatties in order to stimulate the challengers are called gee fighters. If your fight is genuine you just say it's a straight. And the money we get in the collection at the end of a session is called the nobbings."

There were lots of other things to be learned about life in the booths. For a start, you didn't merely box like you did at the permanent shows. You had to become a real fairground man and learn how to raise tents, erect ridge poles, hammer pegs, fit rings together, assemble stages. And know how to take them all down again in the proper fashion afterwards. If the gaffs at which they appeared were only short stays they would have to set it all up in the two hours prior to opening for the evening's fights; and worse, they would often be called on after a hard day's boxing to dismantle everything and stow it in their truck, ready to be on the move first thing in the morning. If it rained the work was twice as heavy for the canvas would have doubled in weight with the moisture and it would be stiff and difficult to fold. It was no place for the weak.

There were good booths and bad booths. The bad ones consisted of a collection of fighters as frayed and flayed as the surroundings in which they travelled and not even the liveliest of barkers could persuade the flatties that these were champions. Len Johnson's booth was the opposite. It was efficient, disciplined and entertaining. Len, smartly dressed, would line up with his men, Chocolate Al Francis, George Bolton, Jerry Wang, Abie Cheetham, Young Siki and Matt Morgan, arms folded, dressing gowns a rainbow splash on the gaily painted stage and when the barker said they were the greatest in the land, you could believe him.

The challengers from the flatties were as varied as the booths themselves. Being fairgrounds and fairtime, many in the crowd would be in high spirits; in all the senses that can mean. A good drink followed by a good fight was a happy diversion for many men and they would turn up, in various states of sobriety in order to try and catch the gloves at the booths. Not usually as drunk, though, as the man Alex Farries remembered in the booth outside the Black Cat cinema in Springfield Road, Glasgow. He was staggering so badly he couldn't negotiate the steps up to the ring and fell from them breaking a leg. But nevertheless, many of them had the whisky courage, although it was Len Johnson's policy not to have drunks in the ring. He would only relent if the man had a local reputation as a fighter and if the crowd were insistent that they accept his challenge. The booth men knew the minds of their challengers and the flatties and if they took on one of their local heroes, under the influence or not, they would be sure of a big influx of paying customers to the ringside. Once in the ring, the booth boxer would "carry" his local challenger. Disposing of them quickly, which was invariably easy for the skilled boxer, was bad for business. If they let the man hang on for three rounds so that he collected his money, he would more than likely return the following day, with less drink in him this time and convinced that he would be the winner. Of course, word would get round the town that our Jim was coming back for another bash and they would be assured of another good audience. Their psychology rarely failed. Often they would get a challenger like this to return several nights and each time they would crowd in to see their local hero in action; and the booth men would cleverly make him look an even bigger hero each time.

If such characters were scarce and challengers reluctant, gee fighters would be placed among the crowd. The "gees" could turn on a fight that had the crowd's yelling. And they could do it without hurting each other. Sometimes, though, a real boxer in the crowd would catch the gloves. He might be someone from a rival booth, poaching for two or three extra quid; he might even be on holiday himself or it could be his own home town. Whatever, they would always be recognised as pugilists and the booth owner would ask them before getting into the ring if they wanted to gee or not.

Usually they would agree to gee and accept a lower purse for doing so. They once got Andy to gee for Benny on a quiet day in order to put on a good show for the crowd. But Andy was told not to speak when accepting the challenge. Benny was always introduced from the stage as the "great Scottish boxer" and, into the bargain, always wore a tartan tammy which had been given him by Andy as a lucky mascot. And if Andy had been heard by the crowd accepting the gloves in a Scottish accent, they would have suspected a "fix". So Andy accepted the fight by playing the role of a deaf mute.

Despite the gee fights, there was always plenty of real action in a booth tour. Both Benny and Andy had numerous real fights during this trip and after he left the booth, Len Johnson felt compelled to write to Elky Clark, boxing writer for the *Daily Record*. Elky was something of a legend in Scotland. He had been a British, Empire and European flyweight champion, a holder of the Lonsdale belt, and only narrowly lost a world title fight in an epic battle at Madison Square Garden with Fidel La Barba. Elky lost his career in that fight. Such had been the ferocity of their contest, the Scot had to have an injured eye removed afterwards. As well as being the boxing writer for the *Record*, Elky helped young promising boxers to fix up with the right managers and promoters. Johnson wrote to him because he was impressed with the performance of Lynch in his tour with him. "Dear Elky," he wrote. "You will perhaps be surprised to hear from me after so many years but I felt I had to write to you about Benny Lynch and Tommy Steele, two Scottish boxers who have been with my booth. Lynch I consider a future champion of the world. He has returned home again and I suggest you should do your best to get him

matched. He won't let you down. I am sure of that. He has everything
that goes to make a real one."

Sammy Wilson smiled when he was told about the letter and asked
about Benny's future. "I don't need Len Johnson or anyone else to tell
me the wee man's a future world champion. I've known that for
years. And there's no need to worry about fights for him . . . I'm
arranging them all right." Sammy was anxious to see Benny back in
action again. While he was sure the booths would have improved
him and given him more experience, particularly under such a
ringmaster as Len Johnson, there was a niggling doubt that he may
also have picked up some bad habits. Many of the booth boxers had
perfected gee fighting to such an art form, landing their vicious
swipes and hooks with powderpuff effect, that it affected them when
they were in a real fight. But Sammy knew in the first round of his
first fight back from the booths that his man was still on the right
road. His opponent was the experienced flyweight, Joe Aitken.

"Look at Benny," said Sammy to a second. "Christ he's fair come
on. See how he's stopped stepping backwards. And look at the way
he's coming out of corners . . . that's a Johnson trick, so it is. And so is
that way he's parrying punches . . . see him, parry and punch in one
movement. Is that no' beautiful. And he's hurting wi' these
punches as well . . . more than he ever did. Look at the way his upper
chest has filled out. His arms as well. Like the bloody boy Adonis.
Christ he hasnae half come on."

He had. The booths had improved him, physically, mentally,
temperamentally. His body was more shapely, pectorals and deltoids
bulkier with the hard physical work packing and unpacking the booth
and all its gear for the gaffs. His neck was thicker, his stomach
trimmer. His ring skills weren't complete yet, there was still more of
the apprenticeship to be served, but his attitude, his approach, his
confidence had all matured. And he was nineteen years of age.

Benny knew himself that he had changed and that the things Sammy
had always told him could come true. He knew now he could be a big-
time champion. And especially so after he had been called by the camp of
the Scottish flyweight champion, Jim Campbell, as one of his sparring
partners. He told Sammy what he thought of him after some sparring
sessions. "Him . . . the Scottish champion? We'll do him all right Sammy."
Sammy told him he knew that. "But it'll no' be this year. You've a few
hurdles to get over yet. There's your old pal Paddy Docherty, for instance.
He's come on since you last met in the ring."

Benny would smile when Paddy's name was mentioned. For there
was no boxer he knew better. He held him in the same affection he
had held his brother. Benny and Paddy were to fight five times . . .

officially. Unofficially, they had lost count of the fights, scraps, scrapes and encounters they had together. Paddy had been with him the night the Protestant had slashed him. And on many other occasions too when there had been danger, real danger, from the men who were not boxers, but fighters . . . street fighters.

Paddy had come from Eglinton Lane, close by Cumberland Lane, a narrow jumble of begrimed tenements, stables and stores. His father old Paddy, was a fruit hawker and well known locally, touring the streets with his hand barrow.

Paddy and Benny enrolled together for their first day in the Penny Buffs, Miss Kennedy's infant class at St John's Primary School. Four of the boys who were at the school at the same time were to have a destiny from the confines of a twenty-foot boxing ring: there was Johnny McGrory, to be the British featherweight champion; Tommy Steele, to be an English areas featherweight champion; Paddy Reilly, to later change his name to Docherty, to be the unofficial British Paperweight Champion. And Benny Lynch.

Benny and Paddy fought in the school playground, in Cumberland Lane, in Eglinton Lane, in Wellcroft Place, in back-courts, in alleys, in closes, in the street, on the pavement; and if anyone dared to lay a finger on one of them, the other was the first to go to his help. Paddy was Benny's big challenge. He could beat all the other boys at school, big ones as well. But Paddy's natural skills as the purest of pugilists were his big test. Paddy was the smallest and most fragile boy in the class. And he was one of the toughest. He was cheeky as well and that was further endearment they had for each other.

"Mind the day you got up to sing for Miss Kennedy and sang *Molly Kennedy I Love You?*" Benny would remind him when they met.

"Aye, an' she gave me a fuckin' tanking for it."

They loved talking about their boyhood days and all the old pals with whom they had shared their first adventures in the Gorbals . . . Bobby Smith and Arthur Green, Willie James and John McQuilter, Tommy Morgan, Eddie, Sam and John Ferguson, Josie Tohill and Josie Parker, Francie Quinn and Snub Reilly, another boy called Paddy Reilly, and the Hynes boys.

"Mind the day we all walked tae Ayr?"

"Aye, an' ended up a' taking hudgies on the back o' lorries."

"An' stealing wood from Ritchie's yard in the Lane and making them into bundles of firewood sticks to sell round the doors?"

"Aye, so we could buy a bottle of Eldorado at Meiklejohns the licensed grocer for one and a penny."

"An' you wanted to be the toff an' get a bottle of VP instead at one and eightpence."

"Well . . . got you steamboats quicker."

"Aye, miraculous."

They would speak too about their new adventures in the ring . . . and on the dancefloor. They were both proud of their prowess as dancers. But the disputes they had about who was the better fighter didn't apply on the dancefloor. For Paddy was the clear winner, even though Benny had a high rating. "You only do it to get the birds," Paddy would joke. "But I'm picking up a few quid on the side now at the competitions. Have teamed up with Frances Fitzpatrick from Florence Street and we've won a few competitions. Got a couple of quid when we won the bantams at the Bedford Parlour."

"Bantamweight?"

"No . . . you bam. The bantam dancing. It's for the under-five-feet. Wee Frances makes it nae bother and I wear my dancing pumps that's got hardly any heels. We entered a few others as well. Won the waltz and slow trot at the Blackburn then got the waltz at the Garngad Hibs hall. Christ, Benny, talking about the Garngad. That's some place. Talk about wild. Then we won a cup at the Tower Palais in Possil. Right big competition it was. Bobby Philp and Ella Scutts, you know the world champions, were judges. But there was this mob there from the Garngad. You know, staring eyes and lets-get-him kind of characters. And they had started a book and put all their money on this one Eddie Philips, one of their chinas from the Garngad. They though he was a walkover. Christ, you should have seen them when Philp and Scutts named me as the winner. They were ready to tear me to pieces. Just then I noticed a tram coming flying down the road . . . so I cut right out and was on it without it even slowing down. Tell you what, you'll no' get me up there again."

Benny told him about an incident at the Tripe, their old favourite when they had started the dancing, and where Paddy used to stand outside with tuppence ha'penny in his pocket hoping to tap someone for the other ha'penny he needed to get admission. "You know the trapdoor in the middle of the floor . . . you know, between the two poles. Well, some daft bastard put out the lights and lifted the door and a couple of dancers ended up in the basement. Christ, they could have been killed. It was pandemonium so it was till big Sweeney got the lights on . . . then chucked everybody out."

They saw the funny side of that and laughed lustily at Benny's description of the confusion in the dark and the screams of the girls.

"They tell me you're getting plenty of fights, Paddy," said Benny.

"Fights! Gees, between them and the dancing I haven't stopped Benny. One week I fought five fights. Five ten-rounders. No' bad eh?"

"Aye . . . an' you still cannae punch!"

Paddy would laugh. "An' you still cannae beat me."

Their score was one fight each. So they had a third. And it went ten rounds, the verdict to Benny.

"Christ, he's a tricky bugger, Sammy. He's that quick you can't plant him. An' all the time he's knocking up the points wi' his tap, tap, tapping . . . and not one of them hurting."

There was a fourth fight, and again it went ten rounds. Paddy got the verdict and that made it two each. Not many weeks later they had a fifth. This time both their hands were raised by the referee at the end of the tenth. The crowd, mainly from Bridgeton and Protestant, were furious at the result. They were convinced their man Paddy had won. Ironically he was a Catholic but because he was Bridgeton they ignored that point; he was theirs. A fight started in the hall, then the bottles started flying and the two boxers scurried to the dressing rooms. "Bit of a stushie that," laughed Benny to Paddy as they changed from their boxing gear. "Aye, and I saw Billy Fullerton right in the middle of it. Know what he told me once? He says, 'You're a great wee guy Paddy. Want to know something? You're the only Catholic I've ever spoken to'."

Sammy came in to help Benny with his gear and they left together. "Well," he said, "that's your last fight with wee Paddy. He's your local bogey man. There's you heading for the stars and wee Paddy, seven-and-a-half stone of him, going no place. Couldnae punch a hole in a wet *Noon Record* but he's that wily and fast you cannae get near him. And it will always be that way."

It was back to The Plan. Sammy told Benny he was arranging a series of new opponents, all with varying styles and skills in order to widen his experience. "There's some great wee Irish boys that you'll need to see to. Blokes like the Warnocks. Have you heard of them? There's a whole family of them and they're hard wee men that would face up to a lion for a bob a round. These are the kind of men you've got to get under your belt before going for Campbell's title. Remember we're going for the world title. Okay, supposing you saw off Campbell tonight . . . you'd be right in there wi' the Yanks, Tallies and Filipinos, no' forgetting a' they English battlers, and there's plenty of them. No, wee man, the plan is that we take it in stages. You'll fight a' these awkward men we have around here first of all. One rung at a time."

The next rung was to be Billy Warnock, the man from Belfast.

The fighting men of Ulster were a breed of their own. Times were hard in Scotland. They were harder in Ireland. And few had it harder than the Warnocks. There were six of them, four boys and two girls, when their father died at the age of thirty-four. It had been hard enough for them before he died for his wages would often be gone in drink before he got home on a Friday night.

The Warnocks lived in Beresford Street in the heart of the Shankill. That meant they were Protestant, for that's what they were—and are—in the Shankill. To a man. Yet the dominant part of their life was exactly like those just two main roads away in the area they called the Falls. There they were Catholics. To a man. Religion ruled and divided them, but what dominated them and what should have united them—but didn't—was the one factor they all shared . . . oppression. In the Gorbals, the human dovecotes were in three storey tenements which, from the outside, belied the horrific overcrowding in them. In the Falls and the Shankill they were one storey terraces, back to back in narrow little streets where the overcrowding was as horrific, and more apparently so. On both sides of the water they shared the same fight for a weekly wage. And those who had one shared the same struggle to make it last from one pay day to the next. Usually it didn't.

Billy was the eldest of the four boys and had to act as father and get a job at the mill when the man of the house died. He was twelve years of age. He worked at the Mill School which meant that one week he would be in the mill on Monday, Wednesday and Friday, going to classes at the school there on the alternate days, and the following week it was in the mill on Tuesday, Thursday and Saturday till one clock and, again, in the classroom on the alternate days. Wages for the Monday, Wednesday and Friday week were four shillings and six pence. On the Tuesday, Thursday and Saturday week it was three shillings and six pence. If they plunked school their wages were docked. No one plunked school.

Young Billy's job was in the machine room where he learned to dress the flax amidst the mad clatter of the spinning looms. The hours were six in the morning till six at night and there were two miles to be walked before and after work, from Beresford Street right to the very head of Shankill Road, then along Woodvale Road and up the Crumlin Road to the big mill at Ligoniel. There were tramcars, but it was a halfpenny fare each way and mother needed every halfpenny badly. So he walked, except on wet days or when he could get what the Glasgow boys called a hudgie, a hang on to the rear of a truck or tramcar.

Like their Scottish counterparts, the Warnocks and the McStravicks and the Smiths and the other great Ulster ring men, were wage fighters. Because the infrastructure of the sport in Ulster wasn't up to Scottish standards, fewer of them could make a fulltime living out of it. Managers and promoters were scarce. Billy was working in the rigging loft of Belfast Harbour when he received the invitation to come to the Parkhead Arena in Glasgow and fight the man he had never heard of, Benny Lynch. The deal was good . . . £10 for a win, lose or draw. There were no expenses, however, which meant he would have to pay his return fare on the Burns Laird ferry, give a few shillings "bung" to the seconds, another few shillings for a meal, plus lose a day's wages. That would come to a total of about £3. Still, that left him with £7 and that was more than two weeks wages, so it was well worth the trip to Glasgow.

Billy left his home that June morning in 1933 to walk into the city and across the Lagan to his workplace in the harbour. It was the day before the fight. That night at 5.30 he tabled his two marlin spikes, one wood for the hemp ropes, one steel for the wire hawsers, packed his dungarees and changed into the sports jacket and flannels he had brought in a small case. Billy Warnock, splicer's helper, was now Billy Warnock, professional fighter, and off across the water for a scrap.

Benny thought him a great character and laughed as he bantered away, joking and telling stories about the fight game in Northern Ireland in his appealing Shankill accent, as broad Irish as Gorbals was broad Scottish, but with its inbuilt capacity to make everything sound funnier, unlike the beligerence of the Glasgow accent. "Do I ever fight me brothers?" he laughed when Benny asked about the other boxers in the family. "Christ, we have a fight every day of the week, so we do. Talk about fighting every day, Benny, we have a man called Jackie Campbell, he's a featherweight now but fought yer Kayo Morgan, the Yank ye know. And d'ye know, Jackie's such a fighting man he once fought a ten round fight every day for seven days in a row. Can you imagine that?"

He told Benny too about his hard times as a boy. "You're what, Benny . . . twenty years of age? Well, I'm twenty-nine going on thirty and I was out working when you were three years of age. See my mother, wonderful ould dear so she was. Not that ould when she died, right enough. But with the ould man passing on when he was thirty-four she had to work the rest of her days as a smoother in the linen mills . . . ye know, smoothing out the linen before they put it on the shafts in the big mill. Anyway, she died about ten years after the ould man and I mind o' the day the doctor came to the house and said she had passed away. 'See her heart' said the doctor. 'See her heart,' he said, 'was as good and as strong as the day she was born.' But her frame was worn out wi' work and starvation . . . working all day at the mill then coming home at night to look after four wee boys and two wee lasses. Aye, that's what killed her, Benny . . . work and starvation. And they tell ye that work never hurt anyone. Make ye laugh that."

They stopped Benny's fight with Billy half a round before the twelfth bell. They said Billy could take no more punishment.

"I don't think much of yer referee," he said afterwards. "There's he saying I could take no more punishment and I'm off right after the show to be at my workbench in Belfast for the morning. How can I be fit enough to go to work the next day when yer man is saying I couldn't take any more? Oh well, maybe ye'll give one of my brothers a fight sometime Benny!"

Benny was progressing. Previously most of his victories had been on points. Now his punching was telling and there were more and more knock-outs against opponents or, like Billy Warnock, the referee would stop the fight or a second would throw the towel into the ring.

A significant victory was beating Boy McIntosh in four rounds.

The crowd were amazed at his performance against Boy McIntosh. The Boy had never had a hammering in the ring. He was from the club in Dalmarnock run by George Aitchison, the veteran manager-trainer who in forty years turned out more champion boxers than any other man in the history of Scottish boxing. And Boy McIntosh, from the mining village of Blantyre, was one of the toughest. They were speaking about him as "the new sensation", which was not surprising as rarely had they seen such a hitter and most of his fight record was littered with two-letter conclusions . . . K.O. Talent like that combined with the experience of Aitchison in his corner presented a formidable challenge.

Sammy warned Benny. "It's 'go' right from the start. That's the way the Boy does it and you'll rattle him if you give him the same treatment right from the first bell." And he did. By the end of the second round, the Boy and his manager knew they were fighting someone in a different class. Lynch was hooking viciously and pistoning into his body with hammer punches to his rib cage. "Right, now you've really got him softened up," Sammy told him at the end of the third round. The bell was still echoing for the start of the fourth and the Lynch fists were threshing again; the Boy had fought himself to a standstill. The knock out punch was inevitable. He was still flat on his back when the referee scissored his arms for the "out".

Benny Lynch was now set for a new stage in his career. Sammy had decided he was ready to take on a different class of boxer. He had fought enough of the ones they called "promising boys". He had taken on sufficient of the tradesmen boxers, the men who were always there; the bill fodder who didn't really care whether they won, lost or drew, just as long as they didn't get a hiding or were incapacitated in some way to prevent them from getting another quick fight and another wage. Now was the time for him to start moving into the championship class, the men whom everyone said "had it"; men who were title holders or former title holders and still in the running to regain the championship or set to move into another division for another title. One of the best of them was Jim Maharg.

Maharg had known the big time . . . the real big time. Three years earlier he had been the flyweight champion of Scotland beating Jim Campbell for the title. That fight had been for a record purse, more even than Tommy Milligan had fought for and he had been the greatest. Jim Gilmour, Sammy Wilson's old pal, was the promoter and the purse was £1225, plus £200 side stakes. And the previous year Maharg had fought Jackie Brown for the British flyweight title and was unlucky to lose . . . on a foul. "Brown jumped," Maharg would say. He meant that a punch aimed at a legal part of his body had been deftly converted into an illegal punch by the recipient jumping just as it landed so that it hit him below the belt. It was just one of the many tricks used by those who got up to tricks.

Maharg, like so many of them, had been around the boxing game since he was a boy, when his dad had asked around for "someone to look after my boy" . . . in other words, make him a boxer. Jim suffered from a bad speech defect and as a result was excruciatingly shy and retiring. The wee houses and wee parents produced wee boys, the industrial revolution's legacy to the West of Scotland. But Jim was smaller and more tragically thin than most. At seventeen his fighting weight was five stone seven pounds. But, as compensation, he had pluck and a determination shared by few and against all the odds he was to become one of his country's most outstanding champions. He got his first grooming in defence and attack in the Oatlands Boxing Club, run by Harry Smith in an old painter's hall in Hickman Street, one of the first streets in Govanhill, the suburb immediately south of the Gorbals on the other side of Dixon's Blazes, whose noises, smells and activity it also shared. The instructor in the Oatlands Club was Donald McNaughton, one-time welterweight champion of Scotland, and he was quick to recognise that the stick thin little boy they called Maharg had more to him than a body that looked like it would snap in two if punched too hard. And Donald grafted on to him the skills that had been his with the mid-heavy men.

Now Maharg once again was having trouble with his weight. This time, however, it wasn't because he was too light. Now he was becoming too heavy and was having to train more rigorously to get down to eight stone. His fight with Lynch was set for eight stone two pounds and he made the weight all right. Fearful that his stamina might be impaired, Maharg carefully budgeted his reserves in the early part of their twelve-rounder, letting Benny do all the running. By the halfway mark, Maharg had the confidence that he would make the twelve rounds and opened up considerably more. The referee made meticulous notes of the points each had scored. He had seen Maharg in action before and greatly admired him. He had heard about Lynch, but had never seen him in action before . . . and he was more than impressed. Both men were still on their feet at the end of the twelfth and the crowd in the Parkhead Arena gave them a great ovation for their performances. Maharg thought the verdict might go to him as he had fought well and scored many good points. But it was the up and comer who had his hand raised.

The referee and Benny met casually in a corridor at the end of the night and he mentioned how much he had admired his style and that he could have a good future as a professional. "In fact," he said, "I would like to have a word with you sometime as I'm becoming more and more involved in all aspects of boxing."

"Aye, fine," said the wee man. "What's your name again?"

"Dingley," replied the man who had been the referee. "George Dingley."

13

Going For Titles

Although he could produce more than £1000 from his pocket at any one time, Sammy Wilson was still of the working people as was his wife Mary. It would have been nothing to them financially to have bought one of the new houses that were all the rage at the time. They called them "semis", two separate houses built within a single villa design, each with their own front and rear garden. William S. Gordon was selling them in Shawlands and Milngavie for £700 on a £30 deposit and John Lawrence, who said he was Rangers' greatest fan, was building a big estate of them at Williamwood in Giffnock with repayments at seventeen shillings and nine pence a week which his salesmen assured covered everything . . . feu duty, mortgage repayments, rates, and insurance. And, not only that, you got a tiled bathroom as well. Sammy could have bought two of them, he told the boys in the street, and still have enough left in the tank to run one of the best books in the South Side. His wife Mary had been fearful at first of Florence Street. She had come from Tradeston, just a mile away. It was quiet there and Florence Street, with its hustle and bustle, commotion and characters, had been overwhelming at the start. But, as with the others, it had consumed her and she became as much a part of the street as the street was a part of her. They loved Florence Street and all it meant to them. Its lifestyle was their lifestyle. They ate their dinner at a time when the people in another class had their lunch. And they had the meal they called their tea at a time when others had what they called their dinner.

It was a Sunday evening and Sammy was at his tea when there was an excited knock at the door. "Sammy . . . Sammy . . . for Christsake, Sammy, ye better come quick." The word that came next had Sammy jumping up abruptly, scattering his knife and fork on the table. "It's the Clintons. They're down at the club needling the wee man and I think he's gonnie have a go at them."

The Clintons and Benny Lynch were bad news. There were three of them . . . Alex, Tommy and Willie. Willie was the oldest. They were fighting men. Not boxers . . . street fighting men. And they would taunt Benny that they were better and harder men than he was. "Gonnie be a champion wee man," they would say . . . then laugh, sneeringly . . . "aye a champion at pullin' yer puddin'." There were other taunts, but Benny had always kept his temper. Sammy knew about them and had warned him never to take them on. "Your fighting place is in the ring . . . no' the street."

Benny had been training at the club when the Clintons came in. "There's Lynch," they said. "Think you're a big man . . . eh? . . . Ony wan o' us could beat you wee fellah. Fancy a go wee yin. C'mon show us how good you are Nancy boy."

It was more than he could take. "Right then . . . you, Willie. But it's in the ring."

"Right wee man . . . but it's bare knuckle."

The fight was over when Sammy burst through the door of the club. It took three of them to carry the doubled up figure on the canvas out of the ring and over to the massage table, where he writhed in agony as Sammy set to work on him, rubbing his chest covered in ugly raw weals to try and ease his suffering, every breath a painful stab.

Benny was drying off after a shower when Sammy confronted him. "You daft wee bastard. I told you a fuckin' hundred times no tae bother with the likes of them. Right, so you gave him a doing. But it could have been you. Bams like him are just wanting to be big men. They want to tell their chinas they gave Benny Lynch a tanking. That would make them the biggest men in their street. And you, wee mug, goes and takes them on. I'm telling you, wee man, you dae that again . . . and I'll sort you out masel'."

The rating of Scottish boxers was world class, even though none had become a world champion. The top men in most divisions were good enough, however, to rival their counterparts in England, the Continent and America. Even men who still hadn't fought eliminators for the Scottish title were considered worthy material to take on champions of other countries. Carlo Cavagnoli was the champion of all Italy and had signed contracts to fight for the European flyweight title. And, as a good test for him, they said he should go to Scotland where a matchmaker had the very man for him . . . a twenty-one-year-old whose reputation was rising fast, though he still wasn't big time; he wasn't even known outside the boxing fraternity in his hometown Glasgow. They called him Benny Lynch.

Hundreds of Glasgow Italians turned out at the Central Station to welcome their home country hero Cavagnoli and his manager Nick Cavalli. They included a delegation from the organisation which

was making a big impact in their native land. It was making the trains
run on time, making life such a misery for thieves that property
vigilance could be relaxed and, in a far-off place called Eritrea it was
practising a new style of warfare called dive bombing, using it to
eradicate mud villages and their innocent inhabitants in order to
show they were the masters. They were the Glasgow *Fascisti*.

For them Carlo meant something else. He was a symbol of a new
nationalism stimulated by memories of a glorious past and thriving
on the promises of an even greater future. To others, he was just an
Italian boy to be welcomed and there was a run on Capaldi's, Risi
Brothers, Cav. da Prato's, and Fazzi Brothers, the string of Italian
grocers, for the best pastas and panetoni, salami and salcicci,
antipastos and vinos. The wives made even bigger pots of sugo. For
win or lose, they had their champion with them and it took less
reason than that for the zestful Italians to celebrate the way they liked
to do.

It was to be the first time that the cavernous Kelvin Hall had been
used for a fight and there was opposition from the Glasgow
Corporation, its owners. There were stories about persuasion money,
but it did help to have an establishment figure like Lieutenant
Commander E.W. Billyard Leake, R.N., of Hollybush House, near
Ayr, a patron of sports and member of the prestigious National
Sporting Club behind the promotion.

Top of the bill was to be Johhny McMillan of Glasgow challenging
Seaman Tom Watson for the British featherweight title. Although it
was kept quiet from his opponent, McMillan's big challenge was
jeopardised in a riding accident at the Dumbreck riding school.
Johnny had hurt his arm while stopping a little girl's runaway horse.
Tried to do a Tom Mix, they joked. But it was no joke to the Scottish
champion who suffered a fissure fracture of the ulna bone in his
forearm resulting in intensive treatment from specialists, including
sessions with the Celtic Football Club trainer Eddie McGarvey who
had a rating among the footballers as being an expert with contused
knees. He gave Johnny's arm similar treatment, his favourite kaoline
poultice, a whole tin of it every day. And they spoke in awe about
that for a whole tin cost four shillings and sixpence. But Johnny's arm
had to be right for the night as there was little chance of re-arranging
the Kelvin Hall date . . . so money was no object.

Benny had never seen a boxing show like it. Neither had Glasgow.
Sixteen huge arc lights illuminated the ring, their powerful rays
searchlighting down through the tobacco fog on the fresh white
canvas. But it wasn't just the big lights that were new to Benny. He
had never seen such an audience at a boxing show. There were more

than 300 stewards on duty. He had often fought to crowds of only
that size. Every one of the 10,000 seats was filled, and hundreds
of others were standing; the biggest-ever indoor gathering in
Scotland. In the first rows there were women in evening dresses with
fresh orchids pinned on them. There were men in dinner jackets and
dress coats. Some were in Highland dress and others in Regimental
jackets with rows of miniature medal ribbons. They had paid two
guineas each for their seats. Two pounds and two shillings. More
than what the dole thought was enough for a man to live on for a
whole week and just a few shillings less than the average man's
working wage. They were the ringside seats and on the floor of the
immense hall; the others behind them were on raised platforms, the
higher the platform, the lower the price; thirty shillings, then twenty two
shillings, seventeen shillings, twelve, eight and four shillings. The
latter two were completely sold out more than a week before the
promotion. They had been snapped up by the city's real boxing fans.

"Hey Benny," said one of the seconds. "Have ye seen a' the fuckin'
penguins that have come to see you? An' their tarts are a' dolled up in
long dresses. Maybe they think y'er gonnie gie them a dance wee
man."

Benny laughed. It was his kind of humour. Nevertheless, he was
impressed at what he saw. He liked style. There was no style in a
muffler over a shirt without a collar because you couldn't afford the
collar or the tie topped by a cloth cap with a greasy skip. That was the way
they had to dress for they had nothing else. But if you had it, why not
flaunt it? Nothing wrong with a bit of effort to look smart, he thought.
And a lot of the new colourful gear men were starting to wear was just
the kind of stuff he fancied.

Despite the ballyhoo for the McMillan and Seaman Watson fight it
was a tame affair. McMillan's arm was obviously paining him and he
suffered several rounds without using it once. Had he been fit he
would have beaten the daylights out of the Englishman, said the
experts. But the crowd inside the hall and the thousands who
congregated outside in Argyle Street, many of them with binoculars
in order not to miss from afar the glamour of the occasion, were to be
given consolation. For they had a new man to enthuse about. Those
who were in the know said they had been aware of him for years.
They knew about boxing, they said, and that was why they knew him.
Others were claiming varying forms of affinity with him. They knew
him to speak to, they said. They lived just round the corner from him.
Their auntie knew his mother. Their pal worked beside his father.
Some said they saw his first fight. Some said they had seen him fight
as a boy. Some said they had seen Jimmy Wilde, the bag of bones

Welsh boxing wizard when he had fought Billy Padden, but the wee man from Florence Street looked even better. Some countered by saying they had seen the great Tancy Lee from Leith, the first Scot ever to become a British boxing champion, and that he was even greater than him.

Benny Lynch had become a household name.

Carlo had come at Benny all crouch and tiger-like which was no surprise to him for Sammy had made a study of the Italian and they were prepared for him. He came on hard, advancing straight, a punch soak, then a piston left shot from the wee man and the confidence evaporated from Carlo. He tried to avoid other similar straight lefts only to receive hooks instead.

Carlo, champion of all Italy, didn't win one round.

They were singing about Benny as they played their street games in the Gorbals the next day.

> I'm Popeye the sailor man,
> I'm Popeye the sailor man,
> If ye gie me a penny,
> I'll fight oor wee Benny . . . I'm Popeye the sailor man.

Others tried a variation, less lyrical, but nevertheless they sang it and the more they sang it the more it spread; from Florence Street to Cumberland Street and Crown Street, up to Caledonia Road and down to Old Rutherglen Road, over to Cumberland Lane, Wellcroft Place and down through Surrey Lane where the Froddies had jumped him.

> I'm Popeye the sailor man,
> I'm Popeye the sailor man,
> If you eat all your spinach,
> You'll can fight Benny Lynich . . . I'm Popeye the sailor man.

The legend was in the making.

The Kelvin Hall promotion had brought a new dimension to boxing in Scotland. Commander Leake and his establishment connections—he was married to Jean Laird of the Burns-Laird shipping line—were the nod of respectibility to a sport which, by and large, had been reserved for the kind of people the top people called . . . the lower elements. The lower elements were bemused. Long dresses and orchid corsages weren't exactly their view of the boxing fan. An Epic of the Fancy had been turned into an Event of the Fanciful. The local politicians had been there, the men from the marbled splendour of the City Chambers. So were the ones who arrogantly spoke of themselves as the city's professional gentlemen, the solicitors and surveyors, architects and accountants. They had a new kick. Two men beating the hell out of each other's brains in a twenty by twenty foot

ring that sixteen arc lights carved out of the Kelvin Hall gloom like a
diamond solitaire. It was a new dance for them, better than anything
they had enjoyed at their new ballroom, the Plaza. It was a new
picture, but with more action than anything they had seen at the
Paramount or Regal. And say, didn't that little boxer in the second
fight, you know the one who beat the Italian Cavag something,
didn't he remind you of the gangster James Cagney? They say he's
from the Gorbals too.

Some newspapers were shaking off their fustian nineteenth
century image and making more of an effort to bring journalism into
the century that had begun more than thirty years before.

The *Daily Record* in Scotland was in the vanguard of them. They
had discovered the "angle". The something in a story that was
different . . . diverting, entertaining, maybe even titillating; and that
hadn't been done before in their newspapers. What better than the
big fight for something different? Lots of something different. The
woman's angle. What a poet thought of the event. Good scene
pictures. Get it on the front page as well for it's not just a boxing
match; it's an occasion. Get some excitement into it. The woman
reporter was told to do a feature on her reactions to the women who
were there. They gave her report big treatment on Page Two, with a
plug for the story on Page One . . . "A Woman Looks At The Fight":

> This is advice to young men about to take their best girls to a boxing
> match . . . don't. Not because it might shock their susceptibilities for I
> doubt if modern women are squeamish. At the Kelvin Hall last night I
> watched one or two of the bright young things happily powdering
> between the rounds and another happily blowing smoke-rings during
> some heated in-fighting.
>
> No, the reason for leaving them at 'iome is that women, because
> they take the technicalities of boxing so much more quietly are able to
> devote much more concentration on the boxers. And even the most
> contented sweetheart cannot help making invidious comparisons
> between her bowler-hatted, sedate and sober escort and the
> magnificent figures in the ring.
>
> I watched the women at the fight last night. They were self-
> consciously few beside the men, and ermine cloaks and organdie
> evening frocks seemed exotic blossoms under the smoke pall and the
> relentless glare of lights.

The poet was equally carried away by it all. He was by-lined as
John James Miller and seemed to take a McGonagall view of the
proceedings. He dedicated his lines.

To Seaman Watson.

> You won and did it fair,
> The twa o' ye tried different roads,

Twas yours that landit—there,
So noo I say richt off the reel
Haud oot your hand, I wish you weel;

To Johnny McMillan.

So Johnny you were beat, Brave Lad!
Ahweel, twas nae disgrace,
There's nane can say your show was bad,
Or you were scaur'd to face
A rowtin' tearin' game licht weichter,
But a' the time a bonnie fechter!

And the crowd.

An' you ten thoosand fowk wha lukit on,
You dinna' often see a fecht like yon!

They had never written about boxing like that before in Benny's country. They had never felt about boxing like that before. They had never been so overwhelmed by it.

Less than a month later there was a down-to-earth scrap in the homely Adelphi Stadium, at the foot of Florence Street, Benny against Londoner George Low, the referee having to stop the fight in the second round in order to save the unfortunate Englishman from the endless and crippling left hooks curving into him. And there wasn't an organdie frock in sight.

"Christ Benny, you were Jimmy Cagney in *White Heat* there the night," said one of the seconds as he unwound the long strips of bandages from his hands. They used the maximum the boxing laws permitted . . . eighteen feet of two-inch bandage; for his hands were susceptible. "Jimmy Cagney," exclaimed Sammy Wilson. "Fuckin' hell. He's no real that yin. I saw *White Heat*. He knocks down these four big guys in a fight and they stay down. Four kayos in a row. Christ, the fuckin world's heavyweight champion couldnae dae that. Lotta fuckin' baloney."

Benny was more than jubilant when Sammy told him later that he was now ready to take on Jim Campbell for the Scottish title. "Sammy, I've been telling you I've been ready for him for ages. Gees, I've sparred wi' the guy and I know I can do him."

By coincidence, the pair of them met days later in Queen Street. It was Sammy who saw him first, neatly dressed, broad slightly rounded shoulders, rugged faced, a boxer. They greeted each other amiably, reservedly. No plans had been announced but Campbell knew he would be their next target and what Sammy said to him came as no surprise. "We're coming for your title, Jim." Campbell smiled. A wry, self-assured smile that needed no words and meant . .

"Well, come and get it." He turned to look at Benny for his reply was a message specially for him. "You . . . you will never be so lucky in all your life getting a chance to fight me. I'm the champion of Scotland." Then he turned back to look at Sammy again. "We'll fight in two weeks time."

Campbell and his entourage left almost immediately for Wick, in the remote north east of Scotland where the countryfolk called a weasel a futrack, where buckie vallies were wild rose hips and when someone fell head over heels they said it was heels ower heid.

Benny went back to the Cathkin Braes. And Sammy set about settling with a promoter. When you're a beginner or a struggling battler, it's the boxer or his manager who has to go and look for the promoter. Sammy and Benny had done plenty of that. But now it was different. The promoters were coming to them. The promoter was an unusual sight in Florence Street and the playing children parted ranks to stare at him. "He's a right big shot," they would say. "Smokes big cigars so he does." And he wore expensive clothes, so he did. Colourful ties, fine nap coats, and the new style American rimless glasses. George Dingley was efficient to deal with. He knew his figures, knew his boxing, knew the money that would make managers nod in approval and knew that nod would be more good news for his bank manager. And Benny was to be the best good news in his life. A horse called White Bud, painted or not, had done it for his father. It had got him the big one at Lincoln. Would the wee Benny man do the same for him? Would he, like Sammy said he would, become the world champion? That would be the real big time for George if he did. For, if he got in with him now, he could be the man who promoted all of his fights. He could be his agent as well so that not only would he make profits from the show, he would get a percentage of his purse. And if he did get that world title all the top stars would want to come to Glasgow. He could bring them in from America even. Wonderful dollars that would mean. Lots and lots of them. He could be as rich as his Dad was when he was at his richest. There could be eleven pleasure cars for him too, and there were plenty of lovely handsome houses around Ayr just like Johnstone Hall. Play them right, treat them right, handle them right and he too could become a part of that little fighting machine from the Gorbals. The best part. The part that dealt with the money.

"Hey Sammy, have ye seen my ear?" It was one day after training, another twenty hard and sweaty rounds at the Polytechnic and he had just showered and was combing his hair, sleek middle shed, in the mirror. "Christ, Sammy, I've got a cauliflower ear. Fuck that, Sammy. I'm chucking it." He was half joking, but there was a tinge of earnestness in his shock at the state of his ear, raw and red, the lobe definitions vanishing with the swelling. Sammy looked at it in mock concern. "Christ, wee man, your right. You've got a cauly ear. Aye, it's a wee fuckin' beauty an' a'. Let me know when you've got two and we'll have a talk about it." The boxers laughed and Benny saw the funny point too. "Bastard, so he is."

One of the seconds consoled him and said he would put a light dressing on it to ease the pain. "You could always get the leeches to it. Aye, leeches. That's what we used to use. You can still get them at Fraser and Green's the big chemist at St George's Cross. You'll get one for about a bob. Comes in a wee box. Take it hame, rub some milk on your ear then put the leech on it. Greedy bastards so they are. Suck a' the blood they can get till they're that swollen they fall off. Then you put them in a tumbler of salt water and that makes them sick and they spew a' the blood out. Then ye put them back on your ear again. You see Benny, it's your capillaries that are fucked. And that's what's made your ear red and swollen."

Benny shook his head. "You want tae scunner me? Tell you one thing. They'll be nae fuckin leeches."

The Scottish title fight was arranged for the grandly named Olympic Sports Stadium at Parkhead.When they read about a venue with that kind of name in Paris, Rome or New York it would be in reference to their biggest and most prestigious stadium. Glasgow's Olympic Sports Stadium was nothing like the name suggested. In fact, few even knew it by that name. For it was the Nelson Lea whippet racetrack, flanking Celtic Football Park. Nevertheless, it was a useful little outdoor stadium for boxing promotions where crowds of up to 10,000 could comfortably watch the bouts.

There were grumbles about Dingley's prices. It was eight shillings ringside and many rows back from there before they lowered progressively to one shilling.

"Tell you what," they said, "they better give us a fight for that money."

They did. Fifteen rounds of it. Square on. No posing. No setting traps. No enticing. No feinting. No cat and mouse. No tentative throws. No hesitation. They got their eight shillings worth. And a new champion into the bargain. Campbell was amazed by the decision and his face showed it before turning to a look of sadness and then, quickly, changing to a broad, sporting smile as he saluted the new champion.

"We'll need to fight him again Sammy," said Benny. "It wasn't the clearcut way I had wanted. And did you hear the crowd booing?" Sammy understood. He would have felt that way himself. "Right then

. . . but we'll keep you fighting and improving till a fight's arranged."

Campbell jumped at the chance of a rematch and a date and venue was set by promoter Dingley . . . Cathkin Park, homeground of the Third Lanark Football Club. It was set for June 27, exactly six weeks after their first meeting. There was no waiting around. Even less for Benny who, as Sammy said, should keep fighting. Eleven days after becoming Scottish champion he was in the ring again . . . and together with the referee had to rescue Welshman Evan Evans as he swayed, battered and defeated, on the ropes to help him back to his corner. He had gone three rounds. And four days after that Peter Miller from Newcastle lasted eight rounds with him at the Parkhead Arena before being given the smelling salts to stir him from prostrate unconsciousness on the cape.

The Earl of Stair, Sir Iain Colquhoun, the clan chief who owned half of Loch Lomondside, and Brigadier General Sir Norman Orr Ewing were among the gentry at the ringside in Cathkin Park for the return match with Campbell. It was more than the bright young things who wanted to see the little fellow from the Gorbals.

They fought the same style of battle as the first fight, action and movement every minute. But there was to be nothing close about the result this time. It was after the tenth round that the real superiority started to show. Campbell was taking terrible punishment but wouldn't take a backward step. That wasn't his style. He was tottering and reeling, drunk-like, in the fifteenth after being down for a short count of two, and had their been a sixteenth round the seconds would have thrown in the towel. Referee Billy Strelley, Geordie Aitchison's old bare-knuckle rival, had no need to raise his hand. Benny had both of them raised in a salute to the crowd, as well as to his game rival Campbell, bloodied and bowed in his corner.

There were no boos or jibes from the 16,000 crowd this time. When Campbell got up from his seat they cheered their loudest for a man who had given his best. And when the Master of Ceremonies announced the victor, they tried to cheer even louder. The former champion had been thoroughly deposed. Long live the new king!

It had been a great night for the old boys of St John's. Like Father Fletcher had told them, if they kept at it, trained hard and lived the good life they would become champions at their sport. Johnny McGrory, on his way to becoming the featherweight champion of Scotland, his nose now as tough as Father Fletcher said it would be, knocked out Albert Roothooft, from Belgium, in the third round, and Paddy Docherty put up a great fight to get a draw with John Carlin of Greenock.

"Well, it's all going to the plan, wee man." These were Sammy's first words when Benny called at his house the following day. But he was there for other than the daily instructions. In his hand was a new gold pocket watch which he handed to his manager. He wasn't good with words, but managed to say it was just "a wee something for what you've done for me". He said he wanted to get it engraved . . . "you know, to you from the Scottish Flyweight Champion". Sammy thought for a minute. "No," he said. "Just make it . . . from Benny Lynch, the Flyweight Champion. There's gonnie be lots more titles and you'll no get them a' on it."

That over, Sammy was outlining their future plans. They had come through all the early stages of the overall campaign . . . competing with all his young contemporaries, moving up to the seasoned battlers, then into the national championship class. From now on there would be only two categories of fighters . . . men in the world championship ratings or ones the promoters thought would make him the kind of purse that he was now worth. "And I've a real beauty for your next fight. Maurice Huguenin the Frenchman." "Fine," said Benny. Who he was or what he was didn't really matter all that much. He was now a journeyman tradesman boxer. Time tested, time served, and well tried. They could put who they liked against him.

Others had different views and Sammy came under attack for putting his man at risk. "Suicide," said the experts. "Lynch is good . . . but not that good." They pointed to Huguenin's record. He had drawn with Valentin Angelmann, the reigning champion of France. And he had beaten Young Perez, the former world champion. He was a seasoned campaigner in the championship class. Sammy countered their claims. He had never hurried Benny in his life. It had been the opposite, in fact. Had Benny been making the decisions he would have been trying it on with such men much earlier in his career.

Huguenin came to Glasgow and went home the loser on points over twelve rounds, with Johnny McGrory getting his Scottish Feather title in the main fight of the bill. Angelmann, the other Frenchman, followed Jim Brady as the next challengers. Both went home losers.

The autumn of 1934 was to be one of Benny's busiest fighting periods. One fight in October, three in November, two in December, all of them scheduled twelve-rounders. Two went the distance, the others ending either in knockouts or the referee stepping in to save the other man from serious damage. All of them were men of the highest calibre . . . Pedrito Ruiz, champion of Spain; Johnny Griffiths, from Wales, in a rare fight in which only one punch was thrown—the very first punch of the contest and down went Johnny for the ten;

Tut Whalley, the dangerous southpaw, and how he hated them, disqualified for a low punch; and Sandy McEwan, who had a record few could equal having beaten both Praxille Gyde, the European flyweight champion, and Young Perez while he held the world title. Benny was on his way up, and getting there fast. But such was the game that as you battered your way up, you battered others down.

Every man who suffered a defeat wondered if it was the start of his decline. Unlike any other sport, it was the participant who killed off the other participant single handed. One man against another and only one could be the winner. They had no time for the losers. It was "hard luck, you did well. Maybe you should take it easy for a while." And for most who got a fingertouch to the Delights of the Fancy, it would be all too brief. The pace was fierce. They didn't mind a fight a week with work in between or else changing their name so that the Means Test inspectors wouldn't have them before a Tribunal. It was their living and they fought as long as the heart and lungs held out. And when the light flickered, it would dim quickly; snuff even quicker. The gamer they were the quicker they could go; for they were the ones who could suffer it through the pain, expose their ribs, their jaws, their skulls to the incessant thump, thump, thumping; wheeltaps and sledgehammers; ones that migrained, ones that sickened. It only needed one really bad mauling to finish a fighter off; three or four would certainly do it.

Alex Farries had gone out like that. Few had been more game, which was why they had liked him the ring; which was why he had faced up to Benny four times, the fourth being his last-ever fight. He was only twenty-eight and retired for just over a year when he went to see his old rival Benny fight Pedrito Ruiz. It would be a tremendous fight, everyone was saying, for the Spaniard had few equals on the Continent. He was also a bit of a character, which endeared him to the Glasgow public.

It was November, cold and sombre, and amidst the hodden Glasgow scene, the flamboyant Pedrito, in tans and checks, had the crowds parting on his strolls through the city. He fascinated them with the adornment which accompanied him everywhere . . . an expensive, shiny malacca walking cane, tipped with an exquisitely carved head of a sheepdog. Pedrito had real style; like Benny thought he too would have when he got into the money.

Pedrito would have got a lot more headlines that week had it not been for another man with a foreign-sounding name who was creating his own legend . . . of another sort. He was Johnny Ramensky, the man the newspapers called "the Lanarkshire convict". Johnny was of Lithuanian descent and, like many others, was to come

and live in the Gorbals. The year before he had been sentenced to
five years jail for burglary . . . his profession. He was an exceptional
tradesman at this art, never demeaning himself by taking from the
poor and specialising in safes from wealthy companies. His other
speciality was to be . . . escaping from prison. And the headlines they
were giving him was for a feat which had everyone gasping, and
mainly in admiration. For Johnny had scaled the wall of Peterhead
Prison, the old blue-grey granite jail fortress on the wild north-east
coast of Scotland where they put the kind of people they thought
might want to escape from prison. No man had ever cleared
Peterhead's high walls before. They were the unscaleable, the
authorities had said. Until the exceptional Johnny Ramensky, that is.

Johnny was the talk—and the toast—around the street men at their
corner haunts and bookie's stances. Sammy Wilson had wisecracked .
. . "Aye, I should have made up a book on him getting away."

"An whit would yer tanner double have been Sammy . . . that they
didnae catch him for a year!"

They remembered his previous escapade at Barlinnie, Glasgow's
very own prison, dominating the northern approaches to the city like
some fearsome and foreboding Tibetan monastery. One of the
gathering at the stance had been there in the summer of 1931 when
he had made his amazing demonstration: "I'm telling you, there's
naebody in Hengler's circus could have done what he did that day.
He gets up on the roof of the big recreation hall, right up the rones
like a bloody fly out for a walk. It's sixty feet up to the roof, so it is,
then he takes off his shoes and socks and entertains us with his
physical jerks, running about on the roof like it was the gym. The
screws were feart tae go near him, no' that he would have used
violence or anything, he's no' like that. They were just feart of the
height. Up there the whole afternoon, shouting down at us to throw
him up hard-boiled eggs. He even made up a pillow and did some
sunbathing . . . an' you know the slope of that roof. Barlinnie has
never seen anything like it."

They were visibly disappointed when, on the day before the fight,
Johnny Ramensky had taken over the headlines again . . . this time for
being caught, wandering minus footwear and headgear in bitter
conditions near the little village of Balmedie. He was twenty miles
away from Peterhead and just eight miles short of a hiding place in
Aberdeen where he had friends.

The excitement of Ramensky over, the newspapers could concen-
trate again on Pedrito Ruiz, cane and all, and Benny Lynch. Their
fight was to be a duel that every boxer and fight fan would want to
see and Alex Farries milled around with the thousands of others

outside the City Hall wondering how he was going to get in. For Alex was broke. He didn't even have the few shillings for the cheapest seats. So he planned to skip in.

Skipping in, as they called it, was a popular practice at places of entertainment in Glasgow. For some it was something of an art form. Confident, courageous, and cunning they would skip in, free of charge, anywhere there was a show with a box office. Skippy Burns, another of the Florence Street characters, was one of the best at it. He was small and fair-haired and in his early teens but his boast was that he had skipped into every cinema up town and treated the ones in the suburbs with a disdain of ease for entry free. They were a doddle to him.

"Take the Paramount," he would say. "Got the smartest commissionaires in town, blue tails, white gloves pinned to their shoulders, and not one of them keeps a watch on the door that you can skip in. For they havenae twigged it. It's the first door past the main entrance in Renfield Street and takes you up a flight of stairs to the cafe. They a' go in there at the interval from the balcony so all you do is walk back into the hall with them for they don't re-check the tickets. Regal . . . through the exit door in Scott Street and that gets you into the hall through the door for the lavvy. La Scala . . . right in the front door and tell the doorman you're only buying sweeties at the shop. The shop is next to the door into the hall and you just flash a bar of Fry's Sandwich at the usherette and you're in. Cinerama . . . two entrances, one for the cheap seats, one for the dear seats. Go in the cheap entrance and ask for a dear seat and they direct you along a corridor to the other pay box. When you get there just say you've been at the lavvy and they let you in. The Coliseum . . . wait at the one-way opening door up the lane. Somebody always comes out it and if you're quick you can be in before the doorman comes to close it."

Skippy's Dad was even better at it. He preferred frontal assault, and even took the wife with him on occasions. His skipping-in attire was his Orange Walk bowler and umbrella and a blue nap coat he kept in the wardrobe smothered in mothballs. He would spend hours brushing and polishing himself up till he looked the complete toff. Even had the commissionaires saluting him when he walked up to them, all plummy-voiced saying . . . "Good e.v.e.n.i.n.g. Are we busy tonight? Takings good?" They assumed he was management and they would "Yes sir, no sir" him then show him to the best seats when he said "I think I'll have a look at the show." He did the theatres as well as the cinemas and was only challenged once, about his identity, to which he replied coolly . . . "Burns. Mr Burns . . . Royal Navy." He had been too. One of Jellicoe's men . . . an Ordinary Seaman.

Alex, of course, wasn't a professional at the skipping-in business. Nevertheless, he was determined to see the fight and thought if he hung about long enough outside the City Hall he would find some way of entering. Sure enough he spotted it. The man at one of the side doors was Jimmy Stevenson, an old boxing pal. He managed to catch his attention and Jimmy gave him the nod. He was inside the hall and sitting in one of the best seats when a girl programme seller came round. Alex didn't even have the threepence for a programme and the girl mentioned this to one of the stewards. "Bet he's nae ticket either," he said. The steward checked and Alex had to shake his head. "Fly man . . . eh? C'mon . . . you're for the oot."

But luck was on Alex's side. Just as he was being shown from the hall, Sammy Wilson entered with Benny's Dad John. "Howsitgaun Alex?" greeted Sammy ever cheerful. Alex was saved by the bell. They took him to the dressing rooms to meet his old protagonist. But there was little time for wellwishing. The dressing room area was in an uproar. The Spanish party were screaming with rage. Pedrito was refusing to fight. He couldn't fight . . . his walking stick had gone. His favourite cane; his loving, adorable, lucky mascot had vanished . . . slipped inside Benny's dressing gown when he had been wishing him luck before the fight.

"You daft wee bastard," Sammy stormed when they discovered it was in his dressing room. "Christ Sammy . . . just a joke," Benny pleaded. Pedrito had his walking stick back within seconds and was quickly pacified. But it wasn't to bring him the luck he needed. After a brave start, he quickly succumbed to the punches coming at him and didn't win a round after the fifth, Benny getting a clear points verdict on the final bell.

14

Texas Jack The Beau

The Fancy, as they had been known, were the cream of the sporting aristocrats. Those who were intensely interested in the art and science of boxing. The patrons of the prize ring. They had been around since the early eighteenth century when John Broughton upgraded basic fisticuffs into a sporting science and handed off all and sundry till he was beaten by Jack Slack at the ripe old athletic age of forty-six years. The Fancy were the followers of all those who dealt in levellers, benders, crackers, nobblers, pepperers and conkers, which, they understood, were the ones who could use their fists with titanic strength. They went with Molineaux the Negro, Deaf Burke, William Perry, the Tipton Slasher, Big Ben Brain, Dutch Sam Gully and endured with Bold Bendigo when he thrashed Young Brassey from Bradford in fifty-two rounds, Charley Langan the Irishman in thirty-two rounds and the endless battle with Bill Looney which went ninety-nine rounds before his rival was humbled.

The Fancy were from royalty, from the titled and from those with personal fortunes who could equate with them. The Fancy were flamboyant and lived with style in their courting of the oldest and most basic of sports. They were the friends of the champions; and the champions were their friends. And when a champion was beaten, they passed on to the next champion, pollinating their own grandeur with each friendship. There were those of them who followed it for part of their life; there were those who followed it all their life. There were princes and princesses of the Fancy; there were Kings and Queens. But the king of them all was Hugh McAlevey . . . Belfastman.

They called him Texas and Texas Jack . . . Mr Who . . . Beau . . . and for those who didn't know how that was spelled just ordinary Bo. It was Texas because he was a millionaire and had odd-jobbed it around America for seven years as a young man, arriving penniless from Ireland and returning with enough dollars and diligence to go into the liquor and bookmaking business. He was Mr Who because when they banned bookies from advertising, he dressed as a Chinese Mandarin and took out advertising space in the newspapers for a photograph of himself in the costume and captioned . . . "Mr Who". Into the bargain he had the slogan "Starting Prices All Races in China" emblazoned on all of his seventeen shops. Everyone got the message for everyone knew Hugh McAlevey and a foolish law was made even more foolish. And the reputation of the flamboyant Beau grew even more.

He was raconteur extraordinary, singer of no mean ability, a bird fancier, City Councillor and tireless traveller. When he crossed the Atlantic it was with a suite on a Cunarder and he was known to all the seasoned socialite travellers on that route; the captain's top table set, people like the Hon. William Waldorf Astor, M.P., Percy Straus, president of Macy & Co, the Maharajah and Maharanee of Bhavnagar, the Count and Countess de Pemgny, Daniel C. Roper, the American Secretary of Commerce, and William A. Julian, the Treasurer of the United States. They all knew and loved Hugh for he was the most companionable of travellers.

"Sure now," he would say, "'I've crossed the Atlantic so many times Dan Parker, the *New York Daily Mirror* columnist wrote that the fish nod every time I go past."

He had been travelling the world to see the top fights since Owen Moran met Abe Atell in 1908. He was there on the night Battling Morgan beat Joe Gans for the world lightweight title. He was at Reno when Jeffries battled it out with Johnson. He was there at the first Gene Tunney and Jack Dempsey fight. And he was back for the second one. He was in Chicago when the man they called the Brown Bomber got the title from Braddock. He saw the great Jimmy Britt fight and was close enough to the ringside to hear Sullivan tell the darting Jake Kilrain . . . "Stand, you son of a gun, stand." He had been to London to see Jimmy Wilde. He had been to Glasgow to see Elky Clark.

"And I've seen the greatest Scotchman of them all," he would tell any Scots he met. "Yer man Tancy Lee. And if ever you want a lesson in perseverance, just look at your wee man Tancy. What a story. There he was, way past his twenty-eighth birthday, and you know what some of them look like at that age, when he achieves the great ambition of his life by going down to London and winning the Amateur Boxing Association bantamweight title. The toast of Scotland he was . . . then yer amateurs discovered he had once taken a few bob in a booth fight to help out the family funds and what do they do? . . . make him hand back the cup and wipe his name from the records. He was nearly thirty, do you know, when he turned professional, gets knocked out in his first fight as a bantam but he's got that much courage and confidence he goes to London to fight at flyweight and beats allcomers even stopping the unbeatable Jimmy

Wilde for the first time and taking his title and Lonsdale belt off him. That was some seventeen rounds that fight. Made him your first British champion. But yer man Tancy doesn't stop at that. He goes right up to featherweight and does he not win the British title and Lonsdale belt at that an' all? And him an old Boer War veteran at that. Jesus, they're not making them like that any more."

And, as he had followed Jimmy Wilde and Elky Clark and Tancy Lee, Texas Jack was to become a follower of another wee Scotchman Benny Lynch. It was after he had beaten Billy Warnock that Benny had come to his attention. Being a fellow bookie, he found an immediate affiliation with Sammy Wilson, inviting him and Benny to Ireland for a holiday. Hugh regaled them like they were Royalty. They were captivated by the big Belfastman with the happy smiling face that looked like it had been created by Botticelli. He was never short of a story for them.

"Do you know what happened the last time I went to Glasgow? I was with my daughter, she trained to be a singer in Florence you know, and there was a little fellow from your parts on the train with us from Stranraer. Well, do you know, we couldn't understand a word he was saying he was that broad. So I says to him after he had talked his head off without us knowing what he had been saying ... 'Sir,' I says, 'you Scotchmen are a much misunderstood race.' Yer man didn't get it, but I'm telling you the rest of the carriage was in convulsions."

They asked him if it was true he had his own grave ready.

"Sure and it's a vault ... beautiful one too right there in Milltown cemetery."

It was a joke around Belfast that he even had laid two phones into it so that he could still get race results when he had passed on. But the vault was no joke. He had engaged the sculptor Kennedy to design it. It was to be one of the grandest monoliths in Milltown ... eleven feet by eight feet and eight feet deep, topped by an ebony-black polished slab surmounted by a cross five feet six inches from ground level, its gate and railings in corrosion proof finish. "Think of the trouble it saves the family when you die," he told them. "There's my place all neat and ready for me when I pass on and nobody had to do a thing. If you choose your own house and make all the arrangements during your life for your family, education and the like, and make your own will, why not do the final thing and get your grave ready?"

He showed them a photograph of it, framed and in a place of pride in his Berry Street offices. Then he said to them, to their surprise ... "How would you like to meet the finest right there ever was?" He bid them to follow him. In a corner of his office he pointed to a glass casket, the contents of which had Benny and Sammy gasping. For it was an arm . . . a human arm. A right arm. Withered and blackened, the thumb outstretched and the forefinger straight, as though in a final desperate point. "The finest right there ever was," said Beau proudly. "There never was one like it . . . and there'll never be another."

He told them its story. It was the arm of the legendary Dan Donnelly, the celebrated Irish bareknuckler of the early nineteenth century, said apocryphally to be the first and only pugilist ever knighted. Dan had been so revered by his followers that they cut his footprints from the turf as he walked victorious from the ring after beating Englishman George Cooper at the Curragh of Kildare in 1815. "And do you know what, they are still there to this very day," said Beau reverently. "What a man he must have been," he said. "They used to turn up in their thousands to see him. Twenty thousand were there when he knocked out Highwayman Tom Hall in twenty minutes in Dublin, Dan's hometown. After he beat Cooper at the Curragh he went on tour with Jack Carter in England and even though they were just exhibition bouts, thousands would turn out to see him. His most famous fight was against Tom Oliver at Crawley Hurst in 1819 and there was more than £100,000 in wagers. You and I would have done all right there . . . eh Sammy? Well, the fight went thirty-four rounds and Danny boy won again. And when he came back home to dear ould Ireland didn't they toast him everywhere he went. Everybody had to buy him a drink, which suited yer man for he liked it. By gees and he did. Just loved the ould whiskey. So much so that when he died of it at the tender age of thirty-two and they buried him at Bully's Acre his epitaph read . . . 'He died at last from fortyseven, Tumblers of punch drunk one even.' What a man. And what a waste . . . dying at thirty-two of the drink."

Dan's arm had been parted from his body by medical students after his burial but it had created such a furore that it was pickled and hidden away, to turn up years later after the death of one of the robbers.

Texas told Sammy and Benny that he was surprised he hadn't fought more Irishmen. "Billy Warnock has a lot of brothers you know. There's Jim, for instance. Grand young lad. Came from the Crusaders boxing club and since turning pro he's won forty and drawn five out of fifty-one contests. Now there's a fine record for you. Mind you, he's a southpaw and I know you don't like them Benny."

"Aye Billy told me all about his brother that time he was over in

Glasgow," said Benny. "They're some characters, eh! Billy tells me they have a fight every day . . . and that's just between themselves.!"

"What about it then, Sammy," asked McAlevey.

Sammy told him he had their present plans worked out. "We're going for that world title first. But tell you what. Once we get it, and nothing's going to stop the wee man here, then he'll come over for a holiday and have a go at your other Warnock . . . Jimmy. Fair enough?"

"Aye," said Texas. "Fair enough. You'll be right welcome in Belfast."

15

Love and Marriage

He was eighteen, she was a year younger. He was a £10 a fight professional boxer, who, his manager was convinced, would be Benny Lynch, world champion; a prediction he took with a shrug-of-the-shoulder philosophy for there was more to life than the sweat-shop tyranny of the puncher. Life also was for living.

She was the eldest of seven children, a twenty five shillings a week machinist in a rubber coat factory and called Anne McGuckian. She had no greater ambition in life than to be like her mother . . . a good Catholic, happily married and settled down with her family around her and her man, a docker, in a steady job.

The fate that brought them together had its beginnings, in his case, at the New Polytechnic Club and his love of dancing and, in her case, at a holiday camp in far-off Campbeltown on the Mull of Kintyre. The McGuckians went there every year with a big tent hired from Blacks of Greenock. For those families who were prudent enough or who were well enough off to save the few pounds for an annual family holiday the tents or the huts were the answer. There were big camps of them all down the Ayrshire coast . . . at Barassie and New Stevenston, at Seamill, the Heads of Ayr and down at the Maidens and Girvan. Others preferred the East Coast, places like Port Seton and Longniddry, or further still up to the Fife Coast to Leven, and the sandhills at Pettycur, Kinghorn, on the High Binn at the back of Burntisland while others still went to farm sites in the Highlands "near where granny had come from".

For Bob and Annie McGuckian and their seven children, Campbeltown was the place. The neighbours had all gone there for years and when they had settled into their two room and kitchen at 141 Paisley Road West in Kinning Park they too joined them in their community holiday.

Mrs McGuckian was a prudent manager with her housekeeping money. She had to be with the long winter periods when shipping was low on the Clyde and the dockers had to go without wages.

These were the weeks when the men would have to assuage their
wives with the hopeful promise . . . "Never you mind, wait till the ice
melts and the St Lawrence opens up. There'll be plenty of wages."
Irrespective, as soon as Christmas was over, Annie would religiously
give one of her friends fifteen shillings a week to put into the Wylie
Barr's biscuit factory's saving scheme. That was their holiday money.
Before the Glasgow Fair holiday—the first Friday after the second
Tuesday in July—Bob would go down to Greenock at the mouth of
the Clyde to Blacks tent factory and order the tents for the holiday . . .
a cottage or a bell for the women and girls, doubling as kitchen and
daytime living quarters, and a small bivouac—their bivvy—for the
boys. Annie would prepare the straw-filled palliasses and pillows
and, together with eight neighbouring families they would all walk to
the Broomielaw on Fair Friday to the pleasure steamers' berth. And
the greatest moment in all the world was when the little *Dalriada*'s
propellers frothed the treacly river, she boomed her steam horn, cast
off the stout hessian hawser, and the little band of melodion, fiddle
and clarinet struck up *Sailing Down the Clyde*. After getting the camp
established and having the first few days with them, the menfolk
would make their way back to Glasgow again, their brief holiday
over, leaving the family to enjoy the summer months under canvas.

Dancing was the big craze and the boys in the neighbouring tents
got together a small group and cleared a piece of ground. It was even
better fun than the Tripe. There were no trapdoors to fall down. They
would dance through the long summer evenings till darkness fell . . .
old-time and modern, new-fangled foxtrots and quicksteps, with lots
of laughs in between and all the current novelty numbers like the
Black Bottom, Boomps-a-Daisy, the Chestnut Tree and Lambeth Walk.
Some could even do the Banana Glide and the other steps they called
Eccentric Dancing and boast, "Hey, look at me . . . am doing my
Johnny Harvey."

"We're opening our own dancehall when we get back to Glasgow,"
said some of the dance-mad boys, a group from Scotland Street, which
boasted the longest tenement block in Scotland, "longest in all the
world", said some. "We're calling it the Villa and it's in Cook Street . .
. you'll need to come Anne," they said.

Dancing was the great communcator. It had glamour, even though
the floorspace might be so small they had to hang the band on a shelf
like they did at the Tripe; it was an avenue to flaunt skills, skills that
were appreciated and could make you a local hero; and boy could
meet girl, girl could meet boy.

The Villa was just around the corner from the Polytechnic and
even though there had been a hard day's training, on the road, in the

ring, there was still plenty of energy left for the dance floor. When the young boxers at the Poly heard about the new dance hall nearby, it had to have a visit. "Better than the Tripe," said one. "More classy," said another. "Aye, but no' as much fun."

Benny had taken a fancy to her right from the first foxtrot. She was petite, pert, alluringly attractive and not all that impressed that he could earn as much as £10 for one night's fighting.

"See you home?" he asked after the last dance, the traditional encounter for popping such a question, or, as they would say "getting a lumber". But there were formalities to be obeyed. She had gone to the dancing with her cousin Tommy Houston as an escort. He would have to be formally asked. "Whit are ye?" he asked Benny. "I'm a boxer," he replied. "That's all right then. You can take her home."

"You'll need to stop sending tickets for my father and I to come to your fights," Anne told him after one fight, the tickets having been sent as a peace-offering and a means of resuming their sporadic courtship. "Did you see what happened when you looked round to see if we were there. The other boxer saw you do it and caught you a right beauty. But anyway, I don't like the boxing. The only punches I seem to see is the ones you receive." It had been nearly forty fights since he had last lost a bout . . . the one to his old pal Paddy Docherty. And the punches that Anne McGuckian could see he was getting were now coming from men of world class. Like Benny, they were the ones who had survived the long road to get near to the top; they were the real punchers, the ones who had a trail of knockouts behind them. They were the ones whose punches told and even though he still scored against them and was always the victor, there were now the agonies of the morning after and the night after that too. Breathe too deeply and you got stabbed. Cough and you felt a red hot needle in our lungs. Shake your head and it buzzed. Then the pains would eventually dissolve . . . and who's next for a leathering?

But if the pains were a problem, there was always a way out for Benny. For Benny, problems never existed. When he was younger and they told him he would be fighting big-time champions, men so tough and grizzled they could break a man in two, he would be visibly unimpressed. Others as competent with their fists would have worried about the prospect of tackling such men; men who, the boxing reporters would write, could stop a man's career in one bout. There were sleepless nights of contemplation when you had to face men like that. Benny never had a sleepless night. And, if there was a problem, like the after-fight pains . . . well he had a way with that too; run; pretend it didn't exist; find a panacea. And, for the right occasion, there was none he knew better than the one his father had found before him and countless others around him had used, if they could afford to. The drink. It was the Great Saviour. The supreme, multi-purpose remedy. It could transcend them from their sepia surroundings to the realm of the rainbow. It could give them courage, if courage was what they needed. Make them happy. It could fortify. Make them fearless. It could evaporate the worry that was tomorrow. Make them oblivious. To each his own reason. To each his own necessity.

Like his courtship, the drinking was sporadic at first. It had begun, as it had so often done, in his younger days as an act of bravado. For a few coppers and shared between them up a close the boys could have a bottle of South African fortified wine, a wine that was cleverly fortified to the point which is the optimum level at which the bloodstream can take in alcohol: even neat whisky couldn't have had a quicker effect. And that's what they liked. Quick effect. Not having to work at it . . . or even enjoy it. Effect was the thing when they were young. Instant good feeling and fortification, that was to be the style of drinking for many of them until they could take no more. Even after adolescence, the habit stuck.

The word had got to Sammy Wilson about Benny's drinking and he was summonsed. "Do you know I've never touched a drop of it in all my life. It's poison and it will go for you. Christ, Benny, don't be a right mug." There were apologies and then long spells without a drink. But, as he got older, Sammy the Svengali was having a lesser effect on the protégé. Once Sammy had been God. What he said, he did. No routine was questioned. No dictat was disobeyed. Benny followed blindly. But the blindfolds were slowly coming off.

He was waiting outside her work that evening and the car in which he was sitting was gleaming. "Just got it from Philip Barr's garage at Brigton Cross. No' bad eh? Twenty pounds down and £10 a month." Earlier that day, in the exuberance of owning his first car, he had driven with his friend Ian Watson down Florence Street, past the Moy corner and Sammy's pitch, with all the usual crowd there, Neillie, John, Josie, Eddie, Tash and Trouble, and the others, shouting greetings . . . and throwing fireworks which had every window up in the street for immediate "hings" to watch the commotion. When they had got to Rutherglen Road they had spun the car round to drive back up the street again, throwing out the remainder of their crackers. Sammy Wilson had gone apoplectic. "You daft wee bastard," he said. "Think you're in the fuckin' big-time. Playing the big man. Tell you what. You get that fuckin' sold. You're no' the world champion yet." Benny left to let him cool off.

Anne, now an apprentice hairdresser in Mrs Shenkin's shop in

Paisley Road West, had just finished her work for the day and after expressing her admiration for the car, was startled at the next question. "Fancy getting married . . . right away? I've got the new car and we can drive to Gretna Green. You don't need to wait there. And we don't need to tell anybody here. We'll just go."

Anne laughed out loud at his surprise question. Then she smiled at him. There was a silence. Then she said . . . "Right then . . . why not?"

The Scots had never stood in the way of young lovers. If they were over sixteen, they could hold hands and declare the vows of solemn marriage with no more formality than having witnesses gathered before them and not a minister or priest in sight. And in the eyes of the law they were legally united. Gretna had become romantically popular as being the first village into Scotland from England where there were facilities for being married with the benefit of Scots Law. The facility at Gretna was a blacksmith who, before his anvil, would unite the young couples from England, and other lands, who flocked there for a marital blessing that ignored the wrath of disapproving parents. It was Great Britain's capital of romance. Although they were over sixteen and could easily have been married in Glasgow, there was much more romance in the prospect of that dash to Gretna.

Without as much as a night's honeymoon, the newly-weds turned the car round at Gretna after taking their anvil nuptials in order to go home and face their parents. The McGuckians were furious. "You, Anne, are staying in this house here and Benny is going home to his father . . . till you're married properly. And there's only one place for that . . . the church."

Three weeks later, on March 8, 1935, at St Margaret's Roman Catholic Church in Kinning Park everyone was satisfied that they were really married . . . the McGuckians, the Lynchs, the Kilcoynes, and Father Feely, the Parish Priest. For this time it was before their God.

George Dingley was there. So was Sammy Wilson. And Elky Clark from the *Daily Record*. And from St Margaret's they went to the Dixon Halls in Cathcart Road, Govanhill . . . "best hall in the South Side," said Benny.

There were reporters and photographers there as well. For Benny was now news. The days of the two-line report on the second back page of the papers were over. Just four days previously he had had another hallmark fight of his career. Most of the challengers had already been disposed of and Sammy had arranged a non-title fight with Jackie Brown from Manchester over twelve rounds. Brown was the reigning flyweight champion of the world. Sammy Wilson's plan for this fight was different from any other Benny had ever known.

"You'll need to hold back with him, wee man. We don't want you giving this yin a tanking or else we'll no' get a quick return for a title fight. Let him think he can beat you . . . then we'll really sort him out." The plan worked out to perfection, although Benny tried to rebel during a few rounds. "Let me finish him, Sammy." But in the ring, he was still impicitly following instructions and as Sammy cooled him between rounds with a white flapping towel he repeated the instructions . . . "Go easy with him. Easy." The result was a draw.

A few days later he was nominated to meet Tommy Pardoe in his hometown of Birmingham as a final eliminator for an official world title challenge against Brown. "And look at the money we're getting Benny," said Sammy. "Three hundred pounds . . . not bad eh? That's just the start of it Benny. That's your biggest purse. But it will be the real big yins after you put Brown away for the title." Three hundred pounds. It was hard for him to grasp that amount of money. His dad earned less than half of that . . . for a year's work walking the line for the London, Midland and Scottish Railway Company. Three hundred pounds for doing the same thing as he had with Paddy Docherty for two pounds and ten shillings, with Alex Farries for £4 and £7 and £10 winner take all. Three hundred pounds for the same blocking and weaving, defending and attacking, hooking and jabbing. It seemed unreal that it was happening to him, Benny Lynch. But then, Sammy Wilson had always said it would happen. The old bastard was right again.

But there were hazards now that he didn't have when he fought Docherty and Farries, Boy McIntosh and Young Griffo. Then he had freewill. He could be off with his old schoolmates, Paddy and Josie, Francie and Bobby and the rest of the gang to the Tripe or the Parlour or go down and hear the patter at the corner, Trouble's escapades, Tash's philosophising. Now it was different. They would come to the house for him. He had to go with them . . . be in their company. For they were the new friends. New friends who claimed they were old friends. There were trainers and men who said they were trainers and who would whisper to him, "Watch Sammy! He could be getting you more fights, more money. He's just thinking about himself." There were promoters who were saying the same— and other things—about Dingley. If they promoted his next fight, they said, there could be more in it for him. Dingley himself and the uptown bookmakers loved him, as they loved all possessions. Rub a bookie and they'll tell you how well off they are. Now the uptown ones had their great new possession. Much better to boast you had wee Benny from the Gorbals in your company last night than take the wife out to show off the new Arctic Fox. Much better to flaunt

Benny at your table in Ferrari's than be seen in your old suburb in the new Humber. Much better to have Benny with you at the nineteenth hole than to tell the members about the big new bungalow you're about to buy. A night with Benny on the town and forever after you could tell them that the wee man was your best friend and, anyway "ah've known the family for years". And, as well as the uptown bookies, the stage comedians, the theatre managers, the impresarios and the others who have a need to talk about friends who are success, clamoured around him.

And in between there were miles to run, punches to be taken.

The £300 for the Pardoe fight included being on the receiving end of a particularly wicked and memorable right hand to the chin which knocked Benny to the canvas in the closing seconds of the first round of their fight. He fell heavily, for falling was something at which he hadn't much practice. It had been years since he had been floored as the result of a punch. And when he went down his head whipped on the cape with a sharp thud then a timely bell ended the round without the necessity of a count. There was no immediate sign that it had caused any damage and Pardoe, in turn, went on to give an immense display of courage by doggedly staying on his feet in face of the worst onslaught of punches he had ever experienced.

Thirty-nine straight fights without a defeat. Benny had beaten the Champion of France. The Champion of Italy. The Champion of Spain. The Champion of Scotland. The best in England. The best in Ireland. And he was a young married man of twenty-two years of age . . . with a wife who had left him.

The new friends and their demands had increased to such a pitch that Anne had become desperately unhappy. She had imagined married life to be something like the style of her own house . . . a hard-working father whose devotion was such that his only pleasure was a bottle of Bass on a Friday night and unhappiness nothing worse than when mother occasionally nagged and he would put on his coat and go out for a walk. And when he returned it was all over. But life was nothing like that for her and Benny. There was no coming home from work and putting the slippers on and listening to the variety on the new push-button radio. Just four months after that happy day when they took their second vows before Father Feely, Anne was back living with her parents.

)

16

Hail The Champion

The Central Station in Glasgow had never seen anything like it. It was never to know anything like it again. The city had four major stations, Buchanan Street and Queen Street for the north and east; St Enoch and the Central for suburban, steamer links, the Lowlands and England. The Central was the premier station. It was the major link with the outside world. If they came from America, statesmen or sportsmen, actors or aviators, they would come via London and then north to Scotland by the L.M.S. to the Central. Buffalo Bill had got his reception to Glasgow there. So had Tom Mix . . . he even rode his horse Tony right into the Central Hotel. And Harry Lauder, Scotland's first knight of the music hall. And Laurel and Hardy. And countless others. But not all of them together were received as were the occupants of the 2.20 express from Liverpool and Manchester when its big pistons came to a slow clanking halt on Platform Two.

They had been crowding into the station that morning since eleven o'clock singing the same songs they had been singing the night before at the Belle Vue Stadium in Manchester . . . *Roamin' in the Gloamin', Loch Lomond, I Belong to Glasgow*. Anything that was Scottish sufficed. For this was a time to be Scottish like it was a time none of them could remember. For one of them had shown the world of what they were made. And they were chanting his name long before he and his party stepped off the train . . . "Benn . . .neee . . .Benn . . .neee . . .Benn . . .neee . . . Benn . . .neee". The word had been flashed round the picture screens and announced at the theatres the night before . . . "Benny Lynch—our Benny—has won the world title".

Five hundred had travelled south with him to be there on his big night. They had never seen such a crowd of Scottish invaders at an English boxing promotion before. The ringside had all the top celebrities of the day . . . Jeff Dickson, the famous promoter, Jack Kid Berg, the British Lightweight champion, Jimmy Wilde, former World flyweight champion, Jock McAvoy, British middleweight champion, Ted Broadribb, the man they called the "well-known London sportsman", and Hugh McAlevey, the man they called the "well-known Irish sports-man". Further back from the ringside and wearing the big woollen tammy with another one clutched in his hands was Andy Smith, his old friend of the booth days. The spare one was Benny's own, the one he had worn when they had paraded with Len Johnson's Troupe at the gaffs. When the pipers marched him into the ring Andy ran up to him; Benny grinned when he recognised him and when he saw the tammy he bowed his head and Andy ceremoniously placed it on him in full view of the huge crowd and the 500 Scots gave Belle Vue a cheer like they had never heard before.

Sammy Wilson fussed over him in the corner, handing him the water bottle he guarded with his life. "You want to get a boxer nobbled and there's no better way than to 'fix' his water," he would say. He made sure that never happened and even had Tommy McLean, one of their camp, drive a special supply of Gorbals tap water to Manchester in case the local supply affected his charge's stomach. They were taking no chances for this one. Sammy stood before him flapping the towel, more a gesture of support prior to the two fighters being called together. Benny sat in his corner, hands outstretched on the ropes showing no more emotion than he would if it were a fifty shilling bout at Tommy Watson's.

When referee Moss Deyong called "seconds out" Sammy Wilson, as he always did, slipped behind Benny, to put his arms round him in order to lift him from the stool at the bell. He had always done this . . ."every ounce saved is another punch," he would say.

Benny didn't need all that much energy this time. Four minutes and forty two seconds later after he had been on the floor eight times, Jackie Brown, the undisputed flyweight champion of the world for the past three years, had to signal to Mr Deyong that he could continue no longer. The King was Dead. And into the ring stormed the Scots fans to chair their new King. Benny Lynch . . . the first Scot to become a world boxing champion.

"Do you think Brown got a surprise?" asked Benny in the dressing room after they had cleared it of the first flush of well-wishers and newspapermen. "Surprise," replied Sammy. "Did I no' tell you what happened? Norman Hurst, you know the big shot sports reporter, well he asked me on the q.t. that time he came up to Glasgow to see you training when I thought you would open up and I told him about half way through. 'You look out for him in the seventh' I says. But I knew he would go right back and tell the Brown camp that. What do they think we are . . . daft bastards?" And the dressing room filled with laughter at the prospect of Brown copping the onslaught the moment he had advanced on Benny in the very first round.

It took the mounted police and foot reinforcements hours to control the joyous cheering crowds that were choking the centre of Glasgow. There were 20,000 of them packed into the concourse of the Central Station, the focal point of which was an artefact of polished World War shells.

Outside in Gordon Street they were jammed from Renfield to Hope Street and around all the side entrances. One woman stood alone. She had gone along not thinking about crowds. Crowds to meet Benny? She hadn't seen him now for nearly four months, but like so many others who turned up that day, Anne Lynch didn't get to see him, and turned to walk home sadly to her parents' tenement home in Paisley Road West.

It had been suggested to the Glasgow Corporation, the governing body of the city, that they give some form of welcome to the new champion. New York would have ticker-taped him. Any English city would have had him on the Council Chamber's balcony, Mayor, Mayoress, robes and all, and in France the President would have kissed him on either cheek after draping him with the Legion d'Honneur. But dour Glasgow authority didn't consider their new celebrity of a category to be honoured. Instead the *Daily Record* newspaper hurriedly assembled a celebration dinner at the prestigious Grosvenor Restaurant for the day of his return, packing it with every available dignatory able to attend at such short notice.

The champion of the world was the toast of the world. He was to be toasted to, toasted with, toasted about. The poets fled to their pens to put him in verse, MacNib of the *Evening News* being one of the first of the mark.

> Tribute I pay to Benny Lynch, who found the championship a cinch,
> He simply did old Jackie "brown" as to the boards he sent him down,
> Glasgow at last with flag unfurled sits right atop the cockeyed world,
> Our Wee Men may honk their klaxon since one of them has laid low the saxon,
> Just take one tip from me old Benny and keep your head!
> By all the omens of the Fates, Glasgow will flourish . . . in the States.

MacNib was no Bard, but astute enough to include a message in his lines of praise . . . "take one tip from me old Benny and keep your head!" Tommy Milligan conveyed a similar message. In his speech at the dinner he referred to the honour of Scottish boxing and turning to the new champion he said in deliberate tones . . . "We champions of the past have deep within us the honour of Scottish boxing. It is up to you to uphold it." Benny had time to work on a short speech before being called. "Thank you from the bottom of my heart. I felt I was fighting for Scotland and my true happiness lies in the fact that I did not let Scotland down. My countrymen were looking to me to triumph and since the referee raised my hand in token of victory I have often thought what I would have done had I failed. I know what the fruits of this victory mean to me personally. I'm very happy, gentlemen, and this function tonight will always remain a very vivid thing in my mind." His words tailed off at that . . . there was a pause as he looked at his notes but obviously could not continue. "That's all I can say," he concluded. He could contain himself no longer when they all stood to face him, cheering and clapping lustily . . . his head bowed and he wept unashamedly.

The celebrations went on after the Grosvenor. There was a cavalcade with police escort to some of the big picture theatres, first to the Paramount, Skippy's favourite for getting in via the side door and through the cafe. The film was stopped and he was introduced to the big audience who rose from their seats to cheer him wildly. It was the same at the New Savoy. Then the cavalcade turned and headed south over the Clyde to the Gorbals. Florence Street was *en fête*, although they didn't describe things that way there. There was bunting and banners from one side of the street to the other proclaiming their world champion. From a second storey window above Knotts to the building across the road was the biggest banner. It proclaimed . . . "WELCOME BACK FROM 'CHESTER TOWN, SAMMY AND BENNY WITH THE FLYWEIGHT CROWN". It was even better prose than MacNib's.

The street was on its biggest-ever "hing". Tash was there at his usual spot, being crowded out at his kitchen window by his wife Mary and their sons and Maw with Nellie, Hugh and old Jake at the other window. Knotts was jammed and they had boiled up extra dumplings that day for they knew they would be feasting themselves on this night of nights in Florence Street.

"Oor Benny," they yelled. "Oor Benny. Gaun Benny . . . gaun yersel son."

They stopped his car as it reached the vicinity of Knotts so that they could stare long and cheer louder. They never had anyone to cheer about in Florence Street before. They never had a hero that the whole world knew about. Not only would the world know him but it would know Florence Street too for when they would write about their Benny Lynch they would always say he was the Gorbals boy . . . the Gorbals boy from Florence Street. So his honour would rub off on them. He had made them world famous. The street that had produced a world champion.

"Oor Benny. Oor Benny. Gaun Benny . . . gaun yersel son."

The money was piled on Sammy Wilson's kitchen table in the house at Florence Street. One thousand one pound notes, neatly stacked in various bundles, some for expenses and other commitments. "That's it Benny . . . that's world champion money. I made them give it to me in cash. Got to watch some of them, you know. But I know about them. They gie you a cheque then when you go to cash it they shake their heids at the bank. Then when you chin the promoter they look a' sad and say the expenses killed them. They got their sums wrong. Or something. Nane o' that for us, wee man. Cash on the nose. And now you're world champ we'll make them pay up . . . before you even fight. But not bad, eh . . . one thousand pounds. And wait till you see what's coming."

Sammy had great ideas for the future. He outlined them, just like he was giving him new training preparations for another fight. "Here's the plan of campaign, Benny. We'll go on a world tour. To South Africa. Then Australia and New Zealand. Then Canada and the States. There's millions of Scots in all these places just dying to see their new world champion. We can give exhibitions, maybe the occasional serious fight. Then, when we're finished that you can step up to bantamweight, and that'll make life easier for you with your weight problems, and we'll go for Sixto Escobar's world bantam title."

Benny stood listening, dispassionately as he always did when Sammy spoke. Sammy hadn't expected him to be excited about the plans. He wasn't like that. But the last thing he expected was what he had to say in return.

"No, Sammy. I'm no' going."

He didn't elaborate. There was no going off to think it over. His mind was set. Benny Lynch was staying in Glasgow. Sammy was shocked, but he knew him well enough not to continue. Maybe he could raise it with him another time.

It was three months till the next fight; three months to enjoy the fruits of the punitive days on the Cathkin Braes; three months without being on the receiving end of a serious punch to the head; three months to let his battered hands stabilise, even though his right hand could never look normal again, the rear knuckles having been gradually and grotesquely hammered back on the rear of his hand; three months without their daily immersion in brine the fishmonger in Stockwell Street kept for him to toughen them; three months to enjoy the conviviality of the new friendships he had, more friends than he ever thought existed; three months without Sammy Wilson giving him plans of campaign.

"You'll be in the real big money now Benny, eh! . . . We'll be calling you hundreds and thousands soon. Thousand nicker for your last fight, eh! How much is Sammy getting you for the Warnock fight?"

They laughed when he said £300. He defended the sum at first for it was the biggest-ever purse that they had been able to raise in Ireland for a fight and Sammy said you couldn't get blood out of a stone. But they still niggled. The uptown bookies said they could have done better by promoting the fight themselves. The men in the pubs told him that when he stood them rounds . . . and more rounds. "Cheers Benny . . . Knew yer faither, Benny."

A week after the world title came to Scotland, there was a diversion for the elated boxing community which confronted them with an aspect of the grim realities of their punishing trade. Ray Bousquet, the Canadian boxer, was sentenced to death at the Old Bailey for murdering his girlfriend. Bousquet was described to the court as a classic case of the punch drunk. Ted Lewis, the former welterweight champion, told the jury that he had great experience of boxers who suffered from punch intoxication. If they suffered it badly they would not be able to stand properly and were easily knocked over. Medical witnesses said symptoms of the condition were a vacant look, far-away thoughts, and general unbalance. Bousquet had been like that, they said, prior to his last fight in which he had taken "terrible punishment". Despite all that, the Judge donned the black cap. The case was to create great controversy among ring men throughout the country as well as their followers, and doubting looks were cast by some at those among them who had seen signs of the condition. Others made light of it. "Best way not to get punchy," they said, "is to make sure you give the tankings and don't take them."

Sammy's plan of campaign for December involved three fights in three consecutive weeks. That would quickly bring Benny back to fitness. They were against Gaston Maton, the French bantamweight contender, Harry Orton, a tough slogger from Leicester, and Phil Milligan from Oldham, each of them men of varying styles and abilities, Orton being a southpaw. He had been specially selected in Sammy's mix as preparation for Benny's meeting with Jim Warnock, the Belfastman, brother of Billy and one of the most awkward southpaws in the business.

The three fights all went the distance, each an indifferent combat, each a points win.

"How much are you getting for the Warnock fight?" They didn't stop. And they all knew better. World champions didn't fight for that kind of money, they told him. "Is Sammy really trying for you?"

They never left him alone. For the first time in his life he had been given problems. There never had been any before when life was simple. Then it was training, fighting, dancing. And if there was a

problem Sammy would fix it; for Sammy always knew. But now there
was mistrust; for they had affected him with their stories. Advice was
everywhere and anywhere, but unlike before there was nowhere to
run. He was soured with Sammy. It showed when he confronted him
in the kitchen of the house at Florence Street, the very place where
all their plans of campaign had been formulated.

"Right, through the room," said Sammy indicating towards the
door leading to a bedroom. Some of the children and Mary, Sammy's
wife, had been in the kitchen. And what they had to say to each other
was not talk for women and children. They raged like friends do
when a friendship is no more. It was son challenging father and
father would not be challenged. They shouted and cursed. "Of course
it's all the money I could get. Nae Irishman has paid more."

"I could have done better ma'sel'."

"Could you fuck."

They had never crossed before and when they did their emotions
soared as their debate plunged to threat and epithet.

"I'm finished wi' you, Wilson. You're no' my manager any more."

He stormed out of the bedroom with Sammy hard on his heels and
still shouting, "I am your manager. You are under contract to me. You
can't fight without me."

The door slammed closed. It was never to open again for Sammy
Wilson and Benny Lynch. A friendship that had been special was no
more. The kinship and affection that had become soured became
bittered. There was just one return visit to the Polytechnic . . . to
collect his training gloves and other gear. Sammy wrote to him that
night. It was a terse note merely to say that he would be there in his
capacity as manager for the Warnock contest. The telegrammed reply
was even more terse. It stated . . . "Services no longer required."
Sammy immediately reported the affair to the British Boxing Board of
Control.

"You'll be better now," the advisers told him, more of them now
than there had ever been. "Sammy was holding you back, you know.
You should have been world champion ages ago."

Dingley had come over to Knotts to look for him. If he wasn't in
the pub, and there were too many of them to start a search, he would
be at the end of a knife and fork cleaning up a plate of Annie Knotts's
mince and totties. He was. He had heard about the split with Sammy,
he said, and he was there to advise. Another one! Benny told him
about taking his training gear away from the Polytechnic and that he
was using the Judean Club, Judi (Judah) Solomon's boxing and
athletic gym in Carlton Place, the Gorbals riverside street. They
discussed the Warnock fight. Who would second him in the ring?

"It's all arranged," said Benny. "I'm taking Willie Lawrie with me." Dingley didn't know him.

"He's one of the men who go about the club . . . he'll be all right for carrying the bags."

Dingley pointed out that he would need more than that for future fights and would need to arrange a proper trainer and manager. "How many fights did you have with Wilson anyway?"

"He mentioned it the other week . . . Warnock would have been the eighty-fifth."

"Well you're just twenty-two," said Dingley, "and you'll have a lot of fights to come before you're thirty . . . but you're not a fifty-bob fighter now. You're big-time so you'll need to get the right men about you to negotiate. There's a lot of sharp people in the big-time and you'll need to be protected from them."

The advice was noted . . . with an order of a slice of Annie's dumpling. Dingley looked at it and smiled. It wasn't the kind of thing he would have been served at Ferrari's or Guy's. "Want a bit?" Benny asked. Dingley stared at the slice they had cut for Benny. It dominated the plate, heavy and thick, a piece sagging over the edge and resting on the bare wooden table. "Eh . . . I don't think I will, thank you."

The crowd at the King's Hall in Belfast were never ones to restrain themselves. "There's yer Scotchman," they yelled when he walked to the ring following the rapturous reception for the local hero, Jimmy Warnock. There were cheers for Benny, but only from the Falls Road fans. Warnock was a Shankill boy. And you didn't get names like Lynch on the Shankill. "Get, ya Taig bastard," they shouted and he heard them. It was the first he had heard anything like that at the boxing.

There were other even worse insults and, for a moment, he wondered about the wisdom of fighting in Belfast. There were plenty of burly stewards around, however, as consolation. Had he known who they were he would have been even more consoled. For they were all members of the Royal Ulster Constabulary's boxing team. Jim Edgar, the promoter, had "made an arrangement" with Captain Morrison of the R.U.C. who supplied the stewards from the Newtonards barracks and every one of them was a member of the boxing team there.

Southpaws are the bane of the conventional boxer. They stand, right foot forward, right hand forward and clobber with their left because, usually, they are left handed. Benny was left handed and had started as a southpaw but had been "cured" at the start of his career, although he retained the great strength of his left hand, particularly in his vicious left hooks, the winner of so many of his fights. He had never liked fighting southpaws. They were his bogeymen. And Jim Warnock was to be the king of all his bogeymen.

It was the first time in eight-five fights that Sammy wasn't in the dressing room with him before being called to the ring and he missed the usual banter. He could imagine what he would be saying had he been there. "Here's your plan . . . keep him busy . . . you watch that left o' his . . . aye his left . . . gie him a couple in the breadbasket; that'll slow him down . . . he's nippy like wee Docherty and he'll make you miss . . . he did Pardoe in two, you took fourteen . . . and don't let him nail you in a corner . . . how's the rub feeling . . . you're in good shape . . . and, mind, watch that left o' his."

There was no massage this time, just a quick dry rub by bagman Lawrie.

No one mentioned the absence of Sammy. There was Euan Wellwood from the *Evening Times* of Glasgow, George Dingley, Joe Aitchison, son of Geordie, a trainer now with the R.U.C., and Lawrie. Benny was cheery and showing no outwards signs that this time it was different. But it was. More different than anything he had known for years. And the crowd went ecstatic. For yer man, as they called him, beat the Scotchman. And in all the pubs on the Shankill and in the Sandy Row and Lisburn and the other places where orange was the colour and green obscene, they were singing for Jimmy. They even had a song made up for him anticipating the victory. It was sung to the tune of *The Mountains of Mourne*.

> There's a boxer in Belfast, oh boy can he fight,
> I seen him in action in the King's Hall one night,
> They brought a great boxer to lower his crown,
> Who had won the world's title from Jackie Brown,
> The fly men they laughed and said this is a pinch,
> And put all their money on the great Benny Lynch,
> And how that fight ended is now history,
> For young Jimmy Warnock it was a great day.
> . . .
> And another great boxer who had fought some great fights,
> Said 'Let me have a go at this glove dynamite,'
> When I mention his name I am sure you will know,
> That he was no mug, it was Tommy Pardoe,
> A boxer from London of fame and renown,
> But he got a surprise just in the second round,
> And he went back to London far over the sea,
> And said no more fighting Southpaws in Belfast for me.

17

Under New Management

Eleven months after they had married and seven months after separating, Anne Lynch gave birth to their first child, a son. The date was February 10, 1936, and Benny had resumed hard training for his first fight of that year, the fateful meeting with Jim Warnock. He registered the birth, naming his son by the tradition of calling the firstborn after the paternal grandfather, John. Despite the happiness of the event, there was no reconciliation. Between appearances in the ring Benny was drinking more . . . and showing it. He would call at Anne's house regularly, but when they sensed where he had been Mr and Mrs McGuckian would send him away again. In the June of that year, however, the couple made a first attempt to mend their broken marriage and together with baby John went off on holiday to the Isle of Man. It didn't work out on that occasion and it wasn't till about six months later that they eventually made a real try at the marriage. He had promised to make a serious attempt to curb his drinking. "Honest, I'll pull my socks up, Anne," he said.

They returned to their first little room-and-kitchen above King's the Tailors in Rutherglen Road, Gorbals, handy for the local boxing gyms and old friends. You had to be "in the know", as they said at the time, in order to get a house. But Anne had an uncle who had helped them get the little flat. Friends had helped them decorate and they had it completely furnished in the latest styles . . . furniture, like cars, was getting rounded and streamlined or "moderne" as they called it. One of the young boxers from the Premier Club nearby had gone up one night on an errand and had gone back to tell his mates . . . "Like fuckin' Hollywood, so it is."

But the money was pouring in by now and a few months after the reconciliation they were able to buy a house that befitted a world champion. It was in Burnside, a suburb of Rutherglen, and in a street called Gloucester Avenue. But in Burnside you didn't say Gloucester as Glow-cester, like they did when they said Gloucester Street in Tradeston, where the Tripe dance hall was. In Burnside they said it properly . . . Gloster. Burnside was upper bracket. The houses there had front doors and back doors, gardens and trees, and some even had garages for their motor cars. The neighbours were solicitors and shopkeepers, teachers and traders. And a world champion boxer who called his house Belle Vue, after the venue where they had first crowned him as the Number One flyweight.

Anne and Benny went on a shopping spree. He wanted Anne dressed as a world champion's wife should be. And one item of clothing more than any other distinguished a woman of wealth and taste . . . .a fur coat. To own one was the ultimate in many a woman's dreams. To know of them was a required item of knowledge, whether you owned one or not. They knew that marmot resembled mink and would be dyed like it but that the fur was much coarser; that lynx was similar to fox, but the fur was longer and denser; that squirrel was hard to tell from ermine; that coney was really rabbit; that beaver lamb could pass for beaver; and that a brown ponyskin trimmed with squirrel would cost about forty guineas whereas a dyed squirrel would be 175 guineas and a genuine Canadian mink 375 guineas, an average man's wages for three whole years. And, like all things of quality, they were always priced in guineas.

They went shopping for a fur coat. There were so many to choose from. One was favourite, a Jaguar, creamy yellow with black rosette markings, the other a wavy patterned Indian Lamb. "Take the two of them," said Benny. And he wouldn't take no for an answer. There were clothes for baby John, the best that could be bought. Stuart & Stuart's of Charing Cross, one of the city's leading furnishers, were given the prestigious order to furnish Belle Vue. "Aye, the lot," said Benny, "from top to bottom." The salesman rubbed his hands and obliged.

After his defeat by Jim Warnock, there were just six other fights that year, the least he had fought in ten years. But the results of them more than compensated for his showing against the Belfastman. The referee stopped three of them to save the opponents Mickey McGuire, Pat Warburton and Phil Milligan, from further punishment. The other three, against Syd Parker, Pat Palmer (Palmer being a defence of his world title), and Eric Jones were decided in the way Benny liked himself . . . knock-outs.

He was a long way from the Gorbals and the men at the corner now. It was a whole new way of life for Mr Benjamin Lynch—"Hey, Benjie, d'ye know you've got thirteen letters in your name; that's bad luck," his young brother-in-law Pat would say. He had a new manager and agent, Mr George Dingley, distinguished city gent. He had a new trainer, Mr Puggy Morgan, ex-Tommy Milligan camp, ex-

Elky Clark camp, ex-Geordie Aitchison club. He had been around the boxing scene for a long time. Puggy was a good bagman. He was a patter merchant and good for the morale in any training camp; the joker in the pack and a vital commodity when training gets weary, tempers get edgy. And he was also the man who made the boy carry away his trademark.

A legal firm were commissioned to look after his legal and monetary affairs. And he had a new training camp. It was far removed from the old Poly, sweaty, stained and spartan. In contrast the new one was select and sylvan. George Dingley had fallen in love with the Red Tub at Campsie and its surroundings when he had first discovered them. It was just the place for a boxers' training camp, he had thought. In effect, they were precision made for such a purpose. They could have their meals in the Inn and at the rear of the premises in a small paddock there was a wooden cabin which the party could use for their quarters as well as indoor training. A ring could be built inside and, if they wanted, they could have another outside. Behind the paddock the ground rose steeply forming a natural amphitheatre and when they became established, thousands travelled from Glasgow to the Clachan at Campsie. It had been their favourite place for picnics for years. Now they could enjoy the hills and streams and watch their own wee Benny as well. For Benny was theirs; their very own. And to see him toil it out with partner after partner made them feel even closer to him; as though they were sharing his sweat and efforts.

"Hey, Benny, did you hear what one of the boys did yesterday?" said one of the seconds one Monday morning. "Well, you know all that crowd that turned up yesterday. He came out to see you training and clocks a' they cars that turned up. Must have been a thousand of them. So he goes into Harley's tea rooms, cadges a big bit of cardboard then writes on it, 'Parking 2/6d.' Then he puts it up on a pole beside that big five bar gate that lets you into the field beside the road and packs it wi' hundreds of cars. Ended up wi' that much money he could hardly walk away . . . then big Tam the farmer turns up and does his loaf for he's got coos in the field and they're a' trapped behind the cars."

When they finished laughing Benny asked if they knew who it had been. "Skinny fellah wi' a long coat and it a biling day. They said he was from the Gorbals." "Might have been the Bandit," somebody suggested. "Aye," said Benny, "wouldn't be surprised." And they laughed again.

Once the urge to train had been easy. He had known that rare quality that came with total fitness, a quality that only those few who reach that body peak of the human machine can appreciate. Running was a joy; legs became tireless, his heavy thigh muscles pushing him up the steepest slopes with gazelle grace; lungs that could bellow huge gulps of air without pain. Training had been a régime of life; fitness had been permanent. But now with the need to fight less, training had become sporadic. He trained only for a fight; before he had trained for fighting. And the longer he didn't train, the harder it was to return to fitness again. The miles became agony, the hills became torture and the prospect of it became hell. So why suffer today? Training could always start tomorrow; and tomorrow could always be tomorrow. Today? Well, that was for living.

They had gone to the Red Tub to train for most of the 1936 fights. Puggy was there in charge, although other trainers came and went . . . Gus Hart, Alec Lambert. There was a variety of sparring partners, good work if you could get it at £6 to £10 a week and your keep— provided you had the ability to suffer the roadwork and be at the other end of the hardest-hitting fists in the country. There was Joe Connelly from Maryhill, Johnny McManus from Twechar, and John Devine from Airdrie, a fifty-bob fighter who had known the booths from Stewart and MacIlbait's in the North of Scotland to Chapelfield's, run by Mrs Copley, in Belfast. John could fight two men in the one night as he often had to do in the booths, and could survive endless hard punching. He was the ideal sparring partner. And young Pat McGuckian, Anne's young brother, tagged along as companion and helper.

Campsie belied the fact it was a mere handful of miles from Glasgow. It had all the appearance of an isolated village at the head of some remote Highland glen. There was only the main street, a scatter of houses and a line of shops. Maggie Brown, an elderly dear with white hair who would be there at every whist drive in the vicinity, ran the Post Office. Bob McLintock was the grocer, his double fronted shop the biggest in the village; where you could buy gas mantles as well as paraffin and where the main essentials of daily life were kept in big hessian sacks in the middle of the shop, oatmeal and flour, barley and sugar, and on white marble slabs behind the counter a mound of butter, a cheese the size of half a barrel, and a big Belfast ham on the slicer. There wasn't anyone made tastier fruit scones and apple tarts than Mrs Harley who, with her husband, ran the cosy four table tearoom, also a beehive for the village children for they could buy their wrapped caramels and lollipops there. Police Constable Gutteridge represented law and authority, commodities which only exercised him at the weekends when the trippers came . . . or somebody tried to take over big Tam's field to make himself some cash. And, as a pointer to the permanency of their village, there was the ancient graveyard around the church ruin at the Clachan, in which there was a vault with the words "Heir Lyis Ane Honourable Man James That Ilk Quha Desist Ye 13 Febrovar Anno 1604."

The needs of spiritual man and spirited man were catered for at the western end of the village. By the Finglen Burn was The Tin Hut, called that simply because that's what it was. Corrugated and painted earth brown, it was topped by a little steeple; a sort of Wendy cathedral. On the Sabbath they held Sunday School in The Tin Hut. Like the village school, both Catholics and Protestants went together, the crassness of religious apartheid being for city people. And on week days it was their community hall, for the ladies of the W.R.I., parties, plays, whist drives, bridge schools, hallowe'en, and dances. None of your foxtrots and quicksteps, though. For life in Campsie was still traditional and for them it was the lancers, quadrilles and eightsome reels. Across the road from The Tin Hut was The Campsie Inn, the village pub run by the Hendry family. But no one locally knew it by such a grand name as that. To them it was . . . The Piggery. It was a small, dark place with brown flock wallpaper, kippered over the years by tobacco exhalations. When the boxers first used it they said it was like somebody's living room and the locals told them it looked like that because that's what it had been till they had got a licence and the room became the village pub.

"D'ye like yer purritch, Benny?" they would ask. "Well that'll get you up the hills quicker than the Johnny Walker." "Aye, especially if he makes it like auld Jimmy Dunnachie. D'ye ken whit he does, Benny? Makes his purritch once a week . . . on a Sunday. Then he pours it into a big drawer in his chest. Then he just slices off a bit every time he needs it. Takes a big slice wi' his piece every day to his work at the Campsie Field. Fit as a fiddle so he is. Says it's his drawer purritch that does it."

They knew that serious training had begun when Benny took the cascara. It had become more a symbol to him than anything else. His personal Styx. An oldtimer had told him that before a really tough training programme was begun the body's system had to be cleansed. "Ye need a right guid guttin' oot," he said. And that's what he did. Like the way he lived and trained, when Benny took to the cascara he did it hard. None of your two teaspoonfuls three times a day, as per the instructions. He would put the bottle to his lips . . . and down the lot in one draught. "Right," he would say, "now we'll get into the hard work."

"Aye, . . . an' we'll keep oot your road for a week."

The road work would begin lightly and they would go in a group,

Benny piled with as many clothes as he could pull on, often as many as a dozen vests, several sweaters, long johns, topped by two sometimes three pairs of woollen track bottoms, long woollen socks, head hooded to retain the sweat, and heavy army boots. The agony had begun. And the more out of training and fatter he was—often up to ten stone—the more the agony. Puggy would forbid him liquids. "It's the fluid we want out of you, no' in you," he would say. So he would chew a pebble to create some comforting mouth moisture. When the pounds came off he would know he was fit enough to tackle the hills. Only Pat could stay with him then. They would be up early, have a light breakfast, then run up the little track that led up the slopes of the steep terrace behind the paddock. The ascent steepened dramatically as they got on to the rough moor grassland of Black Hill, Roman-nosed Blackfaces scattering before them, their wool skirts flying. By the time they had run exactly one mile and had got to the Crow Road, the route that traversed the Hills, at a spot just past Jamie Wright's Well, they had climbed 1000 feet. The fitter he got the harder he ran this first section which took them right into the heart of the Campsies. The road climbed even higher after that to the Muir Toll cottage in the shadow of Holehead, the highest of the high hills that flanked the road. They would leave the road from time to time to splash through the bogs in order to cool flaming feet, the silence broken only by the plaintive cries of the soaring whaups and the shrill of zig-zagging snipe arrowing away from them.

It was seven miles the way they ran before they descended to Fintry, white-washed and postcard dainty and nestling in a sculpted hollow by the banks of the Endrick Water. They would turn at the local pub called The Clachan, and repeat the process of climbing to the high moorland for the grinding seven miles back to the Red Tub. That was the morning work. In the afternoon, after a mid-day sleep there were the sessions on the skipping ropes, ball-bearing handled and which he used like he had been tutored by Diaghilev, periods with the various punch bags and balls, and finally . . . sparring.

Like the road work, everything increased with intensity as the fitness improved. The sparring partners knew about the progress of that. "Hits you like a fuckin' train," they would say. He was the only one they knew who could hit the weighted punch ball, bending it so fiercely that it would knock over its heavy stand. And when his fat was finally trimmed off and he was down to the eight stone that was now getting harder and harder to achieve, he would throw himself from a standing position on to a medicine ball . . . taking the full force of the fall on his stomach. He could also go a full twenty rounds sparring with various partners. And when he could do all of these things with no great discomfort he would know that he was back to the fitness that he had once known all the time. The kind of fitness you had to have to be a world champion.

"Hey Benny, there's an auld tramp at the cabin looking for you," they told him one day.

"Oh, Christ, did he come? I met him this morning when I was out for the run. Great auld guy. D'ye know he recognised me. Imagine an auld tramp knowing me. Shouts to me 'Good on you Benny . . . you're a great wee lad.' Right, let's gie him a good meal and a bevvy." And into the bargain he ordered a whip round to see the old fellow happily on his way, totally overcome at what his day had brought him.

At night the boxers would have long games of cards, Newmarket, pontoons and rummy, and play dominoes. But the best nights were when there was a big championship fight on in the States and they would stay up to listen to it on the Overseas Service. They were particularly interested in a young black boxer who was creating a lot of attention and they were following his career intently. He was called Joe Louis and they were saying he was going to be the next heavyweight champ.

Other nights they would talk about their own varied experiences. John Devine told them about his most embarrassing experience. "I had been fighting at the Kelvin Hall and it was after the bout and I was feeling really rotten. You know what it's like if you've had a bad one. I went to the toilet and this old guy comes in and says friendly like, 'How are you feeling son?' Well, I was feeling rotten and just couldn't be annoyed with anyone and gave him a right mouthful to let him know that. Then another fellah comes in and says . . . 'Good evening Sir Harry.' Christ, it was Harry Lauder."

Benny said he knew him well for he had come to a lot of his fights, even back in the days when he was trying to get the better of Paddy Docherty. "First time I met him he whispered to me . . .'Benny, son. Honesty is the best policy.' Then he paused for a bit, smiling that way he does, and adding . . . 'but AFTER you've made your pile.' "

Another had the story about the night he had come to the Premierland, the club in Bridgeton. "Aye had a half bottle of whisky when he came to the fights and if he didn't bring one with him he would send out for one. This night he asks Sammy Beattie, you know the timekeeper, if he would mind getting him half a bottle and he gives him a ten bob note. So Sammy nicks over to Anne's Bar, get's the half bottle and gives him the change, thinking naturally he's on a good bung. But the auld boy takes his bottle and the change then starts fumbling about in his pocket and slips Sammy what he thought was his bung. Know what it was . . . a peppermint. Sammy says he should have drunk the bloody stuff before giving it to him."

If Benny had taken the cascara treatment he would do his utmost to stay on the tight training schedules, working up to the maximum punishment required of a top champion. If he hadn't taken the cascara and was only in token training, the camp would be on guard in case he be tempted to accept the hospitality that was always on offer from the people who said they were wellwishers.

In the October of 1936 the house in Burnside was ready for Benny and Anne. But they weren't to be together for long. There was a big fight in the offing and George Dingley insisted, as he was to do for all future fights, that for total training Benny should be at the camp. The fight was with Small Montana, who had a familiar title. He was the world's flyweight champion. The New York Athletic Commission and the National Boxing Commission of America didn't accept the rest of the world's verdict that Benny Lynch of Scotland was the world champion. The record books told the full story, however. Montana had beaten Midget Wolgast. Then there was a return match and Wolgast won. Then Wolgast fought Brown, the fight went the full distance, Wolgast winning. Benny had done it in round two. But he didn't need armchair theories to know who was the best in the world. And Montana would know soon too.

He had left the cascara routine later than usual for the Montana fight. Well, it was Christmas. New Year was looming. Did they expect him to be drinking the tangy iron water at Jamie Wright's Well to bring in the New Year? Dingley, who some of them had nicknamed Dingbox, could be good company on the town; he knew all the places where they had style. Anne had the baby to mind so she couldn't join them and, anyway, wasn't it a man's world? A woman's place was in the home.

It was easy to become an alcoholic when you had the constitution of Benny Lynch. For, like the training and the suffering that went with it, he could take it. When others dropped out, he would still be with his favourite company, Crawford's Liqueur Whisky, the one that came in the amber dump bottle, mellow and smooth and without the lead or wooden backtastes of some of the others. He needed it, but it didn't need him. Which was different from all his other nouveau friends . . . for they needed him and he didn't need them.

He had passed the stage where it was the lively tonic, the fortifier, the sunshine that the dour and snell Glasgow day couldn't provide. Quickly . . . alarmingly . . . it had become a necessity; a requirement as vital as food. And life became a seesaw between total training and dedicated drinking. Around Hogmanay, before leaving for their camp at the Dumb Bell Inn in Taplow, Buckinghamshire, in preparation for the fight against Montana at Wembley, he had come home one evening with Dingley, Puggy Morgan and a sparring partner. They had all been drinking and showed it. Anne remonstrated. Benny looked in a mess. He was more than ten stone with the fight just three weeks away. "Don't worry," he said. "I'll make the weight." He did.

That incredible effort alone would have decimated the strength of most men. It affected him too, but such was his physical resilience that he could still shed the weight and put up his fists to the finest fighters in the world. Small Montana, the American domiciled Filipino, was certainly one of them.

It had been torture getting down to the eight stone and Puggy had put such a close guard on him to prevent him taking liquids that he even had to resort to sneaking to the toilet one day . . . and gulping the water from the cistern. For much of each day he spent swaddled in as much clothing as they could get on him in order to melt off the fat and ooze the toxics from his body. Incredibly, they retained a balance of strength, for he needed it. Montana was a strong and experienced fighter and took him the full fifteen rounds; but there was no doubt about the verdict, a clear points win for the man who was now indisputably what his countrymen always knew he was. Champion of the world.

The Bogeyman Returns

He had never had a hammering before. Warnock had beaten him. And before that so had Paddy Docherty back in 1932. But no one had ever really thrashed him. No one could or ever would have . . . but!

Beating Montana after a little more than a fortnight's intensive training had really been something of a miracle. But few had appreciated that, not realising the poor state he had been in only days prior to the contest. And achieving the fighting fitness he had in such a short time deluded him as well. If that was all he needed to do to beat the man the Americans had called world champ he could do even less for men of a lesser calibre. So the see-saw got out of control.

Three weeks after Montana and with only the minimum of training, mainly sparring, there was a non-title fight at the Kelvin Hall, Glasgow, against Fortunato Ortega, successor to Pedrito Ruiz as flyweight champion of Spain. But this one didn't come with a malacca cane! Ortega was a tricky fighter with a solid defence though not in the class of the real top world men. Yet he made Benny look foolish at times, making him miss badly and revealing his timing was out. Nevertheless, he managed to scrape home with a twelve-round points' victory. He was still a winner. He could relax even more.

There were three weeks before the next match, against Len Hampston of Batley at Belle Vue. Hampston, whom they nicknamed Nipper, was a bantamweight; a man with a good enough reputation to provide what the experts reckoned would be a good night's entertainment seeing the world champion in action and, of course, winning. No one was to predict anything remotely like the outcome . . . except those really in the know.

Benny had gone on a real binge. They went to look for him but he couldn't be found. He had told his friends that if they saw any boxers looking for him not to tell them where he was. For he knew they would be after him to get him to the camp. And the camp meant sweat and torture. And worse . . . no drink. They would even raid houses where they thought he might be. Once they got close . . . he was under the bed.

It was Johnny Kelly, friend and regular sparring partner, who found him. He had never known him so drunk. And the fight with Hampston was the next night . . . in Manchester. They tried everything . . . showers and coffee; more showers. Then he went for a long sleep. Because of his state, they approached Hampston to see if he would agree to a gee fight with the promise of a return that wasn't fixed. "No, lads," said Hampston. "It will be on merit." They didn't tell Benny that they had tried to fix it for they knew he would have nothing to do with a gee fight. They had tried before. Gus Hart had tried to get him to lie down for a fight he was trying to arrange against Angelmann, whom he had already beaten, in Paris. He had exploded at the suggestion and had made it clear then that there would be no more similar suggestions put to him.

A boxing match is an exchange of fistic ability which ranges from the amateur to the artist and, in the main, is conducted in a sportsmanlike fashion, despite the root nature of the contest. Lynch's reputation was that of the clean fighter. There were no dirty tricks in his book. He wouldn't bore on the other side of the referee, or eye-thumb, and the like. In the fifteenth round of the Montana fight when the Filipino had been trapped on the ropes it would have been legitimate for the other man to have used the opportunity to his own advantage. Instead, he had gone forward and prevented him from falling, pulled him clear from the ropes, touched gloves and then resumed the battle. It wasn't like that with Hampston. There were dubious low punches from both of them right from the start. Hampston claimed a foul for a low punch when he went down in the first round, but the referee waved them on. Hampston retaliated with a series of punches of doubtful intent. What had started out to be a boxing match had very quickly turned into a fight . . . ugly, brutal, and both men being completely uncompromising to each other.

A left hook to the body and Benny went down for eight. Another to the pit of the stomach, the stomach that could take on the full slam of the medicine ball, the ripple of midriff muscles a belt of steel. But not tonight. The exercising had tapered and the rigid muscle had softened. He was down for another eight. Then another, again in the same area. And he went down again. It was nine this time and he was in desperation when he gained his feet again. Hampston was on the rampage and only the bell ended his unstoppable attack. Nick Cavalli, the Continental agent, had been selected as his chief second for the night and he had to work hard on him in the respite. Benny was in semi-shock. He knew what was happening to him but couldn't bring himself together enough to hold off the menacing Hampston.

"Hampston," he thought. A month ago and he wouldn't have let him share the same ring for longer than two rounds. He was no Jackie Brown, let alone a Small Montana or Pat Palmer. But tonight with the condition he was in and the way he felt, it seemed like those three were there together against him.

A right to the jaw and another straight left which buried itself in his solar plexus and he was down again. Benny Lynch down! Not just once. But in every round. It couldn't be true! The crowd couldn't believe it. But it was happening. And he lay on his back, face contorted, knees bent in pain as he heard the fateful count.

"ONE." . . .

"Mother of God, Holy Mother of God, is this really me?"

"TWO." . . .

"Christ, my guts must be ripped wide open . . . how can there be such pain?"

"THREE." . . .

"C . . h . . r . . i . . s . . t . . . suffering Christ get me out of this misery."

"FOUR." . . .

"How do I get up . . . Jesus . . . get me up!"

"FIVE" . . .

"Roll round . . . yes, that's it . . . roll round . . . lie on my belly and get up that way."

"SIX." . . .

"That's it . . . on my knees now . . . can I push up once more?"

"SEVEN." . . .

"On one knee now . . . I'll make it Hampston you bastard."

"EIGHT" . . .

"Right . . . just one more push, a hard one this time, and I'll be able to stand."

"NINE." . . .

The next round was the fifth. The pattern was the same and he was on his back again. The first was to nine. Hampston crowded in on him the moment the referee signalled to continue. And he was only on his feet seconds when Hampston gave him the most wicked punch of the fight, another sledgehammer to his stomach, again a punch the referee considered not fully below the belt and not a foul. Lynch plunged in a dead man's fall . . . and a man parted the ropes to jump into the ring. It was Cavalli, his second, and he was waving a towel, frantically shouting at the referee that his man had been fouled. The referee ordered him from the ring, but Cavalli bent over his charge, picked him up and carried him to his corner for treatment. The crowd was in an uproar. They thought for a minute their man was going to be deprived of the victory he had legitimately gained in this night of his greatest triumph. But Gus Platts, the referee, was in no doubts about what the outcome should be and the M.C. announced the findings. Lynch was disqualified and Hampston was the winner.

He was still in agony in the dressing room and they had to tape up his rib cage in order to ease the pain and give him support. He sat on the long bench in the room so weak and tortured he was unable to dress himself.

When they did eventually dress him they had to assist him to his feet. "Right, help me round to Hampston's dressing room . . . but leave me when we get there." He winced at every step, each movement jarring the big blue bruise blotches. He was uncut, as usual, but his face hurt so badly he couldn't breathe through his nose, taking short pants of air through his mouth.

Benny had gone to see Hampston to deliver a message. When he got to his dressing room door he pulled himself up and a half smile appeared on his face as though everything was normal. Hampston was surprised to see him but Benny made no move to go into the room. "I'll give you a return within the month," he said. "But I'm telling you something, Nipper. Get yourself fit. The fittest you've ever been in your life." With that, he turned and walked away. The message had been delivered.

They couldn't conceal the agony of the worst-ever night in all his boxing life. Anne was shocked when he got home to see what the punches had done. She had never realised what their bodies could be like after a fight . . . weals that reddened as though there was no skin, bordered by big bruises which were brown and a greeny blue, and a face puffed and so tender it couldn't face food that had to be chewed. He had never thought before about revenge after a fight. The ones he had lost against Paddy Docherty and some others in the early days and, more recently Jim Warnock, were fights to be avenged. And they usually were; the scorecard corrected with a victory. But against Hampston he could only think of revenge for never had a man given him such a beating. Of course it had been his own fault. No one needed to tell him that. He had only been a shell of himself on the night of the fight . . . but had a man to be so humiliated?

He lay for days in agony unable to resume training for the return match, now fixed for March 22 . . . exactly three weeks after the meeting in Manchester.

The venue this time was Leeds. They would be less partisan there. Fourteen days before the match the pains had subsided sufficiently to resume light training. Two days after that it became more intensified and for a full week prior to the date he was in full training, road miles, gym work, and sparring, the sweat rinsing the alcohol from his bloodstream.

They were pleased with him at the camp by the end of the third week. He could outrun any of them, take twenty rounds of sparring in his stride. The only imperfection had been his timing. Once it had been uncannily instinctive, his mind translating every opportunity into instant and precise action; but now there were hairsbreadth flaws in some of his connections, noticeable only to those who had known his target mastery of a year ago.

Hampston was cautious in the opening round, covering himself well and relying on the occasional opportunity which presented itself before despatching a glove. He got one explosive belter in and Benny's face twisted in pain for it had hit him square on the belt. The referee, however, ignored it. It was in the fourth round that the pair of them fell back on the tactics of the first fight; punching viciously to any part of the body, hellbent on turning it into anything but a boxing match. Referee Jack Smith stopped the contest, brought them together to tell them, "Right, lads, none of that stuff with me. You know the rules. Stick to them. As for the fouling . . . cut it out. Right!" They understood.

An aggressive Benny took the fifth and sixth, Hampston gaining confidence to return well to go to the top of the scorecard for the next two. By the tenth Hampston was getting impatient and rushed at his opponent straight from the bell. There are several ways to combat a raging bull in the ring. You can run. Rage back. Cover up. Or keep perfectly cool and apply the ring science you have learned over the years. The first three are easy and reflex. The fourth response is the most difficult and calculated. But Benny knew it was the best tactic. And while Hampston raged and charged, Benny picked him off, bit by bit. A right to the jaw and he staggered on the ropes before collapsing on his back. Up at eight he walked into the most concentrated two-fisted barrage he had ever experienced in his entire boxing career and slowly crumpled on the floor on one knee, his right glove feeling for the canvas as he sank. He rose again, but he wished he hadn't for the left hook that hit him was like no other punch he had ever received. They would often say that a man was hit so hard it lifted him off his feet. It rarely did and a few had ever seen the metaphor in reality. But they did this night in Leeds as Hampston's body lifted right off, his feet rising upwards before falling sharply back on the ropes where he dangled like a wet sheet on a foggy Monday wash line. Jack Smith waved "no more". Benny had his revenge.

*   *   *

They would still speak about Benny at the corner and the betting pitch in Florence Street but the ones who knew would avoid the subject when Sammy Wilson was there. For it hurt. Life without Benny Lynch had affected Sammy Wilson more seriously than they would have imagined. He had been the hard man's favoured son and it was as though the son was now a living death. For he was there, but he was not to be seen, or heard, or helped. Sammy knew his vulnerabilities and how they would exploit them. The thrashing from Hampston had hurt him as much as Benny. And he knew there would be more and although he never said, he dreaded his every fight.

There were three months till the next fight. The cascara could wait. the short-necked amber dump bottle was a better bet. The new friends would be at Gloucester Avenue every day for him. There would be a day at the golf and then on the town at night. They were men of means but so too was Benny. He could match any of them with his wallet and he would show that too.

The alcohol was taking more and more of a grip. He was in a vice he couldn't loosen. The drink wasn't because of the company but because of necessity. He could be the happy drunk, entertaining Anne and any of her visiting family with his antics when he returned from the town. "See me do the Egyptian sand dance . . . nae bother," he would say . . . then scatter sugar on the floor and give them a solo version of Wilson, Keppel and Betty's hilarious dance routine. But the happy drunk had to become the clever drunk for the women would take the Crawford's from him when he got home. "Oh don't do that," he would say in mock disappointment when they took it away. Then he would go into another room and bring out the other bottle he had hidden in a hip pocket. The clever alcoholic has to think of things like that; for although the mind is scattering, it still thinks of preservation and the great need of life . . . more alcohol. So when he returned home there would be the two half bottles . . . one for confiscation; one for drinking.

But, eventually, they discovered that trick and would hide or dispose of the two bottles. One became as clever as the other. "Now don't you tell your Uncle Benny where we've hidden his bottle," they told little sister Alice one night. But there would be an answer for

that too. "Alice," he said, "let's play a wee game. I'm going to look for
a wee brown bottle and we'll play it like hide the parcel. If I get close
you've got to say I'm getting hot and even hotter. And if I'm not near
it you've to say I'm getting cold."

"But I've no' to tell you Uncle Benny where the bottle is."

"But you're not Alice. It's just a wee game we're playing.

"Right . . . am I getting hot . . . hot . . . hotter? Ah, there it is."

And they laughed together. "You see, Alice, you didn't tell me . . .
it's a game we've played."

Although. he was the king of his bogeymen, he again held off his
training as long as possible before his return match with Jim
Warnock. The venue was Parkhead, home ground of the Glasgow
Celtic Football Club and 20,000 including a big contingent from
Belfast, were there. To the great dismay of the Ulstermen, the British
Boxing Board of Control wouldn't allow the fight to be for the world
title, despite Warnock's previous victory over the champion. They
had a series of eliminators in mind for the title and their formula had
to be adhered to; and what the B.B.B. of C. said had to be done; and
be damned to you if commonsense said otherwise.

Two useful southpaws, Tut Whalley and Jim McAloon, were laced
among the sparring pack in order to get Benny used to the wrong-
way-round men. And when the experts saw him handle them they
said they were pleased. Benny would beat Warnock this time. The
visitors thought differently.

They were to have fought at eight stone four pounds but Benny,
uncaring for there was no title at stake, was heavier. The Board
immediately slammed a £150 fine on him and Warnock caused a
sensation by claiming the £1000 prizemoney . . . and refusing to fight.
His logic was that they had signed a contract to fight at that weight,
his opponent hadn't kept his part of the bargain, therefore the
contract was broken in his favour. So there would be no fight . . . and
the money was his, he insisted. Dingley prevailed, however, and
Warnock eventually agreed to put on gloves.

It was another revenge fight for Benny. He had nothing against
Jimmy Warnock, but there were bitter memories of the way the
Belfast crowd had treated him when they last met. However, there
was to be no revenge on that cold June night, black rainclouds
gathering and threatening a downpour. He started well and put
Warnock down in the first round. He thought he had done enough to
beat him too when the bell ended the fifteenth. He had rallied, toe-to-
toed, hooked, put him down, but Warnock had been undismayed
through it all and had fought just as cleverly. Even more clever, said
the referee raising his hand for the victory.

No one could stop their Jimmy Warnock now, said the Irish. And, in theory, they were right. For there was no one around to beat Benny Lynch, except Jimmy Warnock from the Shankill, that was. And twice at that. But first, there was the Boxing Board's dictat to be obeyed. And despite those two convincing wins, the orders were that Warnock was to first of all meet a young blacksmith called Peter Kane from a place called Golborne outside Manchester. If he could beat him, THEN he could fight Benny Lynch of Scotland for the world title.

Kane was a youngster of nineteen and had been a pro since he was sixteen although he had been fighting long before that as a youth in the booths around the market towns of the North of England. The Warnock camp scoffed at the idea of such a young fellow taking on their man. Nevertheless, Kane had won twenty-three of his twenty-seven pro fights by knock outs, no mean feat. And he was now unbeaten in forty fights. The English were convinced he was their answer to Benny Lynch. The Irish knew their man Jim Warnock was. Benny Lynch knew that if he met them at his best, none of them would beat him. But would he ever be at his best again?

If A beat B and B beat C, it should be that A would beat C. They would often apply that logic to the fighters. But it didn't always work. Kane was to meet Warnock in that final eliminator match for the right to share the ring with Benny Lynch for his British, European and World flyweight titles. To the utter astonishment of every Irishman, the young Kane knocked out their man in the fourth round. Warnock had proved superior in two fights to Lynch. Kane had shown he was the man for Warnock. The logic was that Benny Lynch should beware.

Benny and Anne's life together had become something of a trial. Married four months then parted for nearly a year. Together again, a young son then another son eighteen months later; long periods of absence under the orders of his manager; more periods of absence because he was the toast of anyone who wanted to be anyone; and an addiction to drink which even he now knew to be a problem. It had seemed they had never been alone together. The Kane fight was set for the October of that eventful 1937. He would go to the Red Tub long before then. The cascara would be taken in plenty of time on this occasion.

He knew he needed a good victory. It had been a chequered year; that second defeat by Warnock, the terrible beating from Hampston. He had read the stories in the papers about how he might be past it, that the signs were there. And the papers only said what people in general were thinking.

It was yet again another long separation from Anne who had that August presented him with a second son christened Robert and called Bobby. Dingley had insisted that he be at the Red Tub and in strict training and made it clear that she wouldn't even be welcome there as a visitor. Boxing was a man's world and the women just got in the way.

The ragged edges that had been imprinted on him as a result of the whirl that had been his life since becoming world champion were beginning to be ironed out by this longer stay at the Red Tub. This fight against Peter Kane was being treated more seriously than any of his previous title defences. The English boxing writers were openly boasting that at last they had someone who really could beat the Scotch chap. And what a record he had too, they said, counting up all his knock-outs, particularly that one against Jim Warnock, the Lynch bogeyman. Meanwhile, in Glasgow, thousands flocked to the Campsie Hills at the week-ends in order to get a glimpse of their wee Benny in training. They sat on the steep grassy terrace behind the camp for his last sparring session, the Lennox Castle Institution providing an outdoor ring in return for the chance to make a collection among the big crowd for the hospital. The visiting personalities who had come to Scotland for the big fight also took in a tour of the Campsies. There was Jimmy Wilde, the legendary Welsh champion; Tommy Farr, who had come so near to being world heavyweight champion; Victor McLaglen, the burly Irish-American film star who had once been a professional heavyweight and looked it and whose latest movie, The Magnificent Brute, was all the talk, although most remembered him for his classic role in The Informer. They had got W.H. Barrington Dalby to be the referee and Sir Iain Colquhoun as the steward in charge. And the Daily Record signed both Farr and McLaglen to write special reports of the fight.

There were those who knew and those who said they knew; and there were more of the latter. But the ones who really did know and who were not overwhelmed by what they saw or were not out to impress by what they didn't see, had their verdict about the fight. And they said that what they saw that night at Shawfield Park, capacity packed with 40,000 and thousands more unable to get in, was vintage boxing, the likes of which a man would see, if he was lucky that was, only once in a lifetime. It was Kane at his greatest, Lynch at his pinnacle and the best man won. The titles stayed in Scotland. Tommy Farr, who knew, said it was the best fight of any weight he had ever seen. Elky Clark, who knew, rated it the greatest flyweight match of boxing history. And Victor McLaglen, who knew too, picked him up in his arms to announce to everyone that he was holding the Jack Dempsey of the small men. "Oh boy, what a fight," he said. In his commissioned report of the fight he enthused even more.

> It's the most exciting fight of its weight I have ever seen and although Kane was the aggressor until about the ninth round, Lynch seemed to have his measure all the time.
>
> . . . You would notice that Kane's punches had little effect on your boy who seemed as fresh as paint after the fight. Indeed, I was surprised when I met him in Mr Russell Moreland's office afterwards to see how little bruised he was. How Kane weathered the twelfth round I don't know. Lynch had him at his mercy . . . it wasn't a knock out in the accepted sense. Kane was too weak to get up in the thirteenth . . . the gamest loser I have ever seen. And what a clean, fair fight it was. If you can promise me another fight as thrilling and sporting as this one then, boy, I'm certainly coming back to Scotland.

No one ever offered that promise. And there never was another fight like that night at Shawfield Park, although other Scots were to win world titles. It was the fight men were to speak about for the rest of their lives. It was the fight the fifty-bob fighters, the men who knew and suffered their industry, said they never thought they would see the likes of, for they never thought two men could fight like that. Some of them had seen Tancy Lee. Others had seen Jimmy Wilde. A few had seen Montana. But no one had ever produced what they said was the ultimate in the sporting science called pugilism that Benny Lynch produced that night. Sammy Wilson had called him his boy Adonis but Tash, the wise one, had said that the wild boar had slayed Adonis as a youth. Sammy's Adonis was now twenty-four years of age and the king of the boxing world. The wild boar had still to strike.

19

There Were Cheers, There Were Jeers

S cotland hadn't known a legend like him in the twentieth century.
He was the greatest living success story in the country. The boy
from the Gorbals with all the odds stacked against him, who took on
the world with his fists to become the man they said was the finest
flyweight of all time. Everyone wanted to shake his hand. To touch
him. To get to look at him. Scotland had a host of legends through
the centuries. But only one was living and among them. Benny
Lynch.

Nineteen thirty eight. It should have been his year of years. He had
shown in his epic battle against Kane that if he really put his mind
and body to it, he could still make the scales at eight stone, the
flyweight limit, and retain the strength that was required to fight
against the best in the world. There was a fortune to be made against
opponents of his camp's choosing, except when the Boxing Board
would insist on a title defence. Companies wanted him to endorse
their products. Newspapers offered a small fortune for him to write
for them about his life. They wanted him in America to fight for the
bantamweight title, the same title that Sammy Wilson had suggested
two and a half years previously when he had beaten Jackie Brown for
the world championship. There wasn't another sportsman in the
whole of Britain with the same fortune-making potential as Benny
Lynch. Not a footballer or cricketer or car racer had a name to equal
his. The fistic and commercial world was at his feet. He had got to the
rainbow's end. But he was never to touch the pot of gold that lay
there.

A Sunday newspaper, the *Reynold's News*, had asked him to write
about his fighting life, to give his version of his world title defence
against Small Montana, and to speculate about his future as a
professional sportsman. It was a top-selling series and the final
episode was his view about what lay ahead for him.

> I have been asked several times how long I intend to remain in the
> boxing business . . . Whether I shall keep fighting until I get too old for

it or if I shall do as so few have done . . . retire an undefeated champion?.

How can I give any definite answer? Who knows what is going to happen in the glove game? Uncertainty is actually the spice of boxing and although I have the confidence of being able to beat any man at my weight, there is always the chance that some day someone will come along and disillusion me. As I have said before, I intend remaining in the flyweight class and there are sufficient eight stone men in the country to keep me busy.

Uncertainty is the spice of boxing . . .

Who knows what is going to happen in the glove game?

He was under no illusions about the future.

Anne received her first shock about the uncertainty of boxing when she had gone to the lawyer Benny had engaged to look after his financial affairs. It wasn't like the days when Sammy Wilson had put the money on the kitchen table and they had carved it up into little parcels . . . this one for the sparring partners, this one for the living expenses, this one for the tax man, this one for Sammy and this one, the biggest one, for you Benny. There was no cash on the table now. Benny was a business and things were to be done in a business fashion with accountants, lawyers, manager and agent and other mouths. And every mouth had to be fed from one source . . . Benny Lynch's fists. The one source knew everything there needed to be known about his craft; the rest was a mystery. They would look after that for him and see him all right.

Anne had gone to the lawyer because there was a demand from the Inland Revenue. There was £2000 due to them . . . and the news was that there weren't sufficient funds to meet the demand. Unless some money could be produced the Sheriff's Officers, the bailiffs of Scotland, would be calling to impound their furniture. It was the Law of Scotland that if a creditor could substantiate a debt to the Court, an order would be made either against the debtor's wages or his worldly goods, like the furniture of his house. They would come with their Notices of Poinding which they would affix to the goods and from that moment on they were the property of auctioneers who would conduct a warrant sale, the money from the sale to go to the creditors as well as pay the expenses of the Court and its officers. Like a champion boxer, a debtor had many mouths to feed. And, as part of the disgrace of being a debtor, the legal authorities would advertise their name and address in the newspapers. You could make your fortune discreetly; but to lose it and to owe it was to be public knowledge.

The money had come in fast . . . £30,000 to £40,000. It went even faster. The fine for his split with Sammy Wilson and forfeits for not making the weight against a variety of boxers came to thousands. There were the professional people and their fees. There was the retinue, from manager to bagman, sparring partners to helpers. And there was Benny himself . . . the hardest man in the ring, the softest touch out of it.

The spongers knew that. They stopped at nothing to part him from what he carried in his wallet. They would come to the house at Gloucester Avenue to beg from him . . . "Ye see, it's no' for me; it's the weans.'' Barney Noonan, the Maryhill confidence trickster, got him to buy a bicycle for him because of the story he told him. Whenever he went into a bar, every dry mouth in the vicinity gathered round. He couldn't resist them. Anne had to discipline herself never to say, "I would like that" or "I wish we had that." For if he heard, she would get it immediately. Maybe two of them. And such were the professional advisers and experts around him that there were fights to come in which he was not to receive a single penny. But they had their reasons why that should be and there was nothing he could do about it.

They brought a Frenchman called Maurice Filhol to the Kelvin Hall in Glasgow for the first fight of 1938. Most of the fifty bob fighters could have disposed of the unfortunate Filhol, thrown in as cheap punch fodder by agents more interested in the book-keeping than the boxing. The referee put a stop to the pitiful bout in the fifth round and that, wrote Elky Clark, was four rounds too many. The Boxing Board said he had to defend the world title within a stipulated period and a Jackie Jurich from California, the top American flyweight of that year, was nominated. They were to fight at Love Street, Paisley, home ground of the local football club, St Mirren. The date was set for June 29. Somebody better than Filhol would have to be selected prior to that in order to get him back into world trim. There was no better man around than Peter Kane and a contest was fixed for them to meet at the maximum bantam weight , eight stone six pounds. Venue was to be Anfield, Liverpool.

Benny was twenty-five years of age, the flush of youth well gone. It was just five months after he had beaten Kane in that classic match; yet in five months he had aged five years. For the disease had really taken its grip and was relentlessly reaping its terrifying toll. Few, except the medical experts, thought of it as a disease. Some would call them dipsomaniacs, but that was just another way of calling a drunk a drunk. He tried agonisingly to fight it off, but there was no one to show him how; there were plenty to show him how not to. "One'll no' do you any harm," they would say. And he would be off again. He would stay at home at night with Anne and the boys, pacing the floor determined to buck the craving. But the tiger rode him hard. If he could just have *one*. Only that one, that's all, then he wouldn't feel so bad. But it was always that *one* that did it. Maybe whisky *is* better than any of the others. You know when you've had a whisky. Knock it back quick and it flushes down slowly, discerningly; warm and gratifying. But before it has effect, best to get another one down. Why not? If you've had that one, why not another? It will hurry the heightening glow and, all of a sudden the craving has gone and so too has all the anxiety and the insecurity. The tiger is no longer your enemy. He's a friend; the good companion. And Benny was impaled on its juice; the golden flow that came as a friend, left as a foe. Happiness in paralysis. The crippled comfort. Every afternoon became three o'clock in the morning. Every morning was the night before. And the agony would begin all over again.

The monster was not only two faced, it was two headed. It would make him walk the floor in agony craving for it. It would make him walk the floor because of excess of it. The medical men called them the *delirium tremens;* the time when the tiger rode hardest of all. They would occur after a long spell of addiction and they were such that they couldn't be described. How do you describe voices without a soul from a conscience that fragments into a horde of demons? They were worse than all the agony he had gone through with his legs and lungs on the steep braes of Cathkin and the steeper hills of the Campsies. That kind of agony could always have been halted. But there was no stopping these voices. They would come, especially in private moments in the bath or in the lavatory. Sometimes they would be of men, women and children all together ranting at him in a babble; other times they would be of inanimate objects that became animate then animated till they haunted and terrorised. And when they didn't appear the next day, it would be a relief to get that first drink even earlier, for the first quick ones would speedily evaporate the nightmare that had been yesterday. The tiger that gave him its juice was a vampire as well and was sucking the life out of him. And in between it all they wanted him to train and to fight. There were big expenses to be paid and some prizemoney would have to be got.

Just two months after the first Kane fight when he had been a trim eight stone, he had to meet George Bataille, bantamweight champion of France. They were to fight at eight stone six pounds but as he couldn't make that the conditions were rearranged for eight stone nine pounds. Despite being out of condition he was still good enough to better the French champion. Three months after that, and five months after their initial meeting, he was in the ring again with Kane.

Again he couldn't make the weight, this time there being a forfeit clause and he had to pay £100 for being one and a half pounds over the agreed eight stone six pounds. In five months he had gone from magnificence to mediocrity. There were moments in this second fight with Kane that the man with the golden arms fought like it had once been; the distillation of ten thousand sparring rounds was sufficient to keep him on his feet and score enough points for a draw with the man they were saying would be the next world champion.

He was sure it could be like the old days again and that if he dieted and trained hard he could be like he was against Kane . . . the first time. So it was back to the Red Tub and another long separation from Anne . . . and the cascara was taken. Jackie Jurich had better watch out!

It was mid-summer and the sweat flowed as he went through all the old forms of training, this time permanently dressed in layers of the thickest woollens. The weight seemed slower than usual in coming off, although they told him that his progress on the scales was on schedule and that he would make the weight all right. But there were other reasons for the weight not coming off. The alcohol had made its mark on the usual organs it attacks . . . the liver, the kidneys and the heart. When it does that the body begins to retain more fluid than normal because the membranes of the blood vessels toughen due to the damage of the poison and this, in turn, slows down the process of the blood freely flowing either way. When this condition gets to its worst and the blood is unable to circulate properly, the body bloats, first to the ankles, then below the eyes, then the stomach and finally the area around the heart and lungs. The skin becomes stretched so that if you press it on any part with a finger the indentation stays there, just like it would if it were a lump of bread dough. When that stage is reached there comes breathlessness, the energy saps and basic existence can only be accomplished with increasing difficulty. The body becomes prone to infection, such as pneumonia, and death can strike at any time.

Despite the onset of this deterioration process, he was still a remarkably fit man. The fight was scheduled for a Wednesday and on the Sunday, Elky Clark, the boxing reporter, joined the big crowd that had gone to see him do his final hard workout at Campsie. He was still dressed like mid-winter man but despite the bulk of the clothing he went through the strenuous rounds. The partners rotated on a two-rounds-apiece basis. They weren't fifty bob men on this occasion. There was Jackie Brown, former world champion, Jacky Paterson, who they were saying would one day be the world champion, and Tommy Bruce from Edinburgh, three fit, skilled and willing training opponents intent on getting their champion at his peak. At the end of the eleven rounds he went straight into skipping practice with the ropes which always brought the gasps from the crowds as he transformed a fitness and co-ordination exercise into something of an art form that was more theatrical than it was physical.

The weigh-in was scheduled for the regular venue for big fights, the offices of the *Daily Record* newspaper in Hope Street, in the heart of the city.

He had phoned Anne at Burnside the night before and said he was pleased the way training had gone. They had weighed him on the big scales at the camp that night and had told him he was all right. Everything would be okay for the official weigh-in the following afternoon. He had nagging doubts in the closing days about his weight and was sure he wasn't going to make it. When you were at eight stone you knew it; you knew the way the body moved; how much easier it was to run up inclines. But it didn't feel that way this time. Yet they were saying everything would be all right.

The weigh-in ceremonies were conducted, in an atmosphere of official solemnity. The boxers would be called forward, asked to disrobe then formally requested to "Step On" by the clerk of the scales. Two senior Boxing Board officials, Charles Donmall, secretary for Britain, and William Walker, chairman of the Scottish section, flanked the checked and certified scales.

"Jackee Jurich," said the clerk stiffly. "Step On" . . . "Step Off." Figures were entered in the official register and the weight announced.

"Seven stones . . . twelve pounds . . . eight ounces."

"Bennee Lynch" and he stepped forward. "Step On" . . . "Step Off . . . Lynch weighs eight stones six pounds and eight ounces."

The audible gasp was followed by a crescendo of excited talking and a scramble at the rear of the room as the reporters from evening papers dashed to phone their offices in order to get the news fudged into the Stop Press columns.

Eight Stones. Six Pounds. Eight Ounces. Each word was worse than any punch he had ever received; worse than any torture he had undergone in training.

Eight Stones. Six Pounds. Eight Ounces. It had the effect of the Voices . . . the Voices that would come and dement him. But it wasn't the Voices. This was happening for real and other people, not just him, were hearing the words.

Eight Stones. Six Pounds. Eight Ounces. How could it be? They had said last night that he had only been ounces over and that he would lose them, as you usually did, during sleep. It was Puggy himself that had said everything would okay. Puggy had said everything was fine and that he would make the weigh-in at the *Record* "nae bother". Puggy . . .? He looked across at him as the gasps of astonishment filled the air. Their eyes met and they stared hard. Benny's lips moved but he didn't need to say the word. Puggy knew what it was . . . and why it was being said. "Bastard!"

Dingley was summoned to hear the verdict he knew the Board had to make. "Your boxer, Benny Lynch, is no longer the world champion," they said. Then there was a hurried meeting with the Jurich entourage to ask if they would agree to go ahead with a non-title fight at catchweight. Sportingly they agreed, after confirming that they really would collect the £500 default money Lynch had deposited with the Boxing Board as a condition of him meeting the weight.

There were 14,000 at Love Street, Paisley, that night to see him fight. Not many months ago there would have been twice that number with thousands more clamouring to get in. And "skippies" up to their tricks trying to find a bolt hole for a free entry. Jurich went first from the dressing rooms to receive one of the biggest cheers any foreign opponent had received in Scotland.

But there were reasons for big cheers tonight for anyone who was an opponent of Benny Lynch. And he knew that more than anyone. For he had let his country down. The roots were Irish, but he loved his Scots and his Scotland. He had betrayed too his friends, the real friends, who had helped so much in the past and all the real fans who had been so proud of him and had followed him since the time he was fighting around the clubs . . . Anne and the boys . . . the memory of brother James . . . the tramp in the hills that had got the thrill of his life just because he had stopped to speak to him. And it was for these reasons that he wept openly in the dressing room as he sat alone waiting for his call. It didn't matter so much now that they had lied to him about his weight. Had they done it because they knew he wasn't going to make it? Or were there other reasons? Did they have their money elsewhere? You could trust no one in this game. For they were all out to get a bit of you. And the bits were disappearing fast. He would be fighting tonight for nothing. Jurich had got half of his purse, the £500 deposited with the Board. Dingley had given him an advance, but that had gone. He would have been better off as a fifty-bob fighter . . . a drink and some laughs with Paddy Docherty, Sanny Robson and the rest of the boys in the Seaforth afterwards then a night at the Tripe and some more laughs. And there was no shortage of fifty bob fights. Those were the days.

Not like it was now. The big time! Lawyers that tell you there's no money left in the kitty. A manager that was getting richer as he got poorer. And a trainer that fixed the scales.

The seconds came for him and he walked to the ring.

He had never been given boos and catcalls before from his own people. They had done it in Belfast, but that was for other reasons. Tonight it was because he was no longer their great wee Benny.

At the end of the customary formalities during which the M.C. related the events of the weigh-in which brought more derision the chief seconds were introduced and when Puggy's name was announced there was even louder booing and insults. He saw the humour in that and his face creased into its familiar grin. He could have laughed out loud in relief for it was as though the crowd were telling him he wasn't entirely to blame. Others must have had a hand in the dishonour of his most inglorious day.

Had they been at equal weight, Jurich would still have been no great match for the man who had been world champion that morning. It took no great effort for him to show the crowd that they had lost their champion but still had the best fighting machine in the world. And in the twelfth round, when they counted out Jackie Jurich, they were cheering him as wildly as they had ever done in the past. He had been forgiven.

The Boxing Board decided to take a closer interest in the welfare of the man who had become the most controversial fighter in the country. It was obvious for one reason or another that he could no longer make the flyweight division and he was ordered not to try. In future the minimum weight grade at which they would let him fight would be bantam . . . eight stone six pounds. And he would have to lodge yet another £500 with the Board, to be forfeited if he couldn't make that weight.

Life had become a pantomime. Characters came and went, and each unfolding episode became all the more unbelievable. For Anne it was totally incomprehensible. Her husband was sport's diamond solitaire. He was surrounded by the men who said they were the best advisers and counsellors in the business. Yet no one could put a brake on the toboggan on which Benny Lynch was riding madly downhill. Why, why, why, she asked could he be fighting for nothing? Why, why, why, she asked could a lawyer announce they were broke? And why, why, why were they still arranging fights with the likelihood of infringing that strict penalty clause? But the questions were never to be answered. Anyway, what would a woman understand about these things? And the pantomime continued.

Despite the physical condition which was being consumed by the alcohol damage, one of the toughest small men in the world was chosen for his next fight. Kayo Morgan they called him. He smoked cigars, moved with an aura of cocky flamboyance and came from Detroit. And worse, he was a southpaw. Another bogeyman. They knew him in Scotland for he had been before for meetings with Johnny McGrory and Johnny McMillan . . . and gave each of them a Morgan kayo. Then he had returned to his homeland to thrash the reigning world bantam champion Sixto Escobar.

They were to have fought at four pounds over the bantam limit of eight six at Shawfield Park. Johnny McMillan was his new manager-trainer and Neillie McGhie was the promoter. But his fights were now no longer being fought in the ring . . . and if his helpers realised it they did nothing about it. What happened in the ring was a mere formality to what was happening elsewhere. He tried to train, but one liquor bottle could undo twenty sparring rounds; one good binge caused more wounds than one battle. and each binge was becoming bigger and better than the last one.

There were no great surprises to those who knew what was happening when he again failed at the scales. He was heavier than ever, weighing in at nine stone one pound fourteen ounces, nearly six pounds over the agreed fight limit with Morgan. The £500 forfeit money was lost. So too was the fight, Morgan getting the verdict, albeit a close one, on points. And for an unbelievable ending to the unbelievable pantomime, the £1000 cheque the promoter had lodged with the Boxing Board prior to the fight was refused by the bank. The Board, in their wisdom to protect the boxer, had kept the cheque till after the fight by which time the promotor had run out of funds. Not only had this fight been for nothing . . . it had cost him £500. But still they wanted him to fight and six days later he was due in London to meet the Roumanian Aurel Toma.

Sammy Wilson was long gone. So too was Dingley and Puggy Morgan and Neillie McGhie and the others who had come and gone as managers and trainers. But there were always others to replace them. Others who said they knew. Others who, despite what had happened against Jurich and against Kayo Morgan, said he should be up there in the ring fighting. Others who were to ignore the fact that it was now horribly obvious he was beyond redemption as an athlete.

There were just six days between the defeat by Kayo Morgan and the next scheduled fight. The cascara was never contemplated. He was too busy drinking other things. It wasn't merely a binge this time. It was the permanent hook, barbed and clawed and so viciously deep in him that he couldn't even contemplate gutting it from within him;

for each claw and barb were the voices of the *delirium tremens* and, Holy Mother of God, were they not the cruellest things on earth!

Anne pleaded and prayed. She beseeched the Saints for their divine help. But he was beyond their assistance. Pray to St Jude, they said, the Patron Saint of the Hopeless and those to be Despaired Of: "St Jude, glorious Apostle, faithful servant and friend of Jesus, the name of the traitor has caused you to be forgotten by many; but the true Church invokes you universally as the Patron of things despaired of; pray for me, who am so miserable; pray for me, that finally I may receive the consolations and the succour of Heaven in all my necessities, tribulations and sufferings, particularly with my Benny and his problem and need, and that I may bless God with the Elect throughout Eternity, Amen." But St Jude, Apostle, martyr and relative of Lord Jesus Christ, of Mary and of Joseph, hadn't the ability to intercede for Anne on behalf of her husband. Crawford's Three Star was his umbilical to a world where life was hellish without it and hell with it.

He was semi-comatose when they came for him that Saturday. There was Johnny McMillan, the new trainer-manager, and a second and they said he would have to go. "Mirauclous," they said, which was appropriate for it meant miraculous and it was a miracle that anyone was still even in the land of the half-living after having consumed so much. He was due to appear at the National Sporting Club's venue, the Empress Hall, Earl's Court, in London, on the Monday, October 3. "C'mon, Benny old son," they said, "you'll be all right. A wee coffee, a wee walk, then a wee sleep, and you'll be wanting to take on the Brown Bomber." Then they left with him between them for the Central Station and the night train to London. And Anne cried herself to sleep.

The fight had been arranged by Jack Harding, manager of the National Sporting Club. The opponent they had arranged was the Roumanian, Aurel Toma, one-time chauffeur to King Carol. Toma used to spar with the King himself, but they joked that that was to keep him fit for his contests with Maniu, the leader of the National Peasant Party, Codreanu and his fascist Iron Guard, and his lover Magda Lupescu. Toma, dark-eyed and twenty-seven, was two years older than his new rival, and, on record, promised to be a tough opponent. He had an impressive amateur record followed by an equally impressive showing as a professional, outpointing Jackie Brown, among a variety of other international stars, his pinnacle being the European bantamweight champion. He was a clever technical boxer who relied more on points than on punch. But neither was necessary for the man he was about to meet. He had hardly eaten in the six days since meeting Morgan, yet his weight had soared again, the sluggish bloodvessel membranes retaining more and more of the accumulating body poisons. When he stripped, his thighs were jellied and the once hollow stomach had ballooned, his gaunt cheeks rounded. And they couldn't keep the drink from him.

He needed it; he demanded it. And they gave him it. There was a half-bottle in the dressing room, wrapped in a towel, and when he stood on the scales he created another record . . . his heaviest ever. The agreement had been to fight at eight-ten. The scales registered nine stone five pounds four ounces. More forfeit money was lost. Yet he was fit, they claimed. For a doctor had been produced . . . from somewhere . . . and he had given an official statement as a result of what they said was a "rigourous medical test". That statement said that the boxer Benny Lynch was "medically fit".

Ten thousand crowded into the Empress Hall to see the man they had read so much about; the sensational Benny Lynch, the fighter of whom the fighting men said there was none better when he was at his best. And he was about to show them what he was like . . . at his worst.

"Hey Johnny," he said as he sat in his corner waiting on the first bell . . . "I cannae see him."

"You'll see him a' right, Benny, when he comes out. Right, on yer way son."

He came out with all the style and grace of a Saturday night fighter . . . like the kind he used to see occasionally in Florence Street when the Moy closed; feet square on the ground like they were in boots of lead, fists hung low and shouting "C'mon ya bastards!"

"See a man with his feet square on the ground and you know you've got a loser in front of you," Sammy Wilson used to say. Toma dusted him with flurries which rattled off his face and upper chest, both unguarded by the gloved fists slung by his waist. Around the hall there were gasps of astonishment from the mystified fans. Were they seeing right? How could someone they were told was so great appear like some shambling punch drunk? It was an act, of course, they told each other in initial consolation. He's so great he doesn't even have to put up a semblance of a fight. It will be different in the next round, though . . . perhaps.

"Christ, Johnny . . . there's two of them out there. Which one is he?" He slumped in the stool at the end of the first round, baffled by the sight he was seeing in the ring. They wiped the sweat pouring from the face and he gulped big swigs from the water bottle.

"You just hit the right one, wee man. C'mon, you'll be all right,

Benny . . . but cover your face up a bit more. Keep your hands up . . . up . . . up d'ye hear?"

"Aye . . . but what one is Toma?"

"Aw . . . Christ, Benny . . . hit the man on the right, ya daft wee bastard."

The feet shuffled like the old fighters' used to when he went across the ring in a movement that was a mere impersonation of an attack mid-way through the second round, the slung fists in action at last and swinging at something that was in front of him; who, where, what, he wasn't quite sure. "Christ, he's going for the one on the left," Johnny thought to himself. For Benny wasn't just missing by inches. It was by feet. And when he went for the man on the left, the real man on the right, Aurel Toma, came in and was hitting the easiest target he had faced since the big leather punch bag had first swung at him in the gym.

The astonished fans were astonished no more. They knew now. And they jeered, their howls rising to a pitch as the round closed, Benny still bulling in on a shadow that had a body he couldn't find but which was finding him.

"What's that I taste?" he said to Johnny in the respite after the second round was over. "Christ, it's blood." He couldn't remember when he had been cut before. The Harley Street specialists had examined him once and they said he was the toughest and fittest man they had known apart from Jock McAvoy, The Rochdale Thunderbolt who had knocked out 100 men in 150 fights. "You've got skin like a pig," they had said. Which was why he had never cut. "Aye, he caught you with a left on the mouth just at the end of the round there," said Johnny. "You'll get better as it goes on, Benny. Just keep yourself guarded and keep him back from your face. And for Christ's sake, keep your hands up."

"But there's still two of them, Johnny . . . and I keep getting the wrong one."

They rubbed the sallow-skinned Roumanian's shoulders in his corner and could hardly contain their glee at the state of the man across the ring. "Tu il ai . . . du-te si terminal . . . oît poti de repede." "You've got him," they said. "Now go and finish him. Quick as you can," . . . and the bell went for the next round.

He knew that his opponent's stomach was his weakest point. He had hit him there earlier. Once it would have been easier to put a glove through a brick wall. But the breadbasket was soaked and soggy and his glove had sunk deep into it and he had heard his man gasp. So he went for it again when they came out for three. A hard left went in and he could hear him again groan in pain, the sound coming from his throat like a loud gulp. He pulled his left out from the pillowed plexus then returned it harder and, when he pulled that out, followed through with his hardest right which sunk even deeper. The shock waves of the three explosions in the pit of his stomach hit him worst in his legs, and he went into a drunken wobble. He lurched forward, knees together, and the fighter who had been a shadow to him came in again, a glove connecting with his jaw. There was a vivid flash which was a strange yellow and pink and his hearing went peculiar . . . and no longer were there any other boxers in the ring with Benny Lynch.

They jeered and catcalled as he crashed face down on the cape before rolling over on his back, his arms outstretched above his head, his eyes closed tightly. Toma didn't have to wait for the full count to know that he had won the fight. No one had. For there was not the trace of a movement from the unconscious boxer straightened on the canvas. They booed when they helped him to his feet and booed even louder and shouted insults and taunts after they pulled him to his feet and he had recovered enough to make his way, his head bowed beneath the stained towel that cowled his head. "Drunk" . . . "Bum" . . . "Hasbeen" . . . they vented every abuse they thought appropriate at the man who had been transformed into a grotesque version of the fighter that had held everyone who had ever watched him in awe at his grace, tenacity, courage and skill; the man they had called Benny Lynch.

20

A Knock Out With The Monks

The small monk, bearded and with intense blue eyes, sat beside the man lying in the iron-framed bed in room 19. It was on the second floor of the guest house and the Gothic window looked out on a fountained pool in which small red fish swam and which was flanked by gleaming white statues of Mary and Joseph carrying the Infant Child. The room was neat and clean, but spartan and bare. The plastered wall was whitewashed but there was no covering on the scrubbed floorboards. In one of the small panes at the top of the curved window there was a small hole, neat and clean as though it had been drilled but in fact had been caused by a bullet. On the wall over the head of the bed was a small crucifix and on another wall an unframed picture of the Last Supper. The only other furnishings apart from the bed and the chair on which the monk was sitting was a small table on which there was a mirror and a tall delf water pitcher beside a similarly patterned wash basin.

It was autumn and the best of the daylight had gone. The man had been in the bed in a deep, drugged sleep for 12 hours and there was still no sign of his stirring. The monk, Brother Stanislaus, maintained an attentive vigil, wiping the sweat every now and then from the sleeping man's face. He had seen them before like that and had given them similar treatment, a powerful potion he would only refer to as "a sleeping draught" and if he was asked what it was would reply . . . "sure, and that's a secret." And no amount of cajoling would make him reveal his secret.

The man in the bed, deathly still, had a white puffy face and the appearance of someone about forty years of age, although his thick black hair neatly trimmed at the sides didn't have a speckle of grey in it.

Benny Lynch was having the toughest fight of his life. They had brought him to Mount Melleray from Glasgow the night before. His old schoolmate and boxing compatriot Johnny McGrory had been at him for more than a year to go there. He knew they had failed at the special clinic for alcoholics in Chislehirst. But he had to have one last try. Other alcoholics had gone to Mount Melleray and it was said it had helped some. McGrory had been there himself, but for different reasons from what he was suggesting to Benny. He had gone for the same spiritual reasons that thousands of pilgrim Catholics from all over the world went.

The imposing grey limestone monastery had been built by the Cistercian monks over a century before. They had taken the stone from the burned out shell of the Earl of Kingston's Castle. "Well, he wasn't a very good laird," they would say, "and someone decided to do something about it." And after they did the Earl's Castle lay derelict for years until the industrious monks bought its stone and transported it to the site they had obtained on a long shoulder of the Knockmealdown Mountains in County Waterford in the far south of the Republic of Ireland. There they had built their beautiful monastery, the biggest of their thousand-year-old Cistercian Order outside of mainland Europe, its huge cruciform structure dominating the fertile slopes of the high and wild mountains so that it's four-spired bell tower could be seen miles before reaching Cappoquin, the nearest village. The seventy monks lived their life of isolation there. They wore the simple clothes of sixth-century Italian peasants, a white robe topped by a black scapular held at the waist by a stout leather belt, that being the dress at the time when St Benedict had formed the Order from which they were derived.

Their days were long and spent between hours of prayer, hymn-chanting and contemplation and working as farm labourers and herdsmen in the fields around their Abbey in order to maintain their objective of remaining as near self-supporting as possible. If they could have grown their own tea and refined their own paraffin they could have done without the outside world. They thought of themselves as the artists of the world of Christianity rather than the outgoing artisans who were the missionaries and the spiritual shepherds who tended the flocks. And as the artists of their religion they were content in their contemplation and reflection on God and Christianity and life itself.

They gave others the chance to share their experience just as they did at other Cistercian monasteries which was why they had built the big two-storey guesthouse for the pilgrims. They came for a variety of reasons but mainly with a single purpose; to be in a spiritual centre where they could, like the monks themselves, retreat from the world and whatever that world meant to them. Those who had been there spoke enthusiastically of the mental therapy the stay had given them; they returned to the outside world refreshed and stimulated by the experience. Alcoholics had gone there too, friends suggesting that to be divorced from the demon that was destroying them would be sufficient for them to get over the craving. The Monastery officials thought too that the goodness of their surroundings and the understanding which they could offer was a help for the alcoholically afflicted. They meant well but like so many who similarly tried, it was without the scientific understanding for the cruel disease which could wreck the psyche and ruin the physique of the strongest like a cancer of mind and body. It needed more than being temporarily separated from the food on which the disease thrived to provide a cure that had a chance of succeeding.

Benny had come with an onset of another bout of *delirium tremens* and Brother Stanislaus had sat with him as he went through the torture of the voices. They were coming though the fan-light. Yes . . . up there in the fan-light above the door. There were two of them and they were talking to each other and plotting about the man that lay in the bed and was called Benny Lynch; cruel, tormenting voices that were casting up his most shameful secrets, shouting his thoughts aloud at him. They were so real that he had to talk back to them. Then they came in from the fan-light and were on the wall above him, all around the Jesus impaled on the little wooden cross. They had multiplied now; men, women and children all babbling at him in a rhythm which synchronised with his pulse. There was no talking back to them like there was when there had only been two for there were too many of them, jeering and taunting, mocking and teasing, sneering and scoffing. The intensity of the cruel chorus grew; a vivid and insistent torture to which he shrank in cowering and terrified fear, not even aware of the comfort of the devoted monk by his bedside. He wasn't there. The voices were. It was then that they had decided he should be given the sleeping draught which Brother Stranislaus kept such a secret. And for a while he was released from the misery of the pernicious accusers that only he could see, only he could sense, only he could suffer.

It was fourteen hours before he was to waken, this time to a physical onslaught of painful sickness, the after-effect of the sleeping draught, which had probably contained some opium as a medicant. "Easy, my boy," said the monk softly, wiping the sweat from him between the bouts of agonising wretching and vomiting.

It was the next day, more than twenty-four hours after he had been put to bed that he felt well enough to take a few steps around the laurel-fringed gardens which separated the guesthouse from the market garden where there were long lines of dark green savoys and trellises of clinging peas. Accompanying him would be the devoted

Brother Stanislaus, whom the other monks called Brother Stan. Even in
his isolated outpost he was a bit of a Follower of the Fancy and knew
about all the great champions. "D'ye know Benny, you can still make
a bundle. There's your Jack Dempsey. Now he proved you can make
a bundle and hold on to it. I know it's a very difficult thing to jump
up like you have from nothing and sit there on the throne. Not many
get that chance, you know, to sit there, king of their world. But it's
when you get there that you have really to use your head, much
much more than you ever did in trying to get there. That's what
people don't realise. Holding and keeping the victory is more difficult
than getting it. It takes all of a man's diligence to do it. But you could
be like Jack Dempsey, Benny." It was nice to hear that. And especially
when it was with the feeling and sincerity of the faithful Brother
Stanislaus.

Although the monks were not of the material world, they were still
very much worldly. Their silence was strict, but not total and the
word went quickly around that they had such a famous name in their
midst. Brother Robert, the Guestmaster, helped him with the routine
of being a guest at Mount Melleray: breakfast at 8.30 . . . porridge,
two poached eggs and a plate heaped with the rough, wholemeal
bread two monks made in the little bakery at the head of the side courtyard; dinner was when a working man had his dinner, one o'clock, and as
the new season's Kerr's Pinks weren't ready, they had the previous
year's from the store, thick-jacketed and floury matured and with
butter, tastier than any other potato he ever had. There was a heap of
dark cabbage and a slice of meat which the monks shunned because
they were vegetarian but provided for their guests, and there was the
best applecake and custard he had since the days he lived with Maw
Kelter and her big family. There was tea at 5.30, a lighter meal, and if
you went walking outside the grounds, be sure to be back before 8.30
for they closed and locked the doors then and bedded shortly
afterwards. And not to worry about the bell he might hear ringing in
the middle of the night. That was for the monks who rose at 3.15 for
their first vigils which were followed by private mass then community mass at which they would chant some of the 135 hymns sung
by them every week.

Father Aelred became a favourite friend. For Father Aelred Murray
was from Coatbridge in Scotland, had gone to school at St Joseph's in
Dumfries, and he had the same kind of local humour as Benny Lynch.
"He was a right tearaway in his young days," one of the Brothers told
him, and he smiled to himself about that for that was something he
knew about too. "So his father sent him to the school here . . . and he
just stayed on. He became a Brother and then a Priest and is now one

of our most respected members. But he's still a right character." He was. He would joke with Benny in the presence of the other monks. "See this place, Benny. Know the trouble with it? Too many foreigners here . . . and they're all Irish." Their life of loneliness gave them a heightened sense of humour and they would burst into fits of laughter at the banter of the two Scots, one pugilist, one priest.

With the separation from alcohol being complete, the tremens slowly dissipated, but the craving, as it always does, lingered. Nevertheless, the puffiness started to fade and a feeling of some physical well-being slowly rekindled; but it was a mere spark compared to what had been . His old cheer was quicker to return and the monks liked him in their presence. "Fancy a fight," he said to one of the Brothers, and they laughed. "Tell you what, Father Finbar will fix you up with a bout," they said. "He's got a student who's a boxing fanatic . . . so much so he's nicknamed 'Boxer.' "

Father Finbar was the Dean of the College attached to the Abbey at the time and there were some lusty pupils among the senior grades. They too had heard about their famous guest and had joked with 'Boxer' that he should have a bout with the man who had been the world champion. The invitation went out and by the lunchtime of that day it was the talk, when there was talk, in the Monastery, and the word, where there were lots of words, in the school. Two students, Hugh McAlinden and Donald O'Brien, the 'Boxer', were going to have the chance to face up to the man who had beaten the best men that could be found in the world.

The 'Boxer' was first. He was a big strong lad who really did fancy his chances as a pugilist and Benny told him to try as hard as he could against him. He did.

It was amateur against professional and the professional was able to convert the fight into a splendid exhibition bout which had every student on his feet cheering wildly. But they had better entertainment to come. It was the student McAlinden's turn next. Benny had got him aside beforehand. "Do you know what a gee fight is? Well, it means a fix . . . get it? We'll have a real go . . . then you'll knock me out. Okay?" And the students and their monk tutors and the other monks who had sneaked into the back of the crowd from their duties at the Monastery, cheered like they had never cheered in their lives when the referee raised the student's hand in victory after he had counted out the outstretched Benny Lynch, hamming his part like a real pro.

The monks who had got to know him, Father Finbar, Father Robert, Father Aelred, Father Cornelius and Brother Stanislaus, Brother Damien, Brother Gerard and the others who met him more briefly greeted him now in smiling reverence for he had revealed to them his own indominitable character; he was suffering and he now realised the odds were against him but even that couldn't overcome a disposition that always surfaced with a smile.

There were long contemplative walks on his own and others in the company of the monks. They would talk about the Monastery and their work and some of their own characters. Some of them had spent their lifetime there, like Father Aelred who had come as a boy and stayed on and Brother Gerard who had come in 1914, the year after Benny was born. Others had come later in life and lived a worldly and diversified existence before giving themselves up to eternal isolation. Brother Stan had been like that. He had come ten years previously at the age of thirty-five and a veteran of the World War in which he had been a sergeant in the South Wales Borderers. "He's a great character, you know," they would say. "When he was in the trenches at Gallipoli a young Turk came charging at him with a fixed bayonet on the end of his rifle. He was only a lad and despite the fact Brother Stan is only a little man he can be very fierce and when the Turk went for him he shouted in his roughest voice . . . 'Getcher . . . or I'll let you have this,' showing him his own bayonet. And the young lad turned and fled. The same happened when he was on leave in Dublin in 1916. It was the week of the Rising and there were Sinn Feiners everywhere. He was walking in the city with his British Army uniform on and two of them made a go at him. But he calmly took his cap off, put it in his belt and showed he was ready for the pair of them . . . and they made off."

They told him the story of the bullet hole in the window of his room. During the disastrous Civil War following the Anglo-Irish Treaty of 1921 when more Irishmen killed each other than had fallen to the British in the Troubles following the Rising, several Republicans, hiding from Free State raiding parties, had sought refuge in the Monastery after crossing the wild Knockmealdown Mountains. They had included Eamonn de Valera, Dan Breen, Austin Stack and Liam Lynch. "And your namesake was quite a man," they told Benny. "He was on the British death list and they sent a squad to execute him . . . and they killed another man called Lynch by mistake. Dangerous name to have at that time."

He asked about Stack, the man who had hidden in his room and was told that he had been one of the most outstanding of all the Republican heroes. One of the monks, an expert on their history, said that whether or not people believed in Republicanism, Stack had been a splendid example of fortitude and courage. "A bit like yourself, Benny, for he always came up smiling. When he died nine years ago they wrote a fine pamphlet about him and part of it read . .

"He was a man without a crooked twist in him; one who thought straight, acted straight, walked the straight road unflinchingly and expected of others that they should walk it with him as simply as he did himself . . . he went his way, suffered their will, and stood his ground doggedly, smiling now and again . . . compromise, submission, the slave marks, did not and could not exist for him . . . ' Indeed a fine man, Benny . . . and it's courage like that you need for your big fight." He smiled and nodded in agreement.

But the agony continued. And the beauty of Mount Melleray, the contemplative walks, the company of the purest and most humble group of men he had ever met, the prayers, the supplications, the devotions did nothing to alleviate the suffering. He suffered when he bared his soul to the priest in the mustard-curtained confession boxes in the foyer by the chapel. He suffered at morning mass amidst the splendour of the monks chanting their hymns, the morning sun filling the high-roof chapel with the rich magnificence of the colours from the Harry Clarke stained-glass window. He suffered during the early evening Vespers, even through the most enchanting of the hymns, like *Praise the Name of the Lord,* the cantor's clear words lingering long after the conclusion of the service

> *Praise the Lord for the Lord is good;*
> *Sing praises unto his name; for it is pleasant . . .*
> *Thy name,. O Lord, endureth for ever; and thy memorial,*
> *O Lord, throughout all generations.*

. . . He suffered at night when he lay alone in his room in a kind of silence he had never known before and never thought existed. God and goodness had never been so near; the cure and an end to his craving had never been so far. Oh Christ, dear Jesus, Holy Mary, Mother of God, if only he could have a drink. Just one.

Father Robert and Father Aelred farewelled him with smiles and 'God be with you' and they prayed for him when he left with the friends who called for him by car. He told them he felt much better and he looked twice the man that had arrived, haunted by the terrors of withdrawal. And they prayed for him at Mass that evening.

They drove north past Ballynaguilkee, Ballynamult, Ballymacarbry and Ballybeg, all whitewash and thatch, to Clonmel where bold Jim Nugent fired the last shots at the Gashouse Bridge to cover his Republican comrades when they retreated from the National troops. And there was Jackie Lonergan's pub and Tony O'Gorman's, Eldon Morris's and Tony Wrixted's and Hearns Hotel as well and God it felt great to be a drinking man again. For you didn't crave when you were drinking and there were no voices either. And tomorrow was something others could worry about.

Epilogue

The memory of Benny Lynch is that of a great fighter in the ring, not the terrible loser in life. The years after Mount Melleray were mainly those of a lonely and sad figure suffering from alcoholism, deserted by the great band of friends and followers who had enjoyed the limelight of the greatest-ever boxer in Scotland. The contest with Aurel Toma had been his 104th listed fight. It was the first time he had ever been knocked out. It was the last time he was ever to have an official bout, his licence being revoked and then finally withheld on August 26, 1939, because he could not pass the Boxing Board's fitness test. The story thereafter was predictable. His marriage broke and he returned to live with his mother. There was one attempt at a comeback, but *delirium tremens* and physical training don't mix. Thereafter all was gone and life had but one meaning . . . the next drink.

On August 7, 1946, he was taken to the Southern General Hospital in Glasgow, fevered and with respiratory problems. Pneumonia had set in and his resistance was at a low ebb. He died the next day. He was thirty-three years of age.

Postscript

Most of the people connected with Benny Lynch and his story are now dead. But, happily, many are still living. His widow Anne remarried and lives in Bramalea, Ontario, with her husband Frank. Benny and Anne's eldest son John died in his early thirties like his father. Their other son, Bobby, lives near his mother in Bramalea, is married with two daughters and is a manager with a big international company.

Of the principal boxers mentioned in this story, Peter Kane, Jim Maharg, Paddy Docherty, Alex Farries, Johnny McGrory, Bill and Jim Warnock and the champion amateur Harry Dingley, son of John George Dingley, are still living. So too are several of the monks at Mount Melleray Monastery in Ireland, including Brother Gerard, ninety-years-old and working hard, and Brother Stanislaus.

The old family cottage at Meenamault, Carnamoyle, in County Donegal from where James Lynch set out for Scotland, has long since been demolished. There are several Lynch families in the district, however, several of them being second cousins to Benny.

Appendix

BENNY LYNCH'S FIGHT RECORD

Born at Glasgow, April 2, 1913. Died at Glasgow, August 8, 1946
WORLD, EUROPEAN & BRITISH FLYWEIGHT CHAMPION

1931

Jun. 11	Young McColl	w.rsf. 3	Glasgow
Jul. 31	Billy Leggatt	w.pts. 6	Glasgow
Aug. 14	Young Donnelly	drew 8	Glasgow
Aug. 22	Jim Devanney	w.rsf. 3	Glasgow
Sep. 5	Young O'Brien	l.pts. 6	Glasgow
Sep. 12	Jim McKenzie	w.pts.. 6	Glasgow
Sep. 26	Joe Boag	drew 6	Glasgow
Oct. 1	Paddy Docherty	l.pts. 8	Glasgow
Oct. 15	Young O'Brien	w.pts. 4	Glasgow
Oct. 29	Young McAdam	l.pts. 8	Glasgow
Nov. 6	Mick Cassidy	w.pts. 6	Glasgow
Nov. 13	Peter Sherry	w.pts. 6	Glasgow
Nov. 28	Pat Sweeney	w.pts. 6	Glasgow

1932

Jan. 1	Charlie Deacon	w. ret. 4	Greenock
Feb. 5	Young Hardie	w.pts. 6	Glasgow
Feb. 11	Jack Riley	w.pts. 6	Glasgow
Feb. 20	Kid Murray	w.pts. 6	Glasgow
Feb. 25	Jimmy Barr	w.pts. 6	Glasgow
Mar. 11	Scotty Deans	w.pts. 6	Glasgow
Mar. 18	Young McManus	drew 6	Glasgow
Apr. 9	Jim O'Driscoll	w.pts. 6	Glasgow
Apr. 16	Young Griffo	w.pts. 6	Glasgow
Apr. 21	Tiger Naughton	w.pts. 6	Glasgow
Apr. 24	Young Griffo	l.pts.10	Glasgow
May 21	Scotty Deans	w.ko. 4	Glasgow
Jun. 9	Joe Aitken	w.pts. 10	Glasgow
Jul. 8	Freddie Tennant	l.pts. 10	Glasgow
Jul. 15	Tommy Higgins	drew 10	Blantyre
Jul. 29	Jim Jeffries	w.pts. 8	Blantyre
Aug. 20	Tony Fleming	drew 6	Glasgow
Sep. 3	Paddy Docherty	w.pts. 10	Glasgow
Sep. ?	Alex Farries	w.pts. 10	Edinburgh
Oct. 7	Joe Aitken	drew 10	Airdrie
Oct. 17	Freddie Tennant	w.pts. 10	Leith

Oct. 21	Young Beattie	drew 6	Hamilton
Oct. 29	Alex Farries	w.pts. 10	Glasgow
Nov. 4	Tommy Higgins	w.pts. 10	Glasgow
Nov. 10	George McLeod	w.ret. 5	Edinburgh
Nov. 18	Paddy Docherty	l.pts. 10	Glasgow
Dec. 2	Paddy Docherty	w.pts. 10	Glasgow
Dec. 8	Jim Naughton	w.pts. 6	Glasgow
Dec.23	Freddie Tennant	drew 10	Glasgow
1933			
Jan. 13	Dan Conlin	w.pts. 10	Glasgow
Feb. 17	Joe Aitken	drew 10	Glasgow
Mar. 25	Jim Brady	w.pts. 12	Glasgow
Mar. 31	Paddy Docherty	drew 10	Glasgow
Apr. 21	Walter Lemmon	w.pts. 10	Glasgow
May 2	Jim Brady	drew 12	Dundee
May 5	Freddie Tennant	w.pts. 10	Glasgow
May 11	Alex Farries	w.pts. 8	Gourock
May 25	Jim Maharg	w.pts. 12	Glasgow
Jun. 15	Billy Warnock	w.rsf. 11	Glasgow
Jun. 29	Billy Hughes	w.ret. 9	Glasgow
Aug. 17	Alex Farries	w.rsf. 4	Glasgow
Sep. 8	Joe Cowley	w.rsf. 8	Glasgow
Oct. 10	Willie Vogan	w.ko. 2	Edinburgh
Oct. 24	Boy McIntosh	w.ret. 4	Edinburgh
Oct. 29	Bert Kirby	w.pts. 12	West Bromich
Nov. 9	Bob Fielding	drew 10	Liverpool
1934			
Jan. 30	Jim Brady	w.pts. 12	Edinburgh
Feb. 8	Freddie Webb	w.ko. 3	Glasgow
Mar. 21	Carlo Cavagnoli	w.pts. 10	Glasgow
Apr. 17	George Lowe	w.ret. 2	Glasgow
May 16	Jim Campbell	w.pts. 15	Glasgow
	Scottish flyweight title		
May 27	Evan Evans	w.rsf. 3	Glasgow
May 31	Peter Miller	w.ko. 8	Glasgow
Jun. 27	Jim Campbell	w.pts. 15	Glasgow
	Scottish flyweight title		
Aug. 8	Maurice Huguenin	w.pts. 12	Glasgow
Aug. 30	Jim Brady	w.pts. 12	Glasgow
Sep. 26	Valentin Angelmann	w.pts. 12	Glasgow
Oct. 25	Billy Johnstone	w.rsf. 5	Glasgow
Nov. 7	Pedrito Ruiz	w.pts. 12	Glasgow
Nov. 12	Peter Miller	w.ko. 8	Newcastle

Nov. 29	Johnny Griffiths	w.ko. 1	Edinburgh
Dec. 5	Tut Whalley	w.dis. 8	Dundee
Dec. 13	Sandy McEwan	w.pts. 12	Edinburgh

1935

Jan. 7	Bobby Magee	w.pts. 12	Glasgow
Mar. 4	Jackie Brown	drew 12	Glasgow
Apr. 15	Tommy Pardoe	w.rsf. 14	Birmingham
May 6	Charlie Hazel	w.ko. 1	Glasgow
Sep. 9	Jackie Brown	w.ret. 2	Manchester

British, European & World flyweight titles

Dec. 3	Gaston Maton	w.pts. 12	Glasgow
Dec. 12	Harry Orton	w.pts. 12	Glasgow
Dec. 19	Phil Milligan	w.pts. 12	Glasgow

1936

Mar. 12	Jim Warnock	l.pts. 12	Belfast
May 25	Micky McGuire	w.rsf. 4	Newcastle
May 28	Pat Warburton	w.rsf. 3	Holborn Stadium, London
Jun. 16	Syd Parker	w.ko. 9	Glasgow
Sep. 16	Pat Palmer	w.ko. 8	Glasgow

British, European & World flyweight titles

| No. 16 | Phil Milligan | w.rsf. 7 | Manchester |
| Dec. 10 | Eric Jones | w.ko. 2 | Stadium club, London |

1937

| Jan. 19 | Small Montana | w.pts. 15 | Wembley Arena, London |

World flyweight title

Feb. 10	Fortunata Ortega	w.pts. 12	Glasgow
Mar. 1	Len Hampston	l.dis. 5	Manchester
Mar. 22	Len Hamptson	w.rsf. 10	Leeds
Jun. 2	Jim Warnock	l.pts. 15	Glasgow
Aug. 20	Roy Underwood	w.ret. 6	Glasgow
Oct. 13	Peter Kane	w.ko. 13	Glasgow

British, European & World flyweight titles

| Dec. 13 | Georges Bataille | w.rsf. 8 | Leicester |

1938

Feb. 9	Maurice Filhol	w.rsf. 5	Glasgow
Mar. 24	Peter Kane	drew 12	Liverpool
Jun. 29	*Jackie Jurich	w.ko. 12	Glasgow
Sep. 27	Kayo Morgan	l.pts. 12	Glasgow
Oct. 3	Aurel Toma	l.ko. 5	Earl's Court, London

*Title fight, but Lynch overweight and forfeited world title